D1478576

AMA Leadership Series

The Organic Growth Playbook:

Activate High-Yield Behaviors to Achieve Extraordinary Results – Every Time

Bernard J. Jaworski

Robert S. Lurie

AMERICAN MARKETING
ASSOCIATION

American Marketing Association
Leadership Series
Chicago

Copyright © 2018 Bernard J. Jaworski and Robert S. Lurie
All Rights Reserved

Printed in the United States

No part of this publication may be reproduced, stored in or introduced into retrieval system, or transmitted, in any form, or by any means (electronic, mechanical, photocopying, recording, or otherwise) without the permission of the authors.

The web addresses referenced in this book were live and correct at the time of the book's publication but may be subject to change.

The Organic Growth Playbook
Soft | 978-0-87757-368-5
Digital | 978-0-87757-369-2
Hard | 978-0-87757-370-8

Cover Design by Berge Design

Contents

Preface

In the early 1990s, Bob began to notice an odd and disturbing lack of pattern in his work with clients trying to grow or grow faster. They were applying the gold standard methods of marketing: segmenting, targeting, and then positioning products to be differentiated in the minds of desirable customers. But the standard playbook did not reliably result in organic growth. In situation after situation, he observed that well-researched and well-designed campaigns to differentiate products in customers' minds sometimes produced double-digit growth, but often yielded nothing, and sometimes, confoundingly, led to overall sales declines. On the other hand, he noticed that some clients with "good enough" (but not particularly differentiated) products seemed able to achieve consistent growth. This seemingly random distribution of results left Bob with a puzzle—and a dilemma: should he continue to use the widely-accepted standard methods and never be sure he could really help his clients grow, or should he figure out what was going wrong and try something different?

This book is about trying something different—not just for the sake of being different, but in the quest to find a reliable methodology for accelerating organic growth. By the mid to late 1990s, the core thinking—and the first iteration of the tools—was consistently enabling clients to grow faster. In the early 2000s, Bernie began to teach the tools as he and Bob continued to test and refine them in a wide variety of firms—big and small, in developed and emerging economies, in B2B and B2C firms. They worked. In fact, they worked so well that clients began to embed the new approach into their own processes of planning for growth. Over the past five years, the two of us have worked together to further develop the methodology and articulate its core principles.

The result of those years of effort and experience is captured in this book. Its purpose is simple: to provide a comprehensive, integrated method to consistently accelerate organic growth. As we learned in our journey, this requires both a new approach to marketing as well as some key changes to organization-wide capabilities. While firms can achieve significant value by applying the methodology to an individual product or brand, the benefits are vastly magnified when the whole organization is aligned around the approach.

The key audience for this book is thoughtful practitioners who must struggle to achieve aggressive growth targets each and every year. We therefore provide detailed instructions on how to apply the tools and illustrate the process with four comprehensive client stories of organizations in different industries that successfully implemented the approach. A second audience for this book includes academic researchers and teachers. One of our aims is to challenge the conventional orthodoxy of marketing that differentiating products in the minds of customers is the golden key for unlocking growth. Differentiation is necessary, but it's not enough. In our view, organic growth cannot be achieved by changing mindsets, but only by changing behaviors. The focus of our approach is therefore on influencing the few, key customer behaviors during the purchasing process that disproportionately drive growth.

A note on method. This book is based on trial and error in the field. It emerged from what we learned working side-by-side with clients to accelerate organic growth. We were fortunate in also being able to learn from the experiences of several outstanding colleagues who used these methods with their clients. We've had some wonderful successes along the way, some of which are highlighted in this book. We've also learned from some failures at the outset that helped us adjust and fine-tune our approach. All those experiences and the hard work of our many colleagues and clients are reflected in this book.

Chapter 1 provides an overview of the entire book and introduces readers to the core concepts and methods of our approach. Chapter 2 through 10 delve into a detailed explanation of the five principles at the heart of the *Playbook* approach and includes four end-to-end client stories illustrating the methodology. These chapters lay out the tools and techniques needed to apply the approach in your own business. Chapters 11 and 12 cover some of the lessons learned from applying these tools in different types of firms, industries, and geographies. These two chapters are a must read for those seeking to implement and embed the *Playbook* principles within their organizations.

We are excited to share these ideas that we have developed, debated, and refined over the course of many years. We hope you enjoy the book and are able to apply its lessons to deliver stronger, more reliable organic growth in your own organizations.

Bernie Jaworski
Los Angeles
May 20, 2017

Bob Lurie
Chilmark, MA
May 20, 2017

AMA Introduction to Book Series

Welcome to marketing in the twenty-first century—the age of data, social, mobile, automation, and globalization. The field is changing so quickly, it's difficult to keep up. There is increasing uncertainty about the profession's mission and responsibilities. Meantime, the demands marketers face are ever more complex and critical.

This is why the American Marketing Association (AMA) has engaged some of the world's most innovative professionals, academics, and thought leaders to create *The Seven Problems of Marketing*—a seven-book series that introduces and explores a new set of organizing and actionable principles for the twenty-first-century marketer.

Each book in the series takes a deep dive into one problem, offering expertise, direction, and case studies while striking a balance between theory and application. The goal is to provide a contemporary framework for marketers as they navigate the unique challenges and vast opportunities of today's dynamic global marketplace.

Here are the seven problems addressed in the series:

Problem 1: Effectively targeting high-value sources of growth
Problem 2: Defining the role of marketing in the firm and C-suite
Problem 3: Managing the digital transformation of the modern corporation
Problem 4: Generating and using insight to shape marketing practice
Problem 5: Dealing with an omni-channel world
Problem 6: Competing in dynamic, global markets
Problem 7: Balancing incremental and radical innovation

Importantly, the books in this series are written by and for marketers and marketing scholars. All of the conceptual and analytical frameworks offered are born from practice. The authors have applied their tools and methods in client settings, allowing them to test and refine their ideas in the face of real-world challenges. You'll read true stories about how marketers have used innovative thinking and practices to overcome seemingly impossible dilemmas and bring about game-changing success. Theories are explored in a way that busy marketers can understand viscerally. Client stories have been incorporated to illustrate how to apply the analysis frames as well as deal with application and practice-based issues.

Our fundamental aim with this series is to hone the practice of marketing for the twenty-first century. The AMA has asserted that there is a critical tension within every enterprise between "best" and "next" practices. Marketers often choose best practices because they are safe and proven. Next practices, which push boundaries and challenge conventions, can be riskier. Few enterprises, however, transform themselves and achieve breakout performance with best practices alone. The next practices discussed in this series are often responsible for driving outperformance. The books in this series are designed to engage you on two levels: individually, by increasing your knowledge and "bench strength," and organizationally, by improving the application of marketing concepts within your firm. When you finish each book, we are confident you will feel energized and think differently about the field of marketing and its organizing principles. Through the explanation of theory and compelling examples of its application, you will be empowered to help your organization quickly identify and maximize opportunities. After all, the opportunity to innovate and make an impact is what attracted most of us to the field of marketing in the first place.

Russ Klein
CEO, American Marketing Association

Book Series Overview

In 2016, the AMA established its first-ever intellectual agenda. This intellectual agenda focused on complex, challenging, and difficult-to-solve problems that would be of interest to both academics and practitioners. A working team of scholars and practitioners, selected by AMA leadership, identified seven big problems of marketing as the foundation of the agenda. These problems were ranked from a much longer list of challenges. These seven big problems shared three attributes: they were pressing issues that confronted every organization, they were C-suite level in scope, and they could not be solved by one article or book. Indeed, the team felt that each problem could trigger a decade-long research agenda. A key purpose of the AMA intellectual agenda was thus to stimulate research, dialogue, and debate among the entire AMA membership.

The purpose of the AMA book series is to shed a deeper light on each of the seven problems. In particular, the aim of the series is to enable readers to think differently and take action with regard to these big problems. Thus, the book series operates at two levels: individually, increasing your knowledge and bench strength, and at the organization level, improving the application of marketing concepts within your firm.

Given the nature of these problems, no single book or article can fully address the problem. By their very nature these problems are significant, nuanced, and approachable from multiple vantage points. As such, each of the books provides a single perspective on the issue. This single perspective is intended to both advance knowledge and spark debate. While the books may emerge from academic literature and/or managerial application, their fundamental aim is to improve the practice of marketing. Books selected for the series are evaluated on six criteria.

1. Seven Big Problems Focus

Each book is focused on one of the seven big problems of marketing. These problems identify key conceptual issues in the field of marketing that are the focus of emerging academic research and that practitioners are actively confronting today.

2. Audience

The book is written primarily for an audience of thoughtful practitioners. Thoughtful in this context means that the practitioner is an active reader of both professional articles and books, is dedicated to enhancing his/ her marketing knowledge and skills, and is committed to upgrading the organization's marketing culture, capabilities, and results. A secondary audience is academics (and students) and consultants.

3. Integrative Framework

The book provides an integrated framework that frames the problem and offers a detailed approach for addressing it.

4. Field-based Approach

The authors have applied their frameworks in client settings. These client settings enable authors to test and refine their frameworks. Conceptual and analysis frameworks are enlivened via practice and case examples that demonstrate application in the field. Named and/or disguised client stories illustrate how to apply the analysis frames, how to deal with application issues, and other practice-based issues.

5. Academic Literature

The integrative frameworks should be new to the marketplace. The conceptual frameworks should extend existing thinking and the analysis frameworks should provide new ways to conduct marketing-related analysis.

6. Readability

The book should be intelligible to the average reader. The concepts should be clearly defined and explained, and cases written so that a reader can understand the content on a first read.

On behalf of the AMA, I am excited to bring these books to market. I am anxious to hear your feedback—both positive and challenging—as we move the field forward.

Bernie Jaworski
AMA Book Series Editor

Chapter 1

Overview of the *Organic Growth Playbook*

A few years ago, Sam Wilcox, vice president of launch products at one of the world's largest life sciences companies, was in a tough spot. While the company's newest drug, Terrafix,[1] had achieved revenues over $680 million in its first year after launch, its rate of growth had stalled. To make matters worse, the nearest competitor was investing heavily in promoting an alternative therapy, while another competitor was getting ready to launch a third product with a therapy similar to Terrafix. Senior management was pressuring Sam for a new, more aggressive go-to-market plan.

The Terrafix team had invested tremendous effort in developing a clear, differentiated product message—and it appeared to be working. Physicians were aware of Terrafix and it had a solid reputation as an effective, reliable therapy. It was positioned well versus its next best competitor. The drug was claiming a unique space in the minds of targeted physicians. Yet, for some reason, this wasn't driving sales growth. When Sam reviewed the data, it showed that only a small fraction of the patient population at risk for the medical condition treated by Terrafix was getting a prescription for it. He knew something more had to be done.

To better understand the disconnect, Sam's team mapped in fine, quantitative detail the various ways that patients and doctors interacted before, during, and after their annual physical exam. What they found through this study confirmed Sam's hunch: many patients who were at risk for the disease were not receiving a diagnosis that would lead to a prescription. In fact, in most cases, doctors had performed a qualitative, subjective assessment that left them uncertain about the patient's actual risk. And in the absence of a clear-cut diagnosis, most doctors chose not to treat with medication. By contrast, the team found that patients who had taken a newly available objective diagnostic test were four times more likely to receive a prescription for Terrafix. Simply put, when doctors could review an objective diagnostic test with a clear indication of disease, they took action. It became clear that the solution wasn't to build a more differentiated position for Terrafix, but to get doctors to perform the diagnostic test.

In a significant departure from their initial launch strategy, the team made a choice to reorient their marketing and sales from a traditional product pitch extolling the benefits of Terrafix. Instead, they focused on two behavior-oriented campaigns: one to convince more primary care physicians to order the objective test and the other to persuade patients to ask for it. This new choice—to focus on changing a couple of critical behaviors—led Sam's team to rethink nearly everything.

First, they resegmented their patient and physician populations so that they could more precisely identify and target those who would be most likely to ask for or order the test. Then they began a deep exploration of what factors might motivate—or deter—patients in the target segments from asking for a test. This led them further away from their traditional product benefit focus. Instead, these factors ranged widely, from the (limited) physical availability of the test to the importance these patients placed on their own sense of well being. They had little to do with the product itself.

With clarity about who to target, and what shaped their decision to order or ask for a test, Sam's team redesigned and reallocated its marketing and sales in a radically different way. Marketing and sales resources had previously been spread across a host of promotional activities to tout the brand, primarily to physicians. Going forward, the team aggressively funded an unbranded communications campaign encouraging patients to ask for the test, positioning it as a natural, appropriate extension of the kind of "taking care of my health is taking care of myself" behavior on which the exploratory research had shown these patients prided themselves. The team also invested heavily in similarly unbranded efforts to make the necessary diagnostic testing equipment more widely available and economically feasible, and to remind physicians to use it.

We'll return to the Terrafix example in more detail in the next chapter. For now, the important thing to note is how different the team's new approach was from the conventional strategy—and how different the results were. The new campaign led to a 60 percent increase in the number of objective diagnostic tests performed. As predicted by the team's analysis, this growth in tests translated directly into a higher rate of Terrafix prescriptions and increased sales. In the first year of the campaign, total annual revenues rose by 9 percent, while the marketing spend for this more focused campaign actually decreased by $15 million. In the three years after the relaunch, Terrafix's sales grew by nearly 50 percent to $1.31 billion.

Sam's story, while remarkable, is far from unique. Time after time, we've seen this holistic perspective on customers' purchasing behaviors bear fruit by revealing unexplored opportunities for influencing specific behaviors to unlock growth. In this book, we share four detailed stories and dozens of shorter examples of companies that have sparked growth by identifying and activating key customer behaviors. While these examples span a range of product types and industries, they all share certain similarities—namely, a commitment by product teams to make concrete, fact-based choices intended to increase the frequency of high-yield customer behaviors. These choices provide a consistent line of sight for the marketing, sales, and product teams that enables them to align activities in pursuit of common goals.

Senior management's most pressing problem: revenue growth

The challenge Sam faced was one that we've observed again and again: being responsible for revitalizing a good product with an unsatisfactory growth rate. Consistent, profitable revenue growth is the primary goal of senior executives and is generally considered the gold standard in evaluating managers' performance.[2] The reason is simple: reliable revenue growth is the largest single factor influencing a company's stock price and business success. General managers or product managers who consistently achieve profitable double-digit growth are rewarded with significant pay increases and promotions. Legendary CEOs such as Jack Welch (GE), Lou Gerstner (IBM), and James Burke (Johnson & Johnson) significantly outperformed the growth rates of their industry peers. More recently, CEOs like Ratan Tata (Tata Group), Eric Schmidt (Alphabet), and Larry Ellison (Oracle) have built their careers on their ability to generate growth even in difficult economic circumstances.[3]

CEO of the Year and Organic Growth

Many of the most widely admired CEOs have garnered recognition for their ability to drive steady, profitable organic growth year after year.[4] For example:

- Harvard Business Review recently ranked Lars Rebien Sørensen of Novo Nordisk as the top CEO for 2015. When asked about the firm's strategy, Sørensen noted, "Outsiders sometimes come in and say, 'You're dependent on diabetes for 80 percent of your revenue—you should diversify.' But I've always believed that you should do things that you know something about, that you're good at. We've tried a lot of diversification strategies in the past, but we've failed because of the inherent scientific and commercial uncertainty and our own naïveté. So our expansion has been completely organic."[5]

- Fortune magazine ranked Nike CEO Mark Parker their businessperson of the year in 2015. He doubled revenue growth since 2006 and the company took a commanding 62 percent share of the market with 8.5 percent steady annual growth. Nike also reported a profit of $3 billion during 2015—nearly 11 percent of sales.[6]

Our focus in this book is on helping you grow your company more rapidly and reliably—without resorting to acquisitions. Buying another company is, of course, a quick way to grow revenues. And it's often a valuable way of acquiring skills, assets, and access needed for further growth. Growth through acquisition is certainly easier and quicker than growing by outcompeting rivals. Nonetheless, profitable, steady organic growth—be it by taking market share from competitors or by convincing existing customers to consume more of the product—is the acid test for companies and managers. No matter how skilled you are at dealing with the myriad functional challenges of running an organization, if you can't find a way to increase sales from existing or newly developed products, your company will, sooner or later, cease to exist. It will be acquired, dismantled, or shut down. It's that simple.

A cursory look at the business news on any given day reinforces the importance of sustained, profitable, revenue growth. Many of the top stories revolve around firms that failed to achieve revenue targets and the consequences of these shortfalls. The result is typically a drop in stock price and a questioning of the firm's strategy (see The Organic Growth Challenge).

The Organic Growth Challenge

The three short illustrations below appeared as we were writing and are typical of these missed growth expectations:

- Netflix experienced slower subscriber growth in the U.S. as its core market of affluent young to middle age subscribers appeared to reach a saturation point. As subscriber growth slowed to 0.3 percent versus the previous quarter, the stock price dropped by 14 percent.[7]
- McDonald's missed stock market analyst projections regarding revenue growth, stoking fears that the fast food industry was headed into decline. The stock fell 3.8 percent.[8]
- IBM continued to pursue a strategic transformation. It reported sixteen straight quarters of year-over-year revenue declines—with more to come, according to analysts. Other tech giants such as HP and EMC also struggled to accelerate growth, prompting concerns about the future prospects of these industry leaders.[9]

The pervasiveness of the growth challenge is due to the fact that virtually all managers—not just CEOs—face difficult competitive conditions with an inadequate tool kit for growth. Nearly all markets today are characterized by multiple competitors with similar capabilities, talent, and products. Moreover, in all these markets, customers almost always know the product offerings. They've heard many messages about the products and are familiar with the performance of a good number of them.

So most managers in most markets find themselves trying to grow a good (but not great) product. Their product is largely viewed by customers and potential customers as similar to all the others. They know their product has some strong selling points, perhaps an aspect of functionality or perhaps an element of service, in which they're clearly better than competitors. They also know—though they're often reluctant to admit it—that their product has some weak points relative to their competitors' products. Most of all, they know that they're competing in a roughly equal sports league. Everyone is playing the same game, with largely the same talent, product, and offering. It's not easy to carve out a path to sustained growth and success in that kind of competitive environment.

What compounds the intrinsic competitive challenge is that most managers use the same approach to finding a way to grow. This approach has been taught in every business school and reinforced on the job everywhere in the world for decades. It's a four-step process: segment, prioritize and target, position, and promote. The idea is for product managers to segment the market into identifiable groups of customers with distinct product needs, select several of those segments to target, identify a value proposition to position the product in a distinct and compelling way to customers in the selected target segments, and then promote—communicate about the product and make it available—as aggressively as possible to those customer segments. This classic approach is based on the idea that if a company positions its products well, growth will follow.

Except, it doesn't.

The facts are startling. It's common knowledge that a very high percentage of all new product launches (into competed categories) fail—either outright or by failing to achieve a meaningful bump in sales. A recent *Harvard Business Review* article noted that 75 percent of new product launches in consumer packaged goods and retail fail to earn $7.5 million in their first year. And only 3 percent hit the target of $50 million, which is considered the gold standard for a new product launch.[10] The numbers in business-to-business (B2B) industries are equally poor. And it's well known that most of the money spent on marketing and sales efforts to boost growth of existing products earns a poor return, or very often no return at all.

Some of this poor performance could be due to poor work on the part of managers and their teams. In fact, poor execution is the reason given in most companies for failure to achieve growth. But most teams actually do good work, often very good work. We know, because we've watched dozens of them and worked with dozens more. We came to realize that the real root cause of the failure to grow was that these teams were using an ineffective process for identifying how to grow in competitive markets.

It's time for a new approach—a new playbook that is purposely designed to deliver above average growth both reliably and consistently for any manager and any team with a good product.

The Organic Growth Playbook

The central idea of *The Organic Growth Playbook* is that faster sales growth results from designing offers and campaigns that have a relentless, integrated focus on changing one or two high-yield customer behaviors. This is in sharp contrast to the conventional growth approach, which focuses on differentiating product offerings from those of competitors.

Organic Growth Playbook vs. Conventional Approach

Conventional Approach

- Focus on differentiating products in the minds of target customers
- Segment based on benefits, demographics, or attitudes
- Develop customer profiles centered on product use and attitudes
- Develop a value proposition focused on creating a differentiated perception of product
- Spread marketing investment across 4Ps in product messaging
- Fully activate market with a multisegment focus

Playbook Approach

- Focus on changing customer behavior in their buying process that provides most leverage
- Segment based on likelihood of engaging in the key behavior
- Develop customer profiles that reveal critical drivers and barriers of key behavior
- Develop a value proposition that is focused on changing behavior
- Focus investment on behavior change—not product messaging
- Disproportionately and sequentially fund a few segments

The core logic of the conventional approach is that if a brand is sufficiently different and better than competitors' brands, consumers will come to prefer it and will actively seek it out for purchase. But it very often doesn't work out that way. Every customer goes through some type of buying process before purchasing a product or a service. They may talk to friends who've already bought the product. They may visit stores and sample the product. They may look up information about the product or service on the internet. They may articulate and debate the pros and cons of the product. Sometimes their buying process is lengthy, involving multiple activities and iterations. Other times it's short and simple. But, in every customer's process there's an action that *decisively* shapes which product or service they ultimately purchase. By visiting one type of store instead of another, they end up considering only a subset of available brands. By talking to a friend—instead of researching a product on the internet—they're convinced of the merits of one brand over another. Having set out with a notion of buying brand X, some activity—the visit to the convenience store instead of the grocery store, the internet research instead of the talk with a friend—puts them onto a different path, one that ends in the purchase of brand Y. *The Organic Growth Playbook* is built around this important insight. It lays out an approach you can use to change the behavior of customers at critical places in their buying process, thereby shifting them onto paths that favor the purchase of your product or service instead of a competitor's. When your team can impact what customers do during the key phases of the buying process, sales can grow much faster, and with less effort.

The *Playbook* does follow the structure of the four-step conventional approach. It calls for segmenting your market, prioritizing and targeting just a few of those segments, developing a value proposition for each target segment, and designing offers and promotional activities around those value propositions. Where it differs is in the content of those steps, in how the market is segmented and value propositions developed. Its focus is on customer behaviors rather than product. When you segment, target, position, and promote around high-yield behaviors in the buyer's decision-making process rather than focusing on product positioning, you can boost your growth rates by 1.5 to 2 times—and count on doing so reliably. But if you continue to center your growth planning on product positioning—as the classic approach dictates—you'll continue to struggle or fail more often than not.

We certainly didn't set out to create something radical when we began working with our clients to help them drive organic growth for their products and services. Initially, we just wanted to help them produce better results with the conventional process. Time and time again, however, we saw smart, skilled, highly motivated business managers follow the classic approach only to see their growth plans fall short. Over time, we realized that the reason the classic approach failed to generate growth lay, ironically, in its most critical assumption: that once a product is favorably differentiated in a customer's mind—once they've been convinced they like a certain product—they're going to buy it.

In reality, what we observed in market after market was that customers who said they understood and preferred one product's positioning very often bought some other product. Why? Because something they did or saw or experienced during the buying process made the other, initially less well-positioned product a better choice in that situation. Literally, the influence of who they were with, where they could locate a product, or the order in which they looked at products on the internet, shifted their path through the buying process in a way that led them away from purchasing an initially-preferred product toward a completely different product. The point? Even when customers find a product's positioning clear, distinct, and desirable, they often don't buy it. In effect, great product positioning is a necessary condition for growth, but it's not sufficient in and of itself to drive growth. To drive sales growth reliably and rapidly, it's essential to focus relentlessly on shaping the way the customer proceeds through the whole buying process—and not simply on its very last step.

It was working out the logical and practical implications of this seemingly straightforward insight—to accelerate sales growth in strongly competed markets, teams must change pre-purchase customer behaviors—that led us to a new approach that we have summarized in a set of five principles. These principles form the heart of *The Organic Growth Playbook*. Each principle highlights a new way of thinking about some important aspect of growth strategy.

First principle: Map the buying process waterfall

The principles began emerging early on. As soon as we started trying to bring the insight of "buying behavior matters most" into everyday practice, we ran into two interrelated practical problems. The first was that customers' buying processes usually include many activities, and it could be very expensive and difficult to change all of those activities. What we found, however, in every buying process we studied was that there were one or two activities that decisively shaped what the customer purchased. That means you don't have to change *all* customer buying behaviors, you just have to identify and change the one or two critical activities that have a disproportionate impact on what the customer ultimately buys. This is summarized in the *Playbook's* first principle: *map the buying process waterfall* to isolate and focus strategy on one or two critical high-yield customer behaviors. The waterfall identifies and quantifies the various "fall off" or switch points, where customers either exit the buying process or follow a different, distinct sequence of activities. Of course, customers can and do fall out of the buying process at very early stages, in the middle of the process, or late in the process. A natural reaction is to try to do something across the board, addressing all the drop-off points in the buying process. What mapping the waterfall reveals, however, is that there are generally one or two steps in the process where a very high number of customers drop out or switch paths. Even modest changes in customer behavior at those steps can have a disproportionate effect on customers' purchasing paths. The waterfall is essential for identifying the few high-yield behaviors in the process.

Second principle: Use propensity-based segmentation

The second problem was that it was clear that customers' reasons for, or resistance to, changing a high-yield behavior in a certain way would vary considerably across a whole market. Some would change readily; others not. An altered offer or message that would convince some to change wouldn't convince others. This meant that, for reasons of both efficiency and effectiveness, teams would need to segment the market, and do so on the basis of customers' propensity to engage in the high-yield behaviors. This implication is summarized in the *Playbook's* second principle: *use propensity-based segmentation.*

At this point, having made a decision to focus attention on behavior change, it was clear to us that the conceptual tools and tradecraft of the classic approach would be of limited use. By and large, those tools were designed to help teams understand and shape customers' attitudes—or mindset— about how their product differed from competing offerings. We, on the other hand, needed a method to help teams understand and convince customers to change certain buying process behaviors. If you're trying to grow brand X in the furniture business, for example, you would traditionally spend your time trying to understand what colors, shapes, and materials will make your sofas, tables, and chairs more appealing and distinctive to customers, and how best to communicate those product differences. In our approach, having determined that customers who shop at multibrand furniture stores are much more likely to buy brand X, you'd spend your time understanding why customers want to visit multibrand furniture stores and then develop a value proposition, and a campaign, to convince them to make that visit.

Third principle: Unearth the critical drivers and barriers of target behavior

The *Playbook's* third principle involves the need to *unearth the critical drivers and barriers of target behavior*. The logic here is simple. A full and deep understanding of why customers do or don't undertake a target buying behavior is essential because it provides the basis for efforts to influence or change that behavior. As we'll discuss later, achieving that full understanding requires a good bit of data collection, analysis, and synthesis, but the objective is to isolate and articulate what most motivates customers to undertake a target behavior (drivers) and what most deters them from it (barriers).

Fourth principle: Develop a behavior change value proposition

The *Playbook's* fourth principle is to develop a compelling *behavior change value proposition*. Every business must establish a clear product positioning and product value proposition. But having differentiated product value propositions doesn't ensure growth. You must also translate your understanding of drivers and barriers into a campaign aimed at getting customers to behave differently. To continue our previous example, the messages, activities and offers aimed at getting furniture buyers to shop in a multibrand store must motivate them to engage in that behavior by tapping into positive incentives and reducing obstacles. The behavior change value proposition (BCVP) articulates the benefits of engaging in the target, high-yield behavior.

Fifth principle: Invest disproportionately

Finally, we came to realize that, in addition to shifting the focus from products to customer behavior, it was necessary to dramatically change companies' spending habits. The *Playbook's* fifth principle is to *invest disproportionately and sequentially*. It requires serious concentration of effort and resources simply to break through the noise and confusion typical of strongly competed markets. Our final principle articulates the need for a disciplined and systematic approach to conducting sequenced, segment-specific behavior change campaigns.

Taken together, these five principles define a distinctive, systematic approach that will help you overcome the seemingly intractable challenge of accelerating the growth of a good product in a tough, competed market. They represent a distinct break with, and advance beyond, the classic approach. These principles are more than distinctive; they're also reliably effective at boosting growth rates. Regardless of geography or industry, regardless of the size or sophistication of the firm, regardless of how tough the competitive environment, and without the benefit of dramatic innovation, we've found that teams using the approach described in *The Organic Growth Playbook* have been able to boost their historic growth rates by a factor of 1.5 to 2 times for years.

Your team—every team—can get these kinds of results if you're willing to take a new approach to growth planning work, and if you're willing to make and implement the strategic choices that our principle-based approach suggests. As we sketched out above, each principle summarizes a perspective on growth planning work that differs significantly from the conventional approach. The second principle, for example, is about segmenting the market based on customers' propensity to engage in specific high-yield behaviors instead of dividing up customers based on their needs or attitudes. Likewise, the fourth principle is about developing a different kind of value proposition, one focused on behavior change rather than product benefits.

Adopting these five principles will lead to new and different choices for your growth strategy. For example, following the first principle, you'll *map the buying process waterfall* in your category. The insights from this mapping work then form the logic and evidence for identifying the one or two high-yield behaviors that will be the focus of your growth strategy. As shown in Figure 1-1, each principle guides you in making one or more of the key strategic choices that comprise a growth strategy.

The *Playbook's* principles guide you toward making systematic, tightly integrated choices about where and how to grow: you'll end up targeting market segments that are most open to a particular high-yield buying process behavior and tailoring every aspect of the offer, message, and media mix toward convincing customers in those segments to do that high-yield behavior more frequently. We'll explain the insights and logic behind each principle (and its associated choice) in detail in later chapters of this book. However, as is often the case with systems, the explanation of any one part is more readily understood when the whole is grasped. We hope to ease the way by foreshadowing the explanations of the individual principles, and showing how the five principles together create an integrated whole.

FIGURE 1-1

Organic Growth Principles and Choices

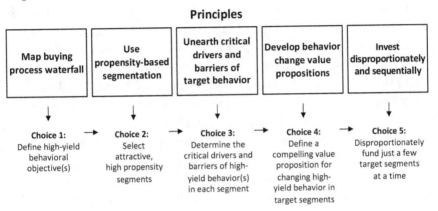

As should be clear by now, we believe the key to faster growth lies in understanding and taking advantage of what customers do, and don't yet do, as they work their way through the buying process. The mapping of the buying process waterfall reveals quantitatively where customers disproportionately drop out of, or shift paths within, the buying process. Your job is to pick from among the customer's many actions and behaviors during their purchase process the one or two behaviors that decisively shape the customer's ultimate purchase decision, and articulate them as behavioral objectives. A behavioral objective is a simple, clear statement of whose behavior should change and in what specific way. We typically frame it as "this "[Specific Person (or Role)] involved in the buying process should take [action X], instead of doing [action Y]."

This first choice is critical. The behavioral objectives are the focal point of all the subsequent work. When chosen properly, the behavior changes specified in the behavioral objectives are the highest yielding throughout the buying process. Even a modest change in the frequency with which customers do them produces a significant change in the frequency with which certain products are purchased or used. Although they may seem unexceptional, and are often early in the buying process, these behaviors exert disproportionate influence over actual purchases.

This choice may seem counterintuitive. You might ask, "Isn't the highest yield behavioral objective just 'buy my product?' After all, if I choose a behavioral objective like 'call a dealer (instead of doing product research online)' or 'go to the multibrand furniture store,' I can't be sure everyone will change their purchase. But if I choose as my behavioral objective 'buy my product,' and manage to convince the customer to change that behavior, I get the sale." This argument sounds plausible, but it has a fatal flaw. It's much more difficult, expensive, and less certain to convince someone to do something different at the point of sale than it is to convince someone to do something different upstream from that purchase—like call a dealer or go to a multibrand store. Put differently, the yield from trying to change people's minds at the point of purchase is intrinsically quite low, especially in tough markets, because they're most on their guard. Targeting upstream buying behaviors is usually a much more cost-effective choice.

Recall the situation most managers face. They're trying to launch or boost sales of a good but not dramatically innovative product. They've followed the classic approach and used every channel and form of media that's relevant to shout the message about their product's virtues as loudly and frequently as they can. In other words, they've maximized their share of voice. But growth has flatlined. Why? Because customers in these competed markets believe they already know their product choices, have reasons why they do or don't want to buy one of those choices, and so tune out the endless annoying buy-my-product messages.

By contrast, customers typically have far less resistance to trying on a new buying process behavior like calling a dealer or going to a store to do some live testing. In fact, it often makes them feel better about themselves. It's usually easier to convince customers to change upstream behaviors than point-of-sale behaviors, and if those upstream behaviors really do shift customers onto a pathway in which they naturally reconsider the merits of different products, then these upstream behaviors are higher yield.

The *Playbook's* second choice involves selecting which subset of customers to target. This "segment then prioritize" choice is structurally the same as in the traditional approach. Customers in any given market vary considerably and it's difficult to arrange messages and offers to suit individual customers. It makes sense to group similar customers into segments, determine the relative attractiveness of each, and create messages and offers tailored to just the few most desirable segments.

So teams typically devote a good deal of thought and effort to segmenting and prioritizing customers. Following normal best practice, they would do so using some combination of customers' stated product functionality preferences, their intrinsic characteristics (for example, customer size), and/or their general attitudes to group them into segments. They would then prioritize the segments in terms of their financial attractiveness (growth rates, profitability, and so on) and how feasible it is to serve them.

The *Playbook's* second principle points you in a very different direction, focusing on the behavioral objectives you've selected. It calls for a new type of segmentation—one based on the customer's propensity to engage in targeted high-yield buying process behaviors. Specifically, customers who call a dealer or visit a multibrand store with similar frequencies, and have similar reasons for doing so, are grouped into propensity-based segments. To ensure targetability, the segments are defined in terms of characteristics that are readily observable to the business' customer-facing functions. Clearly, segments comprising customers with a high propensity toward the chosen behavior—to call a dealer or do a test drive—will be the most attractive, at least for initial campaigns, while customers likely to resist changing their upstream buying behaviors are likely to be targeted later on.

Knowing which high-yield behaviors your want to target and which groups of customers are most inclined to do those behaviors is a great start. But it still isn't enough. You need to know how to change your campaigns—messages, offer, media mix, and so on—in a way that will convince those customers to change their buying process behavior in a favorable way. The groundwork for these redesigned campaigns is laid when you make the *Playbook's* third choice, which calls for the prioritization of the key drivers of, and barriers to, high-yield behaviors.

Every successful growth plan is built on a deep understanding of how customers think and make decisions. In the conventional process, teams focus nearly exclusively on how customers think about products. They conduct many types of research into customers' needs and into their attitudes and beliefs about various products. They typically translate the research into some kind of narrative—a description in story form that lays out what's important to customers—that is used to explain why customers choose to buy one product instead of another. This general process is a good one, but it's heavily skewed toward product and a strong (often implicit) belief that what matters most to customers is which product, offering, or solution has more benefits.[11]

By contrast, the *Playbook's* third principle (and its associated choice) shifts your attention toward understanding the narrative of the customer's thinking throughout their buying process. What the research and analysis typically reveal is that many factors, not just product attributes and benefits, matter in people's decision making. A useful way of synthesizing and articulating these factors is as drivers—defined as the things that motivate customers to engage in a behavior—and barriers—defined as the things that deter or prevent customers from engaging in a behavior. Drivers and barriers can be simple, physical things—such as the availability, or lack of availability of a product, or coming in an inappropriate size. Or they can be subtle, complex, psychological things, like the adoption of a product by a group of people the customer aspires to join. The list of drivers and barriers, which highlights what is foremost in customers' minds as they decide what to do, provides you with the parameters and guideposts you need to design campaigns that can efficiently and effectively change customers' high-yield behaviors. Interestingly, we've found that it's far more fruitful to spend time removing or mitigating barriers to key behaviors than trying to motivate customers to buy by explaining over and over why brand X really is better than brand Y.

This two-sided—drivers and barriers—approach is rooted in a model of consumer decision making that is both more nuanced and realistic than the one-sided product model and based on more robust science. Recent work in cognitive psychology and behavioral economics has shown that consumer decisions and behavior result from the interactive influence of a consumer's situation, what they most want to do or achieve in that situation, and the beliefs and attitudes they bring with them. The model accepts that the preferences and attitudes consumers have formed before starting any given buying process do matter in their decision making. However, it makes clear that what people care about, and how much, is situation specific.

For instance, where customers shop and what products they will consider will change significantly if they go with friends instead of going alone, and change again if they go with their children instead of friends. In fact, what a customer wants to achieve in a given situation strongly shapes and often dominates their thinking about how and where they'll shop, and what they ultimately choose. The age-old comment that "no one ever got fired for buying IBM," succinctly illustrates this point. Even if the buyer knows that another company's product is better, and prefers it, the fact is that buying IBM is likely to appear to be a sound decision to bosses and colleagues, and not upsetting them may be more important than getting the right product. The third principle guides you in analyzing why customers in target segments behave as they do, and synthesizing the insights into a segment-level customer narrative. You can then mine these narratives to unearth what motivates customers to do a high-yield behavior (drivers) and what deters them from it (barriers).

In using the fourth principle (develop behavior change value propositions) to make the fourth choice, you move from the paper world of plans to the real world of offers and campaigns. The drivers and barriers are the foundation for these behavior change value propositions. They delineate the full range of things that matter to customers in a segment. But you shouldn't (and probably can't afford) to simply try to activate every driver and mitigate every barrier. Instead you should draw from among them a coherent, integrated approach to incenting customers to do the high-yield behavior more frequently—an approach summarized as the behavioral change value proposition. And then, you'll have to translate that value proposition into real things—modified products and offers, different messages, shifted media, and so on—that will induce them to change (see Amazon's Behavior Change Value Proposition to Drive Organic Growth).

Amazon's Behavior Change Value Proposition to Drive Organic Growth

A behavior change value proposition is distinct from the product value proposition that typically acts as the design template for go-to-market plans and activities. Indeed, the behavior change value proposition is superordinate to it. Good product positioning is very important, and a necessary foundation for growth. But good product positioning alone won't drive growth reliably. Hence the need for specific messaging and offers to reshape how customers move through their buying process. Let's take Amazon.com as an example. Following the conventional wisdom, we would focus our positioning analysis on such benefits as one-stop shopping, ease of use, convenience, or price versus other web or brick-and-mortar businesses. But target users already know that Amazon is great at providing these benefits. Amazon is already well positioned in the market. However, if the marketing team knew that Amazon Prime users (who pay a monthly or annual subscription fee for free delivery and additional free services) purchase six times the amount that non-Prime users purchase, the team might tailor its message quite differently. A behavior change value proposition would focus on offering customers reasons for changing a specific behavior—in this case, switching from non-Prime to Prime accounts.[12]

The final choice is about investing disproportionately to drive high-yield behavior changes among targeted customers. We're continually surprised in our work with companies at how difficult it can be for them to change their allocation of marketing spend, and especially to focus it decisively on a few segments and on the critical aspects of their go-to-market plans. Partly, this is a matter of making difficult trade-offs. With limited resources, companies must decide what to stop doing as well as what to start doing, or do more of. We often found that marketing spend was often spread across a range of tactics, including both new and old media strategies. We sometimes call this approach "peanut butter marketing" to refer to the habit many companies have of spreading thin coating of cash across a variety of marketing communication tactics.

We observed much greater success when companies made a committed choice to allocate their spending in disproportionate ways—both in terms of sequencing and level of allocation—to compel a specific behavior change by potential customers. Put simply, this boils down to a decision to fully fund targeted segments and behavioral objectives. To return to the Amazon example, converting non-Prime users to Prime customers would require a very different set of tactics compared to getting customers to buy more products or use more services.

These five principles and choices—focus on a few high yield behaviors, define segments based on likelihood of engagement in targeted behavior, articulate customers' drivers and barriers to key behaviors, develop behavior change value propositions, and invest disproportionately in influencing these behaviors in target segments—are the core system detailed in *The Organic Growth Playbook*. While the details of Sam Wilcox's journey with Terrafix is explored fully in Chapter 2, Figure 1-2 provides a snapshot of the principles, choices and decisions that guided him. Following the *Playbook* process, Sam and his team were able to craft a remarkable story of growth.

FIGURE 1-2

Terrafix Integrated Marketing Choices

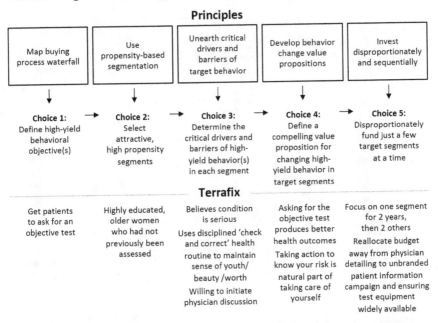

Principles
Map buying process waterfall	Use propensity-based segmentation	Unearth critical drivers and barriers of target behavior	Develop behavior change value propositions	Invest disproportionately and sequentially
Choice 1: Define high-yield behavioral objective(s)	**Choice 2:** Select attractive, high propensity segments	**Choice 3:** Determine the critical drivers and barriers of high-yield behavior(s) in each segment	**Choice 4:** Define a compelling value proposition for changing high-yield behavior in target segments	**Choice 5:** Disproportionately fund just a few target segments at a time

Terrafix

Get patients to ask for an objective test	Highly educated, older women who had not previously been assessed	Believes condition is serious. Uses disciplined 'check and correct' health routine to maintain sense of youth/ beauty /worth. Willing to initiate physician discussion	Asking for the objective test produces better health outcomes. Taking action to know your risk is natural part of taking care of yourself	Focus on one segment for 2 years, then 2 others. Reallocate budget away from physician detailing to unbranded patient information campaign and ensuring test equipment widely available

The path forward

The Organic Growth Playbook was refined over many years through hundreds of engagements with businesses in every type of B2B and B2C market. We checked in with clients six to twelve months after our work was completed to assess the impact on the company's growth. We asked a series of questions related to the comparison of actual sales results to projections before *The Organic Growth Playbook* was implemented. Wherever and whenever the *Playbook* principles were implemented, sales grew—on average by 1.5 to 2 times the prior rate of management's expectations. In some cases, the improvement was much more dramatic. Figure 1-3 provides a list of B2B and B2C companies—three of which we profile in this book (EnServ, Sparkle, Caesar)—and shows the variety of product types and range of growth improvements. Our key finding is that *The Organic Growth Playbook* works reliably. Much like American high jumper Dick Fosbury, who shattered records in 1965 by turning his back to the bar and flopping over it head first, our approach entails a fundamental flip in perspective and methodology, albeit one that incorporates and repurposes some important elements of the conventional approach.

FIGURE 1-3

Selected Results of Using the *Organic Growth Playbook*

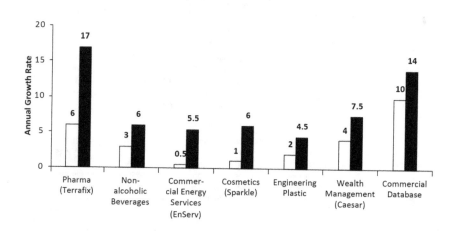

The rest of this book is structured around the principles and choices discussed above. The next section of the book, Chapters 2 through 10, covers four client stories and five principles. The client stories cover a range of products and industries and show how a business leader or team reignited growth for their product or service using the *Playbook* approach. Chapter 2 provides more detail on the challenges confronted by the Terrafix team and the choices they made. In Chapter 4, we describe the growth challenge of a B2B energy services company and how mapping their buying process led them to resegment the market in a unique and powerful way. In Chapter 6, we show how understanding the drivers and barriers to action for teenage girls experimenting with cosmetics products at the point of purchase proved to be the key to unlocking growth. Chapter 8 illustrates how a wealth management firm accelerated its growth by focusing on reducing the barriers that kept potential customers from investing with them.

Each story was chosen because it highlights one or more of the principles in an especially clear way and illustrates how the same system can be applied across very different product categories and industries. Each story is followed by a *theory* chapter, which describes the choices and principles in more detail and offers step-by-step guidance on how to implement the approach. The theory chapters also contain additional examples drawn from our work with different companies.

The final two chapters of the book focus on implementing the *Playbook*. We use Chapter 11 to share key lessons about how to get the most out of using the *Playbook* in different types of markets. In Chapter 12, we complete our journey by focusing on organizational roadblocks that we have observed across almost all of our client engagements. These roadblocks range from issues related to organizational structures (for example, organizational silos within firms), to human resource policies, to the systematic underfunding of market intelligence. For each of the roadblocks, we produce concrete recommendations that have been shown to be effective in practice.

While our objective is to explain the choices and principles that comprise the *Playbook* in a thorough and systematic way, we want to stress at the outset that the *Playbook* is an eminently learnable system. The concepts are easy to absorb, and the approach can be implemented by leaders in any organization. We trained our colleagues to deploy the approach around the world, and they in turn helped us train managers who could embed the system in many of the world's leading companies. Our reason for writing this book is to bring the tools that we've spent our careers developing and refining to a broader audience of managers in hopes that it can help them achieve the kinds of organizational and personal results we've seen so many others attain using this system.

Chapter 2

Terrafix: Reigniting Blockbuster Growth in Pharmaceuticals

Sam Wilcox recalled walking out of his plan review meeting for Terrafix feeling a little dazed. The drug he'd launched nearly three years before had gotten off to a terrific start. Revenues had reached $680 million the first year and grown 11 percent the following year. Since then, however, the rate of growth had dipped to 6 percent, and Sam found himself in the unenviable position of having to answer tough questions from senior managers about what went wrong and how he planned to make it right.

Terrafix was a breakthrough therapy with a new mechanism of action for treating a type of serious chronic condition that—like Type II diabetes, osteoporosis, or glaucoma—is largely asymptomatic until fairly late in the disease's progression. This asymptomatic disease (ASD) would often go undetected by patients and physicians until the patient suffered serious consequences that resulted in extensive medical complications. Terrafix offered physicians a new therapy that could halt or even reverse the progression of ASD—something prior treatments couldn't do.[13]

Sam had run a nearly perfect, textbook pharmaceutical launch that involved heavy investment in sales reps targeting high-prescribing doctors with a strong efficacy message (one claiming that Terrafix could be much more effective than their traditional prescriptions). Additionally, Sam had sponsored or been active at a number of important medical conferences and seminars, so he had generated support from several key influencers. He advertised heavily in well-known journals. Everything seemed on course to deliver the campaign's 15 percent annual growth rate targets.

By the time Sam met with members of the North American leadership team for the annual review meeting, however, it was clear that Terrafix was underperforming relative to growth expectations. The Director of Clinical

Operations presented data to the group showing that physicians weren't prescribing Terrafix as often as the incidence of the disease in the population would indicate. Tracking data showed that doctors were well aware of Terrafix's claimed benefits, but there was a clear gap between this awareness and their prescribing behavior. The management team questioned whether the somewhat cumbersome treatment regimen was deterring doctors from prescribing Terrafix or patients from sticking with it. The discussion of patients' attitudes then led the group to revive a fierce debate about whether the drug was one that would benefit from direct-to-consumer advertising.[14]

The discussion within Sam's team was different. Many advocated redoubling existing efforts to reach physicians with messages about the medicine's benefits. But the company's leadership made it clear that Sam would receive no additional marketing resources until, and unless, he could show more positive results. The information presented in the meeting about the relatively low prescription rate also gave Sam pause. At this point, he got in touch with us to help figure out what might be driving this pattern.

"We decided to take a step back from the problem to see if we could figure out why potential patients weren't receiving a prescription," said Sam. "For the first time, we took a really comprehensive look at the decisions and actions that patients and physicians were taking at every stage of the process."

The buying process and high-yield behavior change

As we dug into the analysis with the Terrafix team, it became clear that we needed to pay attention to a much wider set of activities and behaviors involving both patients and physicians. These behaviors included not only the doctor's decision to prescribe Terrafix, but also the whole chain of actions upstream of that prescription decision, including a review of how patients interacted with the healthcare system in general (Figure 2-1). Mapping the choices of patients through their buying process revealed some unexpected findings.

When the disease was advanced—and harder to treat—both patients and physicians might spot visible symptoms, and diagnosis could occur through symptom-specific examinations and tests. This is represented as Path A in Figure 2-1. However, throughout most of the progression of this disease, there were no visible signs. So, if it was diagnosed at all, it came about through doctors asking patients pointed questions. This sequence is represented as Path B.

FIGURE 2-1

ASD Buying Process (Simplified)

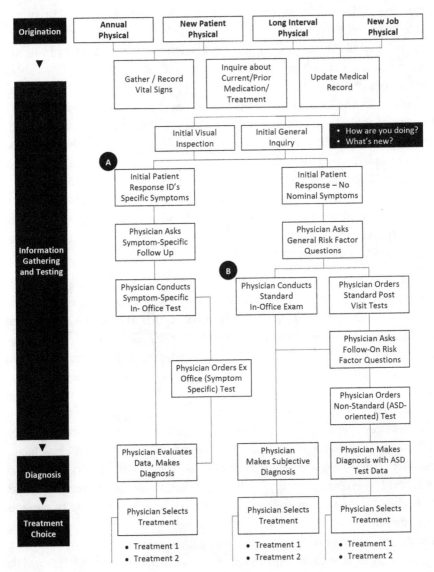

Actually Sam's research indicated that Path B consisted of three basic diagnostic paths: patients received no evaluation or diagnosis, patients were subjectively evaluated for risk factors using their responses to physician questions, or doctors performed an objective test for ASD in addition to assessing for risk factors. The no evaluation path occurred 35 percent of the time. Stated differently, in one-third of all physicals, the physician simply made no attempt to diagnose ASD at all. Most other annual visits—about 50 percent of all physicals—followed the risk factor only path, where physicians reached a diagnosis relying solely on the patient's answers to questions about risk factors. Based on this information, physicians would diagnose patients as not at risk for the disease, at risk, or as having the disease. Finally, in 15 percent of annual physicals, doctors asked the full set of risk factor questions and ordered a newly developed screening test (Figure 2-2). In this situation, doctors didn't make their diagnosis in the examination room, but rather waited until they received the results of the test. Based on the results, patients were again diagnosed as not at risk, at risk, or having the disease. However, using the test meant the diagnosis was made with a much higher degree of certainty and accuracy.

"What we found was pretty surprising," said Sam. "Not only were very few people getting the test that would tell them for sure what their risk was, but more than a third weren't getting any kind of regular assessment at all. Given the overall prevalence of the disease, it was pretty likely that some of these patients were actually at risk, so a lot of folks who might have benefitted from Terrafix were actually dropping out of the process because they weren't being screened."

Two striking facts about physicians' behavior emerged from this analysis. The first was that the diagnosis depended greatly on which path the doctor followed. When doctors relied solely on the patient's answers to the risk factor questions, they diagnosed 85 percent of patients as not at risk, 5 percent as at risk, and 10 percent as having the disease. When doctors had access to results from the objective test as well as risk factor data, only 41 percent of patients were determined to be not at risk, while 21 percent were diagnosed as at risk, and 38 percent were determined as having the disease.

It became clear that subjective disease evaluation (using risk factor data alone) was very inaccurate. More than half of the patients who were judged as not at risk were receiving the wrong diagnosis. The rate of patients who were

FIGURE 2-2

Quantified Paths through ASD Buying Process

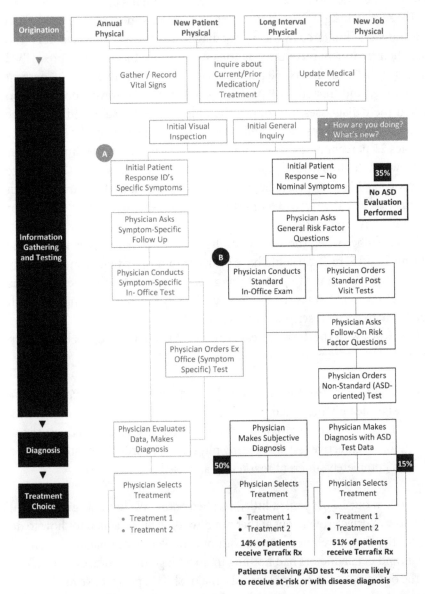

at risk or had the disease was nearly four times higher when doctors used the objective test rather than subjective disease evaluation. In the absence of definitive data about the presence or progression of the disease, physicians tended to be conservative about diagnosing or treating the condition. As Sam noted, "It turned out that without the objective test, doctors couldn't really know whether they were diagnosing or treating patients properly!"

The second insight from the analysis was that treatment recommendations were dramatically altered by the type of diagnostic data available. Doctors who based their treatment recommendations strictly on subjective data prescribed changes in diet and exercise 58 percent of the time, other therapies 28 percent of the time, and Terrafix 14 percent of the time. However, doctors who reached their diagnoses using both the objective test results and subjective data prescribed changes in diet and exercise only 24 percent of the time, other therapies 25 percent of the time, and Terrafix 51 percent of the time. In other words, when doctors actually *knew* the extent of the disease, they were more than twice as likely to prescribe medication as compared to changes in diet and exercise, and they were 3.6 times as likely to prescribe Terrafix than when they didn't have that data.

"I remember when the survey results came in, when we saw this for the first time," said Sam. "You could have heard a pin drop in that room. It quickly became obvious that the thing that was going to give us the most leverage was to get every patient to take the test, because if they did, they were much, much more likely to get a prescription for Terrafix."

Our work with the Terrafix team on the ASD buying process brought up two points:

- Changes to just one or two high-yield behaviors were likely to drive significantly increased numbers of prescriptions and revenue growth.
- Targeting those high-yield behaviors—namely, getting patients to ask for an objective test and getting physicians to order the test—required a completely different marketing approach.

"That's when our hearts sank a little," recalled Sam. "We had this great insight about how to drive growth, but at that point we didn't have a plan for how to do that. All the things we'd been doing with our marketing campaign to promote benefits and detail doctors had nothing to do with getting more tests done."

The outcome of the analysis forced a major shift in perspective for Sam and his team. Even with the data in front of them, refocusing efforts from driving a specific outcome (doctors writing more prescriptions for Terrafix) toward changing the behaviors occurring at an earlier stage in the buying process (ordering the objective test) wasn't going to be easy. While the team believed that targeting those particular activities to produce desired behaviors would drive the desired outcomes, they had focused nearly all their efforts since launching the drug on communicating product benefits to physicians. In this respect, Sam's team was no different than the overwhelming majority of pharmaceutical marketing teams at the time. Concentrating on upstream behaviors—rather than product branding—ran counter to conventional industry wisdom.

The team articulated two concise behavioral objectives: get patients to ask their primary care physician (PCP) for the objective test instead of waiting to receive a recommendation from their doctor, and get PCPs to order the objective test for ASD instead of performing no evaluation or only a subjective evaluation based on risk factors. If achieved, the behavioral objectives would encourage more patients to take the objective test and stop the high drop out that was occurring during the current buying process. As noted earlier, 35 percent of patients regularly received no ASD evaluation at all during annual physicals and thus dropped off the path that might lead to a Terrafix prescription. Growing the overall market by encouraging these patients to get tested could, of course, benefit Terrafix's competitors as well. However, the analysis showed Terrafix stood to gain disproportionately from this change in behavior.

Additionally, increasing the rate of objective screening would lead to more accurate diagnoses of both patients at risk and those who already had the disease but were asymptomatic. Armed with the definitive data provided by the objective test, physicians were apt to prescribe Terrafix at much higher rates. It's worth noting that Sam's team didn't entirely drop its efforts to convince physicians that Terrafix was the best treatment option for actual or suspected ASD patients. What they now understood, however, was that this marketing objective should be secondary to their efforts to get doctors to request the objective test because this was the behavior change that yielded the best results.

Rethinking segmentation

Shifting their focus to high-yield behaviors required the team to rethink their whole approach to marketing and sales, including how they defined and segmented the market. As Sam noted, "In the past, we'd basically segmented the market the same way most of our competitors did. We looked for those doctors who tended to write a lot of prescriptions. That's essentially how we defined a good customer and we spent a lot of our time and resources on getting our messages about the benefits of Terrafix to them through multiple channels. This old segmentation wasn't going to work for us anymore. The question we now needed to answer was, which patients and PCPs are most, or least, likely to ask for the test and to order it?"

To activate the behavioral objectives, the Terrafix team needed to find customers based on their propensity to engage in the desired behaviors. To do this, they researched a number of observable patient attributes that, taken together, correlated with their willingness to ask for the test. "We knew that not every patient would be equally easy to convince to talk to their doctors about getting a test," Sam recalled, "so we wanted to make sure we focused our efforts and limited resources on groups of patients where we thought we had the best chance of success." In addition to looking at characteristics that indicated which patients might be good candidates for Terrafix—for example, patients at higher risk for ASD based on their age or gender—the team also sought to identify attributes related to the desired buying process behavior in order to more precisely segment the patient population. The research they conducted suggested that a patient's level of education, age, and gender were good proxies for how comfortable the patient was about proactively asking for a test, as well as how interested and knowledgeable they were about their own health. The team also found that whether a patient had previously received an ASD test influenced how likely they were to ask for a new ASD test. Using these variables, they resegmented patients with a focus on differences related to the behavioral objective (Figure 2-3).[15]

They found that women between the ages of 55 and 64 who were previously unassessed for ASD and had four or more years of post-high school education were the most likely to ask their doctors for the test. By contrast, younger women with a high school education or less were much less likely to do so. As a result, the team chose to focus on highly educated older women as their target segment for the new marketing campaign. Although this wasn't the largest segment in terms of numbers of patients, the team believed that the messages and media mix selected for this group would also resonate with other nearby segments—such as women who were over sixty-five and had more than four years of education.

FIGURE 2-3

Patient Segmentation

All Patients in Target Age Group 53MM	UNASSESSED			NOT AT RISK			AT RISK			WITH DISEASE		
	College or More	Some College	High School or Less	College or More	Some College	High School or Less	College or More	Some College	High School or Less	College or More	Some College	High School or Less
<55 Years Old F	**Segment G** Unassessed Better Educated 50–54 **15% / 35%**		Segment A 3% / 10%		Segment B 10% / 12%							
55–59 Years Old F	–Target– Unassessed Better Educated 55–64 9% / 45%							Segment C 9% / 14%				
60–64 Years Old F		**Segment I** Unassessed Less Educated 55–64 **10% /38%**										
			Segment J Assessed without Test Better Educated 55–64 Years Old 8% / 35%				Assessed with Test Better Educated 55–64 Years Old 7% /18%			Segment E 3% / 18%		
65+ Years Old M												
F	**Segment H** Unassessed Better Educated 65+ **6% / 40%**							Segment D 12% / 13%			Segment F 10% / 27%	

Key: **Size of segment** / *Propensity to ask for a test*
Grey boxes are spillover/secondary segments

Since the team's second behavioral objective focused on getting PCPs to order the test, they also created a physician segmentation that sought to differentiate doctors based on their willingness to engage in the desired behavior.[16]

The team put the behavioral objectives at the heart of its new segmentation. This enabled them to identify patients who were more likely to respond to a new campaign directed at encouraging doctors and patients to use the test.

"This was a very different approach for us in thinking about how we segmented the market," said Sam. "Focusing on the behavioral objectives, we came up with some nonobvious groupings of doctors and patients we wished to reach. However, now that we knew who we wanted to target, we had to understand what we could do that would be most effective in changing their behaviors."

Drivers and barriers to behavior change

Once again, Sam's team had to try to understand something it knew little about: what caused a patient or doctor to ask for (or not ask for) an objective test. Using the framework we provided them, they took a look at three factors that shaped patients' and doctors' thinking: beliefs and attitudes they already had about the disease and its treatments, the situation or context they believed they were in, and how they defined a desirable outcome in that situation. The framework helped the team create two main outputs: a concise customer narrative describing the target segment and a list of drivers of, and barriers to, the desired behavior. The customer narrative was different from most conventional customer narratives that focus on a day in the life of the customer to elucidate their needs and wants. Rather, the narrative focused specifically on the behaviors that Sam and his team sought to change and the customer's thought process related to these behaviors (Figure 2-4).[17]

The set of drivers and barriers (Figure 2-5) was essentially a summary of key insights that emerged from this detailed narrative. Drivers were the psychological and physical factors that, if reinforced, could encourage patients in the target segment to ask their doctors for the test. Barriers were obstacles— also psychological or physical—that stood in the way of this desired behavior.

Several behavior drivers related to the target segment's desire to maintain their youthful appearance, which they believed as enhanced by a proactive, "stay healthy" routine. On the other hand, many of those in the target segment associated the disease with frailty related to aging. Since these women didn't

FIGURE 2-4

Customer Narrative for Target Patient Segment

This woman is in her early sixties. Health has become an increasingly important aspect of her life. This stems, in large part, from the fact that she and her husband recently retired. She wants to be healthy so that the two of them can enjoy all of the activities they have been planning to do for so long, like traveling and visiting family. However, being healthy also has important implications for her self-esteem . . . it makes her feel younger and causes others to see her that way too. Therefore, she is highly motivated about caring for her health. She makes sure to do all the "right" things, like eating well, taking vitamins, and getting enough sleep. She visits her primary care physician — a General Practitioner — nearly three times a year and gets a general check up, as well as a mammogram, pap smear, and cholesterol exam on a regular basis. She views her doctor as a primary source of health care information and thus is more willing than other women to initiate discussions about symptoms with her doctor.

Although this patient is better educated, she doesn't feel she is especially knowledgeable about ASD (in actuality, she knows more than she realizes). It's not something that runs in her family, nor does she believe she has symptoms of the condition. That's not to say that she wouldn't be concerned about ASD if she developed it. She knows it's a disease than can cause serious health problems over the long term. But, at her age, it's really not something she believes she needs to worry about. What's more, she is confident that if she keeps taking good care of herself, eating right and exercising regularly, she does not really need to be too concerned about developing ASD.

At this point, this woman has no experience with ASD testing. She and her doctor have not discussed it (presumably, the fact that she doesn't have any specific risk factors is a key reason why her doctor has not suggested testing) nor has she had an actual test. She is not opposed to the test but already has a crowded health care regimen. She would certainly agree to undergo testing if she or her doctor felt it was necessary (and, of course, the procedure was covered by her insurance). However, up to this point, there hasn't been any real reason for her to consider it.

FIGURE 2-5

Drivers and Barriers to Desired Behaviors

Drivers for Asking for ASD Test	Barriers to Asking for ASD Test
• Staying healthy is key to feeling younger and being seen that way by others • Feels that she is as responsible as her doctor for making sure she gets tested for potential health issues regularly • Feels it is her responsibility to initiate discussion about health issues with her doctor • Believes that ASD is a serious condition and should be addressed	• No obvious symptoms or risk factors • Believes she is too young to suffer from ASD • Wants to believe that an absence of symptoms means that she is not at risk • Has a crowded health care regime, i.e., does a lot of tests and activities • ASD test requires additional/special visit and cost

consider themselves old, there was some resistance to thinking about their own risk for ASD. To address this resistance, the team needed to create a greater sense of urgency about the risks of ASD. The team's goal became to develop messaging that motivated this segment to action without triggering some of the fears and stigmas associated with the condition. "We used these customer narratives to help us understand what actions we could take that would be most effective with these customers. In this case," said Sam, "we found that we could have the greatest impact by helping people overcome some of the things that stood in the way of getting tested. So that's where we invested."

Behavior change value proposition

The team found that linking ASD testing to a disciplined routine of other positive health behaviors could be effective in motivating the desired behaviors of this target segment. In particular, they leveraged this segment's long-held belief that taking care of one's health helped maintain or improve one's looks. Specifically, the team leveraged existing attitudes about early detection of silent killers—a mindset that had been nurtured by earlier marketing campaigns related to cholesterol and heart disease in which people were urged to "know your number"—in other words, take a cholesterol test to learn your number. Terrafix tapped into this belief system by making the case that women should take an objective scientific test to understand their ASD status, just as they had to learn their cholesterol numbers.

The team took a similar approach to motivating physicians to order the test. They found that doctors typically didn't realize the extent to which the disease was being underdiagnosed due to the use of subjective risk-factor screening questions alone. Presenting doctors with underdiagnosis data and information about more accurate results that could be obtained from an objective test helped support the message that cutting-edge physicians who wanted to do the right thing for patients should order the test. The company also worked with medical associations to develop new testing protocols that established objective diagnostic testing as the gold standard of care.

In addition, the team recognized that a number of basic factors needed to be put in place to incentivize the right behaviors. For example, practical impediments to ordering or taking an ASD test (a limited number of testing locations) threatened to nullify the effectiveness of the team's new behavioral messaging. To address the issue, they mapped out both patient and physician journeys to look for areas where they could facilitate uptake of testing. Importantly, not all of these touchpoints were under their direct control.

Their analysis identified four major testing impediments that made it more difficult for physicians to prescribe Terrafix. When they first launched the drug, the diagnostic equipment needed to perform an objective test for ASD was available in only fifty or so teaching hospitals in the United States. Sam's team began working with the manufacturer of the testing equipment on multiple fronts to expand availability. These initiatives were highly successful. Over a three-year period, testing became available at several thousand sites across the country, to the point where 90 percent of the country's population could conveniently access a testing site. Next, the team worked with hospitals to increase the supply of technicians who could operate the testing equipment. Finally, at $100 to $200 per test, the price was a barrier for many patients. Getting the test covered by insurance would make doctors more likely to order it and meant more patients could have it covered by insurance. The company therefore began a concerted campaign to convince payers (insurance companies, and so on) that it was in their interest to cover these tests because more accurate and earlier diagnosis and treatment would lead to better health outcomes and lower costs in the long run.

Finally, one of the subtler barriers to doctors' willingness to order the ASD test for patients was their lack of familiarity with how to interpret the standard output from those tests. The Terrafix team worked with key professional associations to set up a working group to create an easy-to-understand index of a patient's ASD status based on testing data.

Disproportionate investment

"We now had a very clear view about how to get these doctors and patients to get the test and the things we could do to encourage these behaviors. Even then," said Sam, "it wasn't a simple matter to get everyone to agree on how to invest our marketing dollars. We were so used to spreading our marketing spend across a bunch of different things to promote the brand. It was all good stuff to do, at the margins, but we knew it wasn't going to give us the growth we were looking for. We had to stop doing some things to do the more important things. And, of course, no one is happy to see you when you're coming to tell them that you're taking budget away from some initiative they care about."

The team shifted the bulk of its marketing resources toward an unbranded campaign designed to encourage the target patient segment to engage in the desired behavior—getting the ASD test. Again, this approach was a radical departure from the team's intensive, product-centered branding efforts of the past. They split the rest of the resources between a revamped campaign aimed at getting high propensity doctors to understand and order the test, and to working with test equipment makers, insurers, and medical associations to bring down barriers to testing.

Interestingly, Sam and his team actually decreased their overall marketing spend due to the precise focus of their campaign. They sequenced their approach, focusing their efforts first on older women who were likely to ask for the test, and physician segments identified as most likely to prescribe the test. Over time, as these new behaviors took hold and programs were rolled out to reduce physical barriers, such as the lack of testing equipment, the campaign was expanded to secondary segments as well.

Epilogue

Figure 2-6 summarizes the five *Playbook* principles and the specific choices made by Sam's team. As a result of the team's targeted marketing efforts, the volume of ASD tests drove an 18 percent increase in prescriptions for Terrafix the first year, 30 percent the second year, and 40 percent the third year. In turn, sales increased more than 50 percent over 3 years, resulting in over $400 million higher annual revenues, even as the marketing spend was reduced by $15 million. "After scrapping our entire launch strategy and actually spending less money on this new campaign, I suppose I should have been feeling a little nervous," remarked Sam. "The truth is, I knew it would work. Why? Because we believed the data from mapping the buying process. It told us clearly what the high-yield behaviors were and what we could expect from changing them. Everything else we did was connected, link by link, to that insight."

FIGURE 2-6

Summary of Terrafix Choices

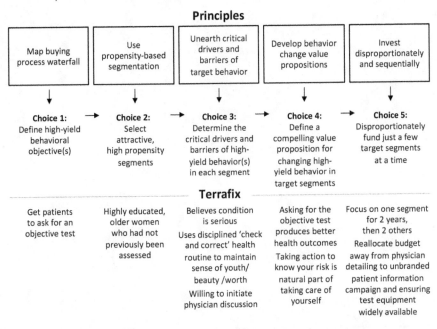

Principles

Map buying process waterfall	Use propensity-based segmentation	Unearth critical drivers and barriers of target behavior	Develop behavior change value propositions	Invest disproportionately and sequentially

Choice 1: Define high-yield behavioral objective(s)	**Choice 2:** Select attractive, high propensity segments	**Choice 3:** Determine the critical drivers and barriers of high-yield behavior(s) in each segment	**Choice 4:** Define a compelling value proposition for changing high-yield behavior in target segments	**Choice 5:** Disproportionately fund just a few target segments at a time

Terrafix

Get patients to ask for an objective test	Highly educated, older women who had not previously been assessed	Believes condition is serious Uses disciplined 'check and correct' health routine to maintain sense of youth/ beauty /worth Willing to initiate physician discussion	Asking for the objective test produces better health outcomes Taking action to know your risk is natural part of taking care of yourself	Focus on one segment for 2 years, then 2 others Reallocate budget away from physician detailing to unbranded patient information campaign and ensuring test equipment widely available

Chapter 3

First Principle: Map the Buying Process Waterfall

The pivot point in our Terrafix case study was when Sam Wilcox decided to reexamine his go-to-market strategy despite pressure to make quick, traditional changes. In particular, his reanalysis demonstrated that the biggest source of growth for Terrafix would result from the treatment of undiagnosed or misdiagnosed patients—an approach that would actually increase the size of the patient population. More importantly, Sam uncovered something that had previously gone unnoticed: the behavior with the most influence on growing the category was the doctor's decision to use an objective test. This choice occurred early in the prescription process. When doctors determined— through use of an objective test—that a patient had ASD, they were much more likely to prescribe Terrafix than if they made the same diagnosis subjectively.

Sam's decision to switch from traditional marketing (asking doctors to prescribe Terrafix) to a more targeted, upstream campaign in which doctors and patients were encouraged to make a key behavior change (ask for the test) led to a *doubling* of Terrafix's growth rate with a significant reduction in marketing and sales spend. Most doctors already believed Terrafix was the superior treatment. What boosted their willingness to prescribe the drug was the certainty provided by the results of the objective, disease-positive test.

This story illustrates the strategic importance of our first *Playbook* principle: *map the buying process waterfall* to focus on a few high-yield behaviors. It also shows the need to identify and influence high-yield input behaviors in addition to output behaviors in the buying process. *Output behaviors* express customers' decisions to purchase or exit the buying process. A high-yield output behavior is one that, if changed, produces the most growth for a product or service. In Sam's campaign, a doctor prescribing Terrafix was the high-yield output behavior. *Input behaviors*, on the other hand, are buying activities or decisions that lead to the desired, high-yield output behavior. Convincing doctors to conduct the objective test and having patients ask their doctors for the test were the input behaviors with the highest probability of getting those patients properly diagnosed. By focusing his marketing campaign on this high-yield behavior change, Sam set in motion a sequence of actions that drove significant revenue growth.

Conventional wisdom

For decades, marketers have been taught that customer behavior can be captured and understood using a simple, linear, four-stage model:

- Customers with a need are made *aware* of potentially relevant products.
- Customers *consider* the relative merits of those products.
- Customers *purchase* one of the products.
- Customers *try* the purchased product.

In some versions of the model there's a fifth stage, in which customers *repeat* purchase the product. Given this model, the conventional wisdom held that the job of marketers and the salesforce was to develop and execute plans that ushered the customer through each stage.[18] Marketers ensured that potential customers became aware of their product, convinced them to make the product part of their consideration set, and persistently asked them to purchase the product.

This traditional awareness-consideration-purchase-trial-(repeat) model was the template for Sam's team when they drew up the launch plan for Terrafix. Early on, they spent heavily on creating awareness using every possible channel and approach, from sponsoring conferences and trade advertising to distributing top-of-mind collateral (branded pens, prescription pads, and so on). Although this awareness spending tapered off later in the campaign, Sam still spent a good portion of his budget on it. He also spent a lot of time and money trying to ensure that doctors had Terrafix in their consideration set. For this, he used a wide range of channels and materials to present them with data explaining what Terrafix did and convincing them it was better than competitive drugs. Finally, Sam funded a big, steady push by the Terrafix salesforce—having them call on doctors multiple times each month and asking doctors to prescribe Terrafix instead of other therapies.

The plan was less effective than it could have been, and eventually stalled because the traditional model behind it was flawed in two ways. First, the traditional model emphasizes the *stages* of the customer-purchase process above the activity within each stage. This led Sam's team to spend a lot of time and money on each stage as they tried to usher doctors along to the next one. It's a phenomenon we've seen many times. We call it *peanut butter marketing* because teams tend to spread their marketing and sales dollars across the whole process—even worse, across all the possible activities and channels within each stage.[19]

In fact, a customer's progress through any buying process is *path dependent*. Certain stages and activities are significantly more important than others. As we'll describe later in this chapter, what a customer learns or does in one activity can strongly impact what they seek to learn or do in the next. This means that the odds of a customer purchasing a particular product are disproportionately affected by which activity or information they experience early in their purchasing journey. In the Terrafix case study, doctors who ordered an objective diagnostic test followed a different path through the buying process and ended up making a different purchase decision than those who didn't order the test. The Terrafix story demonstrates how some parts of the purchase process—both stages and activities—matter more than others. Marketing and sales plans need to recognize this reality.

The traditional model's second flaw is that it's highly abstract and inward oriented. The stages are high-level labels for complex and essentially unobservable processes or states of a customer's mind. We have a lot of sympathy for marketing teams that flounder when asked to make customers aware of their products, because it's not at all clear what awareness is, or what's involved in achieving it. Moreover, the stages in the traditional model more accurately reflect what businesses *wish* customers were thinking and doing (being aware and considering their product) instead of describing what customers actually *do*. In short, the traditional model isn't an accurate depiction of how customers—in the Terrafix case, doctors—discover, evaluate, and choose products. This makes the traditional marketing model a poor guide for selecting media, channels, messages, and so on (see "The Limits of the Traditional Buying Process").

The Limits of the Traditional Buying Process

While the traditional model still thrives in the business world, academics have begun to address its shortcomings. For example, most current models advocate a five-stage process: problem recognition, information search, evaluation of alternatives, purchase decision, and post purchase behavior.[20] This more recent characterization is considerably more activity- and customer-oriented than the traditional model.[21] However, it still assumes that the stages and activities within each stage are independent of one another, indicating that businesses must continue to devote significant resources to ushering customers from one stage to the next. As the Terrafix story demonstrates, this approach can be expensive, wasteful, and unproductive.

The *Playbook* approach:
Map the buying process waterfall

While traditional marketing plans appear to diversify risk by spreading money across several segments, sources of growth, and phases of the buying process, in actuality they can be riskier. Because these plans don't focus resources on specific behaviors that produce the highest economic returns, they not only waste resources but also can mask information about the few activities that are driving growth. As the Terrafix case study illustrates, when a company possesses evidence-based knowledge about customer behavior (not just attitudes or motivation), it can focus its marketing firepower more efficiently and effectively.

Our view is that commercial plans should be designed to induce high-yield behavior changes in a customer's buying process. This can be accomplished only by taking a deep dive into the entire buying process—and quantitatively identifying the drop-off points in the buying process waterfall. Specific changes in customer behavior—such as getting a patient to ask for a test instead of simply answering a doctor's questions—should be the *golden thread* running throughout all go-to-market plans. These golden threads should be the basis for segmentation and the subsequent campaign within chosen target segments. When marketing campaigns are designed this way, the identification of high-yield behaviors *precedes* segmentation. Thus, the targeted high-yield behavior change becomes a critical consideration in designing offers, communications, and promotions.

What characteristics determine a high-yield behavior?

Three specific characteristics determine a high-yield behavior. First, *the behavior occurs relatively early in the buying process and strongly shapes what customers do later or whether they stay in the process at all.* For instance, a mother going into a sporting goods store will see a different selection of winter coat brands than she would at a department store. If she goes to just one retailer, that initial choice of where to shop strongly shapes what she will eventually purchase. In the financial sector, by contrast, the critical high-yield behavior is getting people to schedule a *second* appointment with a financial advisor or revisit the company's website. A large percentage of people who are notionally interested in financial planning simply don't reach out. Sometimes they find the first interaction with a financial planner so intimidating they never go back. However, once they're over the hump and decide to visit the planner or site a second time, the odds of a purchase increase substantially. Clearly, certain activities that are early in a buying process can have profound effects on purchase outcomes.

Second, *the behavior is linked to a source of growth that disproportionately benefits a given company versus its competitors.* Generally, the value of potential sources of growth—increasing share, reducing the rate of share loss, increasing share of wallet, and/or bringing new customers into a category— depends on the company's strategic positioning. For example, a company with a high market share and strong distribution coverage is likely to benefit more than others from inducing behavior changes that increase the rate of new customers entering their category. All else being equal, the company with high market share is more likely to capture a disproportionate share of new category revenue. Conversely, a company lacking strong distribution channels, high market share, or visibility would waste money trying to influence category entry. For this type of company, leading customers to change suppliers might be a more valuable behavior change.

Companies can benefit even more if identified behaviors orient customers toward types of purchase behaviors that are more strategically valuable to the company than to its competitors. For example, in industries with high customer-acquisition costs, companies might seek to grow by cross-selling new services and products to existing customers. This may involve inducing customers to change their behavior regarding the channels they use to gather information about these additional offerings as well as purchase them. For example, Vistaprint successfully used its offer of free, customized business cards to acquire customers through its website and display a range of linked offerings, from checkbooks to personalized coffee mugs to small-business websites.

Third, *the behavior is one that the company believes it's capable of altering for a reasonable return on investment.* Some customer activities early in the buying process may have profound influence on later purchase decisions but are simply too difficult or expensive to reach. This return on the investment assessment is a crucial component of targeting the right high-yield behaviors.

These three characteristics determine whether a behavior change is high yield. Before we explain the detailed methods for identifying and selecting high-yield behavior changes, it's worth briefly foreshadowing segmentation, which we'll cover in Chapter 5. Once the high-yield behavior change was identified for physicians in the Terrafix buying process—conducting the objective test for ASD—it became important to ask, "Which physicians are more likely to conduct the objective test?" This simple question enabled Sam's team to consider important variables for segmenting the market. Targeted behavioral changes and segmentation choices are thus tightly linked, not independent, choices. This is also the reason you must start this process by identifying high-yield behaviors in the buying process. Sorting customers based on their propensity to engage in targeted behaviors often leads to unique and nonobvious segmentation schemes. Thus, logically, the buying process analysis must come prior to market segmentation.[22]

The first principle explained

To understand why high-yield behaviors matter so much, we first need a way to see and measure what really happens during the purchase journey. We capture and structure that information through a buying process diagram. The diagram lists all the activities performed and decisions made by any customer from the moment a need surfaces in the customer's mind until the product is purchased (or not purchased). These activities and decisions are arrayed in the sequence(s) of their occurrence. We then overlay this information on the diagram, capturing the frequency with which those activities and decisions occur—both absolutely and contingent upon an earlier activity occurring. With that data in hand, we can now readily isolate high-yield behaviors by mapping a buying process waterfall diagram. While the waterfall is discussed in more detail below, the quantification enables one to isolate behaviors that may represent high leverage opportunities. To illustrate how a buying process diagram works and show how this diagram can help identify high-yield behaviors, let's examine the buying process for wine in the United States (Figure 3-1).

What catches the eye about Figure 3-1 is how busy and crowded it is, even for what would be considered a relatively straightforward purchase. Even with so many elements, there's a structure to effective buying process diagrams. The diagram is organized sequentially, with the earliest activities and decisions at the top and the last activities and decisions (actual purchase behaviors) at the bottom.[23] As you can see, a customer's wine buying process starts with activities or events that originate, or trigger, the buying process. The customer then proceeds through stages involving research, channel selection, and channel visits, and then ends in the selection of a variety or brand of wine to buy.

Note that both input and output behaviors are listed. Remember, input behaviors influence a decision to buy or not buy. For wine, these activities might include hiring a catering company, talking with friends, looking at published wine rankings, checking current wine inventory at home, or having an internal mental process ("I feel like shopping for wine today"). Output behaviors express a customer's decision to purchase or exit the buying process. Because customers can exit anytime, such behaviors are listed at every stage. Purchase, on the other hand, happens only at the end of the process. Purchase behaviors should record the various ways purchases can occur, because each has different consequences for a company's growth. A customer's purchase, for example, may be a repeat buy (same amount of product/brand for same use) or an expansion buy (same product/brand intended for new uses). Or it may represent a switching behavior whereby a customer purchases a new brand.

The activities in the diagram are typically grouped by their stage or phase in the buying process. These stages are indicated by the labels on the left side of Figure 3-1. The stages reflect different sets of customer activities that we found customers use for a similar purpose and that happen more or less at the same time.

FIGURE 3-1

General Buying Process for Wine (for Personal/Home Use)

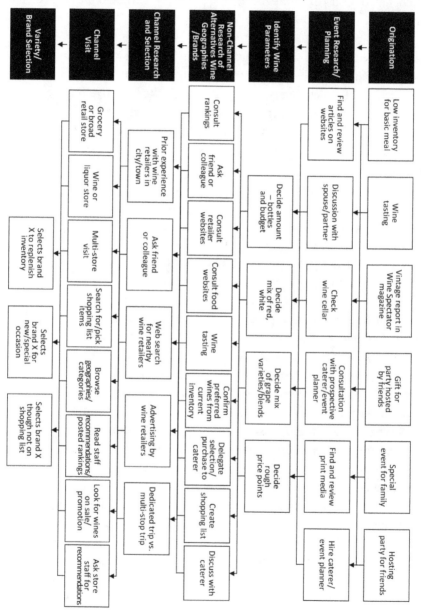

For example, the non-channel research stage includes such diverse activities as attending wine tastings at a store, talking to friends, reading articles on websites dedicated to wine, and reading articles in newspapers or magazines. The stages group together sets of important activities that customers perform. Few customers do all of them, because most are just different ways of getting the same thing done. The stage groupings are therefore somewhat artificial but should reflect the breadth of activities that are unique to particular markets and industries. Except in a few business-to-business markets, customers don't consciously break their buying processes into explicit, distinct phases. Despite their limitations, the stage groupings are valuable. Visually highlighting activities that share a purpose and occur at the same time helps reveal the essence of what's going on and where marketing intervention might be valuable.

The structure of good buying process diagrams also allows us to track and measure how customers typically *flow* through them. Conceptually, there are thousands of ways customers could work through the buying process for wine. At the extreme, each customer could follow a distinct sequence, or path, through the diagram, like the balls in a classic pinball machine do. In reality, there are a limited number of distinct buying pathways used by the majority of customers in a market. Our experience suggests that fewer than ten pathways capture more than 90 percent of customer journeys. For the wine discussion, we'll isolate two such common pathways (Figures 3-2 and 3-3). Moreover, customers perform some activities and follow certain paths more frequently than others. It's the path dependency and uneven frequency of behaviors in the buying process that create opportunities to find and exploit high-yield behaviors for accelerated growth.

Buying processes tend to be path dependent because a customer's actions at an upstream stage will point that customer toward a specific action in the next stage. For example, if a wine purchaser notices that they have low inventory of everyday wine at home, they tend to follow this inventory assessment with a discussion with their spouse/partner. However, if a buyer is purchasing for a special family occasion, they next tend to calculate the number of wine bottles needed for the event. Ultimately, upstream actions can have a huge impact on the probability of a purchase or what kind of purchase the consumer might make—a repeat brand purchase versus a switch to higher-end brand, for example. Consider the significantly different buying pathways associated with a buyer of vintage wines for long-term cellaring or investment versus a consumer who is replenishing their inventory of everyday wine. In Figure 3-2, the vintage buyer pathway could be triggered by the consumer reading about a new vintage in *Wine Spectator* magazine. After this first upstream action, the consumer might check his or her wine cellar to see if this wine would fill a need. This is followed by multiple research activities: wine tastings, looking at specialist websites, and perhaps consulting other friends who know wine. If this research reveals that the new wine doesn't pass certain screens, this stage might encourage an exit from the purchasing journey. On the other hand, if the new wine passes these screening and research activities, there's likely to

be a store visit and purchase. For this consumer, confirming evidence from multiple websites and respected critics may be the key lever that influences whether and where later activities occur.

For the replenishment of everyday wine, the buying process is markedly different. Path dependency may be determined largely by evaluation of product and channel price points. Unlike a wine enthusiast, the average consumer isn't triggered by news of a new vintage, nor does this consumer's purchase journey involve deep research into the product itself through specialist sites. Instead, product research activity takes second place to channel research and evaluation. The consumer tries to identify a channel that will offer the best prices for acceptable wines by comparing prices and promotions across retailer websites, drawing on past impressions of price levels from visits to channels for other reasons, and so on. Indeed, what's striking about Figure 3-3 is how little overlap there is with the activities in Figure 3-2.

FIGURE 3-2

Buying Path for Vintage/Investment Wines

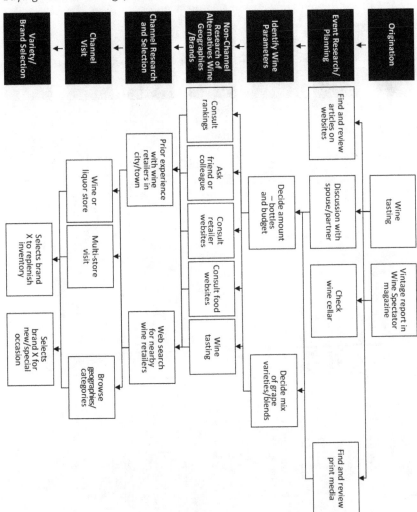

FIGURE 3-3

Buying Path for Replenishing Everyday Wine Inventory

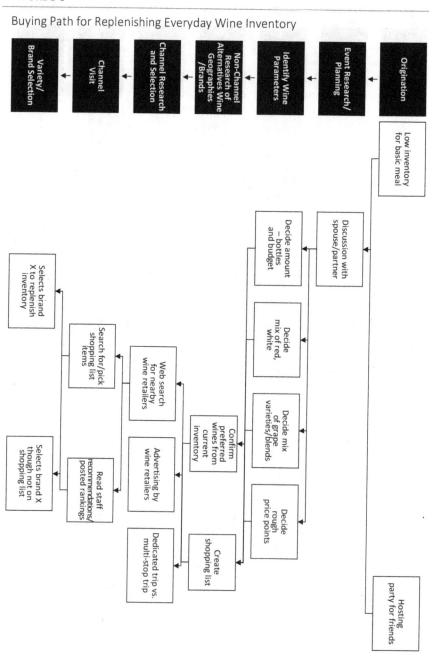

There are three different ways to quantify the frequencies of buying process activities; each is important in its own way. One way is stage frequency, which shows what percentage of customers who entered each stage through some origination activity were still active at a later stage in the purchase process. For instance, of all the customers who had a reason to buy wine, 80 percent eventually proceeded to the stage of identifying wine parameters, while only 40 percent of the original number reached the channel visit stage. Stage quantification reveals that the drop off can be considerable between stages as customers exit the buying process. It can also be highly uneven. For example, as shown on the right side of Figure 3-4, there's a 5 percent drop in the number of customers remaining in the buying process as they move from identifying wine parameters to non-channel brand research. However, there's a 35 percent drop in those consumers moving to channel research.

A second way to quantify a buying process is within-stage frequency. This is the frequency with which customers who participate in any given stage of the buying process perform an activity involved in that stage. Thus, of those customers who made it to the channel-visit stage, 80 percent visited a wine or specialty liquor store, whereas only 20 percent visited a grocery or retail outlet. This data is important during the construction of the media-mix stage of the analysis. As you might expect, these frequency patterns within a stage vary markedly depending on which pathways a customer follows. Note that the percentages across an individual stage don't always add up to 100 percent, because customers may perform more than one activity at each stage.

The third type of quantification examines the frequency of distinct buying pathways—in other words, the frequency with which customers reach a particular purchase decision through a particular sequence of activities in prior stages. For instance, the buying path that originates with a special event where an outsourced caterer makes the wine selection occurs only 8 percent of the time. However, this may be an extremely valuable path as there's little drop off from start to finish. Research may reveal that while this pathway accounts for only 8 percent of purchase occasions, it results in 13 percent of all purchases. In some cases, it may be helpful to identify certain path dependencies *within* a given stage. For example, if asking staff for a recommendation occurs only when customers visit specialty wine shops, not in grocery stores, then they're not truly independent activities, even though they're both listed at the channel-visit stage.

FIGURE 3-4

Quantified Wine Buying Process

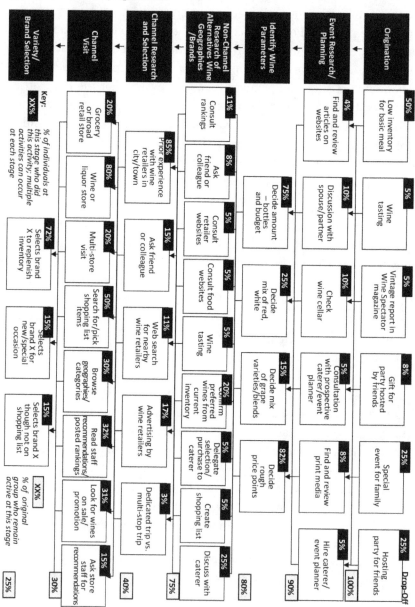

Why Standard Purchase Funnel Analysis Is Insufficient

A buying process diagram's high level of detail may seem like over analysis, but it's essential to identifying high-yield behaviors. This precision can drive simpler implementation and, ultimately, faster growth. Simple analysis typically isn't better—it can be misleading and sometimes dangerously wrong. Traditional models of purchasing behavior that look only at broad stages such as awareness, consideration, purchase, trial, and repeat ignore the critical details of real shopping behavior. Too often, incomplete analysis contributes to peanut butter marketing efforts that waste money and fail to drive faster growth.

The buying process diagram and quantification aren't the end goals. Rather, the hard work of analysis uncovers and targets the one or two specific high-yield behaviors that disproportionately accelerate growth. However, conducting in-depth analysis to get to this targeting requires a different type of market research than most firms perform. To be clear, we've served clients who've collected *some* of the data needed to construct a comprehensive, detailed buying process, but we've yet to come across a client who had *all* the needed data. Most of the time, clients have some qualitative data on buying behavior and some quantitative data on the frequency of various activities. Rarely, however, can they quantify detailed purchasing pathways or drop-off rates across stages.

The process we're advocating requires a two-stage market research approach involving both qualitative and quantitative analysis. The first stage is *qualitative analysis* that identifies all customer activities and behaviors needed to build a comprehensive buying process diagram. Our experience has shown that this qualitative research needs to be conducted in a particular way—through one-on-one interviews that focus on the story and the context of customer behaviors. The focus should be a detailed description of a recent, specific buying situation. For example, if we're interviewing consumers regarding the purchase of an air conditioning unit for their home, we need to know if it was an emergency purchase or a considered purchase during the winter months. The details of their step-by-step activities would likely be different. The key is to identify many diverse situations and let the customers tell the story in their own words. The interviewer probes to insure the story is complete and rich in detail. The sample must be highly diverse to comprehensively map the various pathways. But this phase of research doesn't require a large number of interviewees—twenty to thirty are sufficient. Focus groups won't work since they don't allow participants to tell their full stories in sufficient detail. Based on these interviews, we can construct a hypothesized buying process with the necessary degree of detail.

The Special Case of B2B Waterfalls

For those readers who are wondering whether the buying process and the waterfall diagram apply to B2B markets, the short answer is "absolutely." In Chapter 4 we describe the buying process for EnServ, an industrial energy products supplier.

In Chapter 11, we provide a number of concrete recommendations for B2B marketers. Foreshadowing this conversation, there are a few things to keep in mind while mapping the B2B buying process waterfalls:

- There is often a very small number of important customers, so it is important to conduct in-depth qualitative interviews with these clients.
- More often than not, there are four to seven people that are important to talk to in the B2B process. Teams should identify key procurement decision makers, buyers, users, and influencers to understand their perspectives and behaviors.
- Conventional wisdom and the common belief among the salesforce that they know the customer often gets in the way of novel insight in B2B markets.
- B2B marketers and sales personnel often underestimate the number of stages and steps in the buying process.
- The product development cycle of B2B customers often has a strong influence on how they conduct their buying process. Teams need to look beyond product purchase decisions to more upstream behaviors.

The second stage is *quantification.* At a minimum, this phase quantifies the flows between stages (and each stage's drop-off rates) as well as the frequency of behaviors within each stage. Figure 3-5 shows the stage-level quantification in the buying process waterfall for wine. This type of research isn't statistically complex, but the questions need to be carefully designed in the right order to reveal buying patterns. Since marketers are looking for the various pathways that groups of customers follow, this requires a large enough sample to insure that the universe of potential pathways has been adequately quantified and ordered according to importance.

FIGURE 3-5

Mapping the Buying Process: Drop-off from Stage to Stage

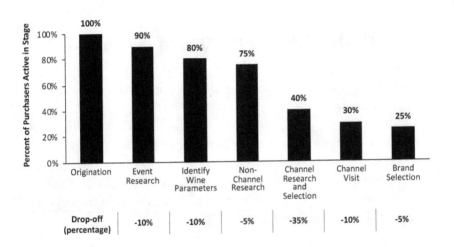

Making the choice: Picking and defining the behavioral objective

The detailed mapping of customer activities throughout the buying process inevitably uncovers critical, previously overlooked or unknown details about what customers do, who they do it with, and when. This research can also shed light on why consumers do what they do in their purchase journey. It's a treasure trove of practical insights for the team. Buying process research often clarifies the subtle but key influence patterns governing customer choices. It can provide invaluable information to your company's salesforce. It contains clues for marketers regarding the types of media or specific websites that customers find most credible. It can even provide hints that help product managers design or modify offerings. The real value of mapping and quantifying customer buying behavior, however, is its ability to help you target the critical, strategic, high-yield behaviors around which your team will build a growth plan. For example, the Figure 3-5 waterfall shows a significant drop off between non-channel search and channel research. All else being equal, these large drop offs upstream in the buying process are obvious candidates for selection as a leverage point. We've found that teams who get this right and target high-yield behaviors early in the buying journey see a dramatic acceleration of growth—even if their overall execution isn't particularly inspired.

Diagnostic Questions Regarding the Waterfall

There are several diagnostic questions that one can ask once a waterfall diagram, like Figure 3-5, is constructed. We recommend that the team explore a few key questions:

- Why did the drop off occur between stages (for example, why do 35 percent of potential customers drop out of the buying process between non-channel research and channel research)?
- If we shift the behavior at this drop off stage, do we disproportionately benefit—or do all competitors benefit also?
- Is the opportunity large enough to pursue?
- Will competition respond to our actions? If so, how?
- Can we drive this behavior change at a reasonable cost? Does the return on investment make sense?

The best operational format for choosing high-yield behavior changes is something we call a *behavioral objective*. As shown in Figure 3-6, the general format of a behavioral objective specifies the desired behavior change in a simple way that you can easily observe. Stage N in Figure 3-6 simply means that the behavioral objective can be at any stage in the process, not just the brand choice stage.

FIGURE 3-6

Defining a Behavioral Objective

The **person in role X...**

does **activity or action A (at stage N)...**

instead of doing **activity or action B (at stage N)**

This format highlights three specific sub-choices you must make when specifying a high-yield behavior as a strategic foundation of a growth plan. First, you must identify one *person or role* in a purchase process whose behavior is the most important to change. In B2B markets, the behavioral objective is identified as an organizational role—design engineer, brand manager, VP of sales, procurement manager, and so on. In B2C markets, a combination of a role with a demographic description with respect to the purchaser or the consuming unit is used—mom as influencer, dad as shopper, or teen as end user.

Second, you have to choose *where* in the purchase process a change in behavior would have the greatest impact. As previously noted, buying processes are usually complex, with many stages. This part of the choice involves identifying whether to target the key person's behavior during an early (upstream) stage or later (downstream). Third, you must decide which behavior *change* should be targeted. In other words, you have to describe in detail both what *new behavior* you want the target person/role to do and what behaviors you'd like that person to *stop* doing.

The Terrafix team defined its behavioral objective for physicians in the following way: the primary care physician (PCP) will order the objective ASD test while interviewing the patient about risk factors instead of simply interviewing the patient about risk factors. A simple but thorough formulation served as the North Star of the team's revised marketing plan. Their three sub-choices were:

- Zero in on PCPs, as opposed to specialists or nurses.
- Try to change PCPs' behavior in an early stage—right after they begin the conversation with their patients—instead of later in the buying process.
- Add a behavior (ordering the test) to what PCPs were already doing (asking patients about risk factors).

For another example, recall the wine buying process. In that case, the team identified a significant drop off between the non-channel research and channel research stages. Looking more closely at the data, the team was able to pinpoint product sampling during the non-channel research stage—in particular, joint sampling by influencers and decision-makers in the process—as a high-yield behavior. Their behavioral objective might have been: "A wife planning a big party should convince her husband to come to an in-store wine tasting event instead of doing the tasting by herself." Their behavioral objective might specify other purchase occasions and behaviors, such as: "The wife carries out an informal, in-home wine tasting with her husband by bringing home several wines for them to taste instead of directly purchasing what the store sales person recommended." In both of these cases, the team specifies the wife, in the lead purchasing agent/shopper role, as the person whose behavior they most want to change. Additionally, the team identifies an early, information-gathering stage in the buying process—in this case comparing wines—as the critical stage for influencing behavior. Finally, the team describes a particular action (or set of actions) they want the wife to take.

It's the specificity of the behavioral objective that makes the concept actionable and efficient. It helps everyone on the team see the target with absolute clarity. The efficiency derives from the way this process dramatically reduces waste. As we pointed out earlier, the traditional marketing approach addresses all stages—and, by implication, most or all of the activities within each stage. As a result, teams try to reach customers during every stage and activity that they can. If they have smaller budgets, they spread their money so thin that it's simply ineffective; if they have larger budgets, they spend a significant portion reaching out to and interacting with customers in stages and in activities that don't actually matter much. This phenomenon is, of course, the proverbial "(unknown) half of advertising spend that is wasted." If your team can accurately identify the key high-yield behavior(s) and concentrate resources on that stage, on that person or role, and on effecting that particular behavior change, you can spend less to achieve the same sales—or spend the same and get much higher growth.

The ideal way to identify customer buying behaviors that strongly shape subsequent activities is to quantify the buying process in a way that tracks how customers flow between stages and activities. The Terrafix and wine examples illustrate this. When the Terrafix team studied the buying process for ASD, they used qualitative research—interviews—to identify and map all the stages and activities in each stage. Then they conducted a large-scale survey that helped them quantify how many doctors went through each stage, how many participated in each potential activity in a stage, and, critically, the sequence of their activities.

Each of these types of data—stage participation, activity participation, and activity sequence—provided a meaningful clue to the presence of a high-yield behavior. The stage participation data—in particular the drop off in participation by stage—highlighted *where* in the process such a high-yield behavior might be. The Terrafix team's first clue to its high-yield behavior was the discovery that many patients were never asked about ASD, because in the first stage of the physical the doctor uncovered symptoms of another condition that had to be addressed right away. In effect, about 35 percent of patients dropped out of the buying process. That high dropout rate alerted the team that some activity during the diagnostic stage might be a high-yield behavior. The activity participation, and especially the activity sequence data, often point directly to behaviors that are critically important. A high-yield behavior, by definition, is one that strongly shapes what the customer does next. So, for example, if activity sequence data shows that every customer who participates in an activity—like visiting the website of a credible testing agency like Consumers Union, publisher of *Consumer Reports* magazine,—visited only those stores or sites offering the top-ranked products, tested just those products, and eventually purchased one, marketers might conclude that visiting the website of a credible testing agency is a high-yield behavior because when consumers visit this site, their subsequent behaviors follow a distinct path that typically leads to purchase.

Upstream vs. downstream behavioral objectives

In the Terrafix case study, the desired behavioral change—getting physicians to order a test—occurred during the diagnosis stage of the process. In the wine example, the desired behavior change—going to a wine tasting—occurred during the information gathering stage of the consumer journey. For B2B customers, the desired behavior change often is related to the companies' pattern of information search and gathering. That a desired behavior change occurs at a particular stage has a lot of practical significance for businesses, because when you focus on a behavioral objective that's upstream (as the Terrafix team did), it usually means a major change in spending patterns. We've observed that companies spend most of their money—usually 70 to 80 percent—on the stage where they think the purchase decision is made. The Terrafix team was typical of this pattern. The team assumed they were most at risk of losing the sale at the moment when the physician made a choice between specific brands, which was at the end of the buying process. Because of this misconception, they spent 85 percent of their marketing and sales budget at the end of the buying process. But their research found that they were losing far more customers upstream in the process than they were downstream. As a result, they had to dramatically shift their focus and their spend.

Conventional downstream behavioral objectives—convince person X to buy your product instead of the competitor's—have a strong hold on most marketing teams. Even when detailed quantification of the buying process shows that most customers leave the process or move away from a given brand due to a choice or activity early on in the buying process, teams argue long and hard about the wisdom of shifting their sales and marketing focus away from the traditional "asking for the sale" approach. Not doing so feels risky. In fact, the opposite is true. It's nearly always *less* risky to choose an upstream activity as the behavioral objective.

The reason for this lies in the nature of the strategic situation of the team. You have a good product or are about to launch one in a heavily competitive market. Centering efforts on a direct appeal to buy your product means fighting an uphill battle. Why? Because customers familiar with your product already have—buried in their subconscious—solid reasons for not buying it. Unless and until the offer actually changes the way the customer views the product, they're not going to change their minds. Customers are most wary when confronted with these types of campaigns, and the marketing team's selling pressure is met with mental shutdown. Resistance is high. Yield is poor. Money, time, and resources are wasted.

Conversely, when teams focus upstream on high-yield behavioral objectives—typically input behaviors—two things go right. First, customers resist changing their behaviors less at this point in the buying process and the behavior change typically leads the customer to see the product in a more favorable light, which makes them more likely to purchase it. Additionally, it costs less to get a unit of upstream behavior change versus a downstream change. Second, focusing on an upstream behavior change isn't an all-or-nothing choice. Some money must be spent on communicating product positioning. It's only good basic business hygiene to make sure customers know what your good product does well. That means you should still always dedicate some portion of your marketing and sales resources to direct appeal.

Conclusion

The key message in this chapter is that you should bet heavily on high-yield behavior changes. You can accomplish this only by carefully mapping each stage of the buying process, the activities within each stage, and the exit points. This collective analysis helps you construct a buying process waterfall. You then need to quantify this waterfall to uncover growth opportunities and build a business case for targeted behavior change campaigns. In contrast to the conventional wisdom, which advocates spreading resources across several sources of growth and multiple stages in the buying process, we recommend a targeted approach that focuses on one or two sources of growth and one or two high-yield behaviors to change.

Chapter 4

EnServ: "Everyone Sees the Market the Same Way"

Susan Gomez was a rising star at EnServ, a leading manufacturer of commercial heating, ventilation, and air conditioning (HVAC) equipment, and building management systems. EnServ's incoming CEO was concerned that sales in the $400 million energy services portion of the business had remained flat for nearly four years while competitors continued to gain share in this growing and profitable piece of the market. One of his first actions was to appoint Susan as the VP in charge of the energy services business unit.

Susan knew that slow growth wasn't due to EnServ's core capabilities or the market itself: the company had been a leading manufacturer of HVAC equipment for decades and had an outstanding product line. Moreover, the salesforce was widely regarded as one of the best in the industry. The market was broad, diverse, and stable. Every owner of a building, whatever its use, was a potential customer. Building owners had to provide tenants with comfortable working environments, which, in turn, meant they had to have well-functioning heating and cooling systems. The market scope had been rapidly expanding over the past decade to include all types of products that could help a building owner reduce the cost of providing a comfortable environment, including better windows and insulation, as well as more sophisticated control systems and energy audits.

Over the decades, EnServ had developed a distinctive approach to the market. Like most companies in this space, EnServ defined the market by industry verticals (state and city governments, public school systems, retailers, manufacturers, and so on) and tailored messages and product bundles to the needs of these different customer types. This view of the market was strongly ingrained in the company's operations and organizational structure, which reflected these divisions by industry verticals. This approach had remained largely unchanged for more than thirty years.

The company's sales representatives tended to focus on responding to RFPs (requests for proposals) from larger customers. Salesforce compensation was driven almost entirely by commissions, so the rewards for winning large contracts for major equipment—such as rooftop chillers—could be considerable. EnServ salespeople prided themselves on their knowledge of the local markets they served and on their ability to compete for these types of large-scale projects.

This approach had not translated into success in the market for energy services. Susan's predecessor had largely doubled down on the historical approach of industrial vertical segmentation, an aggressive salesforce, and market-specific product marketing support. Susan knew she had to take a different approach.

As she took over as VP of energy services, Susan asked us to help her team perform a fresh analysis of the market to better understand EnServ's customer buying behaviors. "To be honest," she said, "I was pretty sure I knew what we would find. After all, I had been doing this work for a long time and basically accepted the idea that we needed to push harder to replicate the success we'd had in other parts of the market. I wasn't fully prepared for what we discovered and its implications. It was actually pretty humbling."

The buying process and high-yield behavior change

We went to work with Susan and her team to map the entire end-to-end buying process. First, we used qualitative research to determine the basic structure of the buying process, the range of activities at each stage, and the participants in each stage. We then surveyed more than eight hundred customers to obtain quantitative data on what happened during 1,500 distinct buying occasions. The survey asked a variety of questions related to the stages in the process such as where a prospect dropped out in the buying process, what activities they engaged in at each stage, the solution they ultimately purchased, and their supplier choice.

Figure 4-1 provides a sketch of what turned out to be a complex buying process. As shown in the left column, the research identified thirteen distinct steps. The first five steps concern the preliminary research facilities managers undertake just after they first conceive, or are introduced to, the idea of reducing energy costs in their building. This early research phase, which usually includes consulting with one or more vendors, leads to either dropping the idea (self-termination) or the first of two formal go/no-go meetings with senior management (Step 6). If the idea is supported by senior management in Step 6, the facilities manager designs and runs a formal process to request and evaluate quotes from vendors (Steps 7–10). This phase also ends in self-termination or a second formal meeting with senior executives (Step 11). Finally, if the recommendation is approved, the facilities manager oversees implementation and measures success (Steps 12 and 13).

FIGURE 4-1

Thirteen-Step Process to Purchase Energy Services

Steps	Detail of Step 4: Information Gathering Activities (About Offers and Providers)		
0 Pre-Origination	**Information Gathering**		
1 Origination of Interest		**Provider**	
2 Interest Confirmation	**Offer**	**Primary research focus**	
3 Specification Definition			
4 Information Gathering	Sales reps interaction	Property manager	Internal stakeholder recommendations
5 Research Synthesis	Secondary sources (Internet research, Industry reports)	Facilities manager/ supervisor	Secondary sources (Internet research, Industry reports)
6 Prelim. Management Review of Opportunity	Utility	Building engineer/ lead operator	Familiar contractor
7 Provider Set Selection			
8 Onsite Provider Evaluation	Familiar contractor	General contractor	Peer network
9 Provider Decision	Internal stakeholders	Architectural contractor	Sales reps interaction
10 Offer Decision	Peer network	Building owner	Regulation/ rebate documents
11 Capital Outlay Approval			
12 Capital Outlay Execution & Installation	(or) Not actively researched	Sustainability manager (for owner)	(or) Not actively researched
13 Usage & Evaluation			

Note: Each of the unshaded boxes is an actual activity that could be pursued by the customer (e.g., call utility, talk to general contractor, reach out to peer network)

These thirteen steps are a highly compressed representation of a complex, nuanced process. Indeed, it was much more complicated than the Terrafix case study. There is a range of possible activities within each step, with many different routes that a buyer could follow. As shown on the right side of Figure 4-1, even in the process of doing informal, preliminary research, a facilities manager can (and often does) undertake a wide and diverse set of activities. These information gathering activities can be related to the offer or the provider. Offer activities, for example, include meeting with a sales rep or collecting data from secondary sources, while provider activities include talking to internal stakeholders and meetings with familiar contractors.

As shown in Figure 4-2, EnServ's buying process involved different stakeholders at each stage. As in many business-to-business markets, there were multiple participants including owners, financial officers, facilities managers, facilities operators/engineers, and other experts. These individuals dial up (or down) their decision rights depending on the stage in the process. The facilities engineer, for example, is significant only in the early stages, while the building owner or CFO participates and makes decisions at only two stages of the process, although both are important go/no-go meetings. The EnServ team was surprised to discover that it was the facilities manager who turned out to be the key buyer. They drove the entire process and made the final purchase recommendations.

FIGURE 4-2

Stakeholder Influence Varies Across the Thirteen Steps

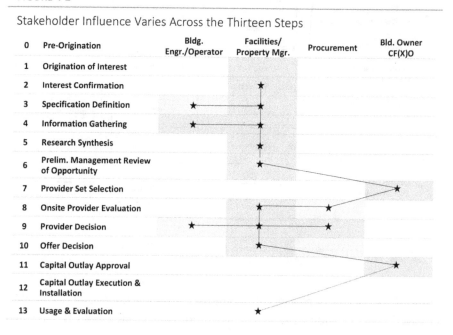

While the buying process and the stakeholder influence maps are foundational, EnServ's survey helped the company quantify exactly where—and in what numbers—potential customers were dropping out. Figure 4-3 shows that the biggest loss of potential customers was occurring before a formal RFP was issued by prospective clients. Reading from the left to the right, it's clear that of one hundred facilities managers with an idea of reducing energy costs, nearly all—96 percent—did some informal research. But only seventy-eight continued their research by calling a trusted vendor to discuss solutions or gather more data. Of the prospects who talked to a vendor and then recommended a solution to their boss, only sixty-four received approval to launch a formal RFP process to select a vendor. Hence, another 14 percent of the original 100 dropped off at this stage. By contrast, relatively few customers self-terminated the process once they had committed to gathering formal bids from suppliers. "Our biggest competition in this market wasn't the other energy service providers," Susan observed, "but the fact that our customers were dropping out before signing a contract!"

FIGURE 4-3

Mapping Buying Process Waterfall for Energy Services

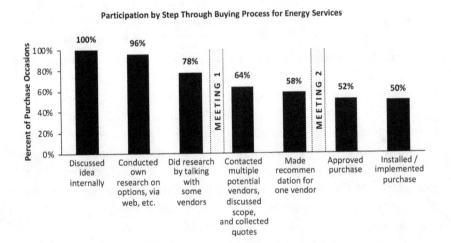

Participation by Step Through Buying Process for Energy Services

The analysis also revealed the critical importance of being consulted early on in the buying process. As shown in Figure 4-4, customers who went through the entire process were *five times* more likely to buy from a vendor who interacted with them in Step 3 or 4 that is, who consulted with them early in their information gathering process than from vendors who were only invited in for the formal RFP process (Steps 7–9). Moreover, customers who didn't consult with a vendor early on self-terminated at a much higher rate.

FIGURE 4-4

Importance of Consultation Early in the Process

Of	100	Potential purchase occasions
	78	Consulted at least one vendor
	64	Ran a bid process
	52	Selected a vendor
	44	Of those selected were the vendor originally consulted in stage 2

INSIGHT | Customers who actually buy are 5X more likely to buy from the vendor with whom they originally consulted than from a vendor who only responded to their RFP

As Susan recalled, "It was a bit of a shock to see these numbers coming in. We had a lead qualification process that led us to focus on the big RFPs as they came down the pike, but we were basically ignoring the decisions that were taking place before that point and didn't recognize the impact this had on who gets chosen for the work."

Analysis of the survey uncovered one other major counterintuitive result. EnServ's strategy emphasized selling bundles of services: the bigger the bundle, the better. The energy services marketplace, however, was actually dominated by one-off sales for individual services, rather than bundles. That is, in any given year, about 85 percent of energy services were purchased one at a time, usually one type per building per year. Only about 10 percent of all customers bought an energy services bundle, and did so every three or four years. "At that point, we had to acknowledge that we were swimming upstream by pushing bundles," Susan noted, "searching for a behavior that was actually pretty rare in terms of number of transactions."

Based on the data, Susan and her team felt that a fundamental change in strategy was needed. The team decided to make two recommendations to the CEO. The first was to reverse its earlier focus on bundles and address the larger market opportunity for one-off energy service projects. The second was to focus on two behavioral objectives. Based on the research, it was clear that the primary high-yield behavior change involved building a trust relationship with facilities managers that would lead them to consult EnServ *first* at an early stage of the process, increasing the chance that EnServ would eventually be selected for the work. "We boiled it down to a single phrase: Be consulted to be selected!" Susan explained.

The secondary behavioral objective was to grow the market by encouraging facilities managers to consider and follow through on energy services projects. In effect, trust-based relationships could be leveraged to help grow the market by using early conversations with facilities managers to consider and follow through on energy services projects. While growing the market in this way could also benefit its competitors, EnServ stood to gain disproportionately by establishing relationships early in the process.

As she prepared to present the findings and recommendations to the CEO and executive team, Susan realized the dramatic implications of what she was proposing. "In the past, our definition of a good customer was a CFO of a big account in a vertical industry segment who would consider a bundle. That's how we saw the market. Unfortunately, this meant we ended up going head-to-head with our major rivals over what we now realize was only a slice of the potential market."

Rethinking segmentation

Like others in the energy services industry, EnServ used a simple demographic approach to segment its market. They tended to distinguish among customers based on account size and by industry vertical. These verticals were quite standard: commercial offices, government offices, schools, health care facilities, retailers, industrial sites, and so on. "The good thing about this segmentation was that it was obvious where each customer fit (Figure 4-5). And, to some degree, customers in different businesses or with larger facilities *do* have differing needs when it comes to energy services," commented Susan. "The problem was that the segmentation didn't tell us anything about the behaviors we wanted to target. It didn't give us a way to find the good customers in terms of influencing their buying decisions before they got to the RFP."

What Susan wanted was a new segmentation scheme that would be as obvious and easy to use as the industry vertical approach, but would reveal a customer's propensity to consult with a vendor. Significantly, Susan chose not to delegate the work to an internal or external market research group. She knew that she was going to be changing significantly how her team went to market and needed to ensure their buy-in from the start. Instead, she pulled together a cross-functional team of senior players from marketing, sales, and customer service and told them they were going to be hands-on responsible for creating the segmentation.

FIGURE 4-5

Existing Segmentation Frame

Industry/ Vertical Account Size	Commercial	Government	Schools	...	Retail
Large Accounts				...	
Midsize Accounts				...	
Small Accounts				...	

This team's process was straightforward. First, they needed to develop a broad list of readily observable customer characteristics.[24] Next, they would screen that list to identify which variables were most highly correlated with a facilities manager's propensity to consult with vendors. The team began by brainstorming a list of customer characteristics beyond industry vertical and size. These characteristics would help their organization more easily target the right prospects. They focused especially on the most readily observable characteristics—or those that could be easily learned by asking—and created a long list of more than forty.

The second step was to identify the customer characteristics that were most highly correlated with a prospect's likelihood to consult a vendor. To study this correlation, the team took advantage of the quantitative survey we noted earlier, which had also gathered information on a larger number of customer characteristics.[25]

Figure 4-6 displays a sample of the output from this correlation analysis. Across the top are eight of the forty customer characteristics, such as age of the building, tenant composition, and energy tracking. Down the side are the behavioral objectives the team was considering at the time. The figure shows that some customer characteristics are correlated with a propensity to consult, while others are not. For example, facilities managers who have sophisticated, real-time energy use tracking systems at their fingertips are highly likely to consult early on with vendors when considering energy services projects. On the other hand, there's little or no correlation between the age of a building and that facilities manager's propensity to consult a vendor.

FIGURE 4-6

Testing the Correlation of Customer Characteristics and Behavioral Objectives

| | **CUSTOMER CHARACTERISTICS** | | | | | | | |
BEHAVIORAL OBJECTIVES	Individual Building vs. Part of Portfolio	Energy Tracking	Facilities Dept. Independent Budget	Project Experience	Building Operations (Owner vs. 3rd Party)	Geographic Region	Age of Building	Tenant Composition
Consulted with Provider	Y	Y	Y	Y	N	N	N	N
Ultimately Selected Provider (Any)	Y	Y	Y	Y	Y	N	Y	N
Considered Provider (Any)	Y	Y	Y	Y	Y	N	N	Y
Same Provider Consulted & Selected	Y	Y	Y	Y	Y	N	N	N

Note: 40 customer characteristics were tested for correlation with a potential behavioral objective

In the end, the team used a combination of five characteristics that showed the highest correlation with two key behavioral objectives: consult with a vendor in the initial phases of an energy services project and proceed with recommending that an energy services project take place (instead of self-terminating). These characteristics included:

- Whether the facilities manager tracked energy consumption on a daily/weekly basis.
- Whether the facilities manager had personally completed two or

more energy services projects.
- Whether the facilities manager supervised multiple buildings or just one.
- Whether the customer's building was located in a state with stringent energy conservation requirements written into its building codes.
- Building size.

The team delved into finer detail around how to define the parameters of each characteristic. For instance, they decided it was sufficient to classify the stringency of state building codes simply as high, medium, or low to yield meaningful differences in terms of customer behavior. They adopted a more fine-grained approach in categorizing building size, where small, for example, was defined as anything under 25,000 square feet. The key was finding the tipping points where the relevant behaviors started to diverge.

The next step was to arrange these characteristics in what we call a *segmentation frame,* a simple, two-dimensional chart that maps the entire market as a grid of intersecting variables—a process we'll explain more thoroughly in Chapter 5. Creating this frame required Susan's team to nest some variables within others. The approach was to place the dimensions with the broadest explanatory power at the outer edges and to use other variables to provide more granular insight into differing behavioral propensities. The team found that they could eliminate some detail to simplify the graph without sacrificing accuracy. They also arranged variables in such a way that similar types of customers fell into contiguous areas and could be grouped to form a single segment (because they knew that not every box on the grid would be its own separate segment).

It's important to note two key points about these segmentation frames. First, they have a general pattern. On one axis are general customer demographics, or demographics of the firm in the case of B2B firms (Figure 4-7). Situational variables are on the other axis. Second, the goal of creating this type of frame is to observe the collective correlation (of all variables in the frame) between the customer characteristics and the behavioral objectives. After trying out several different configurations, the team settled on a frame that effectively reflected the distribution of behaviors they wanted to map. The frame had firm demographics on one axis (for example, building size) and situational/usage variables on the other axis (for example, how closely facilities managers tracked energy use).

FIGURE 4-7

New Segmentation Frame for Energy Services

		Track energy usage on a daily or monthly basis		Do not track energy usage on a daily or monthly basis (track utility spend only)
		High stringency energy-related building code states / 2 or more projects completed	**Medium to low stringency energy-related building code states** / ≤1 project completed	
Part of portfolio	**Bldg Size < 25k sq ft**	(1) Consult: 60%; Select: 77%		
	Bldg Size 25k-200k sq ft	(2) Consult: 91% Select: 77%	(4) Consult: 91% Select: 85%	(5) Consult: 83% Select: 77%
	Bldg Size >200k sq ft	(3) Consult: 95% Select: 70%	(6) Consult: 74% Select: 60%	
Individual building	**Bldg Size < 25k sq ft**	(7) Consult: 53%; Select: 76%		
	Bldg Size 25k-200k sq ft	(9) Consult: 79%; Select: 78%	(11) Consult: 53% Select: 47%	
	Bldg Size >200k sq ft	(10) Consult: 72%; Select: 81%	(8) Consult: 45% Select: 60%	(12) Consult: 42% Select: 58%

"The a-ha moment came when we put the variables together in a way where we started to recognize particular customers in the grid," recalled

Susan. "We had salespeople on the team saying, 'I can tell you five actual customers right now who belong in that box.' After fiddling around through trial and error with these dimensions, we got to a place where we started to recognize distinct customers and where they fit in the segmentation. That's when we knew we were close."

Taken together, these variables described market segments with different propensities to consult or engage energy service providers. At one extreme were customers responsible for more than one medium-to-large building located in states with stringent energy conservation requirements who tracked energy use regularly (Segments 2 and 3). Based on data from the buying process research, these segments showed a propensity to consult with a vendor more than 90 percent of the time and select providers more than 70 percent of the time. At the other extreme were customers responsible for a single, small building in states with moderate regulation who tracked energy consumption infrequently (Segment 8). Other segments lay in between and exhibited different behavioral propensities based on the combination of factors included in the frame.

This was clearly a new way of dividing up the market for the EnServ team. In this new approach, industry verticals weren't included. However, the segmentation variables were still clearly observable and actionable for the regions and sales districts. It was a straightforward matter, for instance, to determine a building's size and whether it was in a jurisdiction with stringent energy requirements. It was also a relatively easy ask for a salesperson to discover whether a facilities manager was responsible for just one building or a larger portfolio. EnServ's team could also readily discover how frequently a facilities manager reviewed energy consumption data and pinpoint the number of energy-related retrofits a manager had led. It might require a visit or two, but this was information that salespeople either knew or could get easily.

The team quickly zeroed in on a couple of segments. They reasoned that the richest opportunities lay with customers that already tended to consult with vendors early in the buying process, where EnServ could actively engage with facilities managers and convert those early stage relationships into sales. Another consideration was the size of each segment—the number of potential customers it represented. For these reasons, they identified Segment 3 as a key target for the new strategy. This was a large segment spanning multiple industry verticals of facilities managers who had experience performing energy services projects and were apt to consult with vendors early on when considering new projects. The team confirmed that customers in this segment tended to do smaller, one-off energy retrofits, rather than buying comprehensive service bundles.

Drivers and barriers to behavior change

The key for Susan and her team was that the new segmentation not only differed from that of EnServ's competitors, but also provided her salesforce with specific, concrete guidance on how to identify and activate key segments. While competitors were single-mindedly focused on large buildings in particular business verticals, Susan and her team realized that other factors were stronger predictors of the choice to consult with a vendor early in the decision process—a behavior that they knew from their research would lead to better sales outcomes for their company. The new segmentation also focused attention on a specific individual in the buying process—the facilities manager—and enabled EnServ to narrow its activities to influence the high-yield behaviors of these key prospects. If Susan's team moved quickly, competitors would not only be caught off guard, but also would find it difficult to replicate a strategy that was grounded in EnServ's proprietary insights into customer buying behaviors.

The next step for the EnServ team was to create a customer narrative with two purposes. First, the team had to construct a comprehensive narrative that explained why a target segment had or didn't have the propensity to engage in the targeted high-yield behavior. This exercise helped the team uncover why the facilities managers in the target segment behaved the way they did. Creating a customer narrative shifted attention from EnServ's products to the task of trying to understand why facilities managers would seek consultation about energy services. Second, the team needed to isolate the four or five factors that would motivate or prevent targeted prospects from consulting with EnServ. These drivers and barriers would subsequently be used as key inputs to create a go-to-market strategy.

With respect to the first objective—the construction of the narrative—the team mined the quantitative survey, conducted new qualitative research with facilities managers, interviewed key salesforce personnel, and used prior research. In Chapter 7, we'll describe the set of guiding questions that were helpful here, but for now think of the team as using a structured interview process to reverse engineer the factors that went into the facilities managers' decision-making process. We've found it helpful to group these themes into three categories: social and physical context, desired experience, and beliefs and attitudes.

Following this approach, Susan's team developed a detailed customer narrative describing the needs and motivations of facilities managers in the target segment. One of their strong findings was that facilities managers regarded themselves as professionals who sought opportunities to develop and advance their careers. Many had studied and held degrees in property management and devoted time to staying current on industry trends. They read professional magazines and blogs frequently, attended local and national trade shows, and sought to build their professional reputation by staying at the leading edge of industry practice.

Among the demanding set of responsibilities they faced was a mandate to reduce facility costs year over year in the properties they managed. Property owners typically set goals for them requiring annual cost reduction of 3 to 5 percent. While accomplishing these reductions, they had to work within their organizations' capital budgeting processes. The facilities managers were keenly aware of the difficulties of getting capital approval for activities and equipment that weren't directly related to the business mission or capable of generating revenue. They therefore thought hard about how to make projects doable by breaking up and/or stretching out implementation.

This detailed understanding of the facilities managers' experience, beliefs, and motivations allowed the team to address specific drivers and barriers to the desired behaviors (Figure 4-8). Many of the subsequent specific marketing and sales tactics were aimed at the stage in the buying process where the second big drop-off occurred: when facilities managers moved from selecting a vendor to getting approval from their companies to move forward with the purchase of energy services. Helping facilities managers sell the benefits of the project to their employers increased the likelihood that they would stick with the buying process rather than self-terminate.

FIGURE 4-8

Segment 3: Drivers and Barriers to Consulting with or Selecting EnServ

Drivers	Barriers
Influences that lead to "Consult with" or "Select" EnServ	*Obstacles that impede "Consult with" or "Select" EnServ*
• Non-normal performance of equipment	• Large capital expenditure and/or long payback period for what seems to be a pure cost reduction effort
• Ability to show improvement in consumption and cost over time	• Not being on their "preferred" list (which is less a formal designation than being trusted/reliable and perception of expertise in a type of energy project)
• Confidence that project can be implemented smoothly, i.e., with minimal disruption	
• Ability to break project up into manageable pieces (chunks), for both budget and control/implementation reasons	• Finding room for the project in the capital budget "after" all the revenue driving projects are funded
• ROI/payback period	
• Belief that project will restore/add to professional standing, either internally or externally	• Belief that project will be highly disruptive or difficult to implement
• Belief that project will deliver on cost and operational targets in a way that has a clear link to improved business performance other than cost	

Turning to Figure 4-8, we can readily observe the drivers and barriers to consult with or select EnServ. It's interesting to note that the drivers were related to a facilities manager's beliefs (belief that the project would restore/add to professional standing, belief that the project would deliver on cost and operational targets), context (the current equipment wasn't working properly), and desired experiences (ability to break the project into manageable pieces to fit yearly budget constraints, the project could be implemented with minimal disruption). Conversely, barriers for this particular segment were largely related to situational context (not proposing a revenue enhancing project) and desired experience (project is difficult to implement). It's important to stress that Susan and her team worked to maintain a disciplined focus during this stage of the analysis. They didn't want a laundry list of non-actionable items; they wanted to isolate a short list of drivers and barriers that could be the basis for their subsequent go-to-market plan.

Behavior change value proposition

At this stage of the process, Susan and her team were in uncharted territory.

They were comfortable developing product-centered value propositions. Indeed, they already had product value propositions (PVPs) developed. It wasn't that the product value propositions weren't necessary; they just weren't sufficient to grow, as evidenced by the flat sales. In response, Susan and her team shifted their attention to defining a behavior change value proposition (BCVP) focused on changing behaviors upstream in the buying process. The BCVP wouldn't supplant the PVPs that EnServ already had in place; rather, it would complement existing PVPs.

For Susan and her team, the primary behavioral objective was to consult with EnServ. The secondary behavior objective was to select EnServ. As we'll describe in more detail in Chapter 9, BCVPs focus on identifying the specific behavioral change companies want target customers to engage in and how they can enhance the value to the customer of engaging in the desired behavior. Susan's team created the following statement summarizing the value of the new behaviors for the target segment:

Talking to EnServ regularly and early in their process (versus not consulting with EnServ) will enable a facilities manager (in Segment 3) to rapidly identify and design highly fundable, minimally disruptive energy projects that will enhance their internal (and external) reputation as a savvy, results-oriented facilities manager.

Let's look at a few key points about this statement. First, it requires identification of the target segment, since BCVPs vary by segment. Second, this is a value proposition about behavior changes. So you need to be explicit not only about the desired behavior, but also about current behaviors that need to be changed. In EnServ's case, the current behavior was not consulting during the early phase of the buying process. Third, since BCVPs identify behaviors that need to change during the buying process, you need to selectively isolate the most important drivers and barriers to bring about that change in behavior. For EnServ this meant that the project needed to be cost effective, minimally disruptive, and fundable.

As you can imagine, delivering on the new BCVP meant EnServ had to rethink every aspect of its strategy: products, approach to marketing, and sales activities. The new go-to-market strategy focused on four key elements that supported the goal of persuading facilities managers to engage in the desired behaviors.

First, EnServ's research into consumer behavior of their target clients revealed that if a proposed project offered significant improvements and could demonstrate a clear return on investment without major disruptions to the building's tenants or operations, facilities managers were more likely to act. If the project could be broken down into manageable chunks for these managers—preferably chunks that fit within discretionary operating budgets or didn't require a major capital expenditure review process—then the uptake rates were even higher.

Second, EnServ also rethought and restructured its product line in two ways to make it more buyable. The company's long-standing focus had been on a particular type of bundle, preferably anchored around big-ticket products like chillers. The company's first change to its product line involved adding and giving more visibility to inherently smaller and less disruptive products and services, such as audits, lighting, buying group access, and so on. EnServ also modularized all the bigger products and services so customers could purchase each at different scales without paying a penalty in efficiency. This made EnServ more buyable because it put all of the company's products in a price band that fit comfortably within a facilities manager's typical discretionary budget. EnServ also made it easier for the facilities managers to demonstrate both the value of a project and the smoothness of its implementation. Finally, EnServ made it easier to run proof-of-concept pilots for energy services, which helped facilities managers overcome doubts or skepticism within their organizations.

Third, with respect to marketing communications, the EnServ team changed their message, their profile, and where they met and worked with the client. They began actively helping facilities managers boost their visibility and credibility in the facilities management community by turning their projects into speeches or white papers that could be presented at trade group meetings. In effect, they began boosting the career visibility and prospects of the facilities managers that engaged EnServ.

Finally, the EnServ team made a number of changes to their salesforce development and execution model. They began fostering more consultations between facilities managers and EnServ representatives much earlier in the buying process. EnServ invested more heavily in thought leadership in energy conservation, both at the company and individual levels. EnServ also invested in research and the publication and documentation of key issues in energy usage and facilities management. They also built up the thought leadership profile of their individual salespeople by having them sponsor local webcasts, create mailings to key customers, and participate in local trade associations to which their customers belonged.

For EnServ's salesforce, there was a radical redesign of the force's size and coverage model. The salesforce had traditionally been big game hunters—passively waiting for RFPs before springing into action most of the time. As such, their interactions with customers were focused on the specifics of the RFP at hand. The new model called for frequent, information-rich visits, where most of the conversations would not be concerned with a specific project. Instead, the new approach entailed a mix of visits in which EnServ's salesforce would check in with the facilities managers, provide new insights on facilities management, relay information in response to any service inquiries, and/or help the facilities managers make sense of all the data EnServ had gathered on a potential energy project.

Finally, EnServ began helping its salesforce create a *living energy management roadmap* for each existing customer. These five- to seven-year roadmaps showed alternative ways to start, phase, and fund energy services projects, which enabled salespeople to have regular conversations about energy services with facilities managers. They also demonstrated EnServ's commitment to helping facilities managers achieve their own professional and career goals.

Disproportionate investment

The above changes marked a completely novel go-to-market strategy. The salesforce, which consisted of highly trained and experienced energy engineers, had historically been given incentives based on aggressive revenue and margin targets. Consulting with potential customers ahead of an RFP had not been recognized or rewarded as part of any incentive plan. Since the new approach depended on mobilizing the salesforce to act differently, Susan persuaded management to invest resources to realign sales compensation. Under the new incentives plan, part of sales reps' reward would be based not only on outcome behaviors (making a sale), but also on activity behaviors that included efforts to build and cultivate consultative relationships with customers in the target segment.

Additional resources were also dedicated to the development of thought leadership, such as writing white papers and producing research on energy management topics. EnServ also set up a dedicated sales support team—initially five people—to assist the sales team in preparing for client conversations, designing offers, pricing, and answering frequently asked questions. In some cases, members of this team would accompany representatives on sales calls, design or write proposals, or facilitate the sales process in other ways.

Susan also took a multistep approach to rolling out the new strategy, focusing first on the segments that were already most likely to consult with providers about energy services. As EnServ's salesforce gained familiarity with the new approach and incentives structure, they planned to extend the new program to other segments. The pilot phase for the new program proved so successful that they started the second phase nine months earlier than originally scheduled.

Epilogue

The new strategy was not easy to implement but by year 2 it was clear that Susan had the business moving in a better direction, and by year 3 she had a smashing success. All the changes took time to pilot, refine, and rollout. Susan wisely chose to focus on only a couple of segments early on. Despite this carefully planed and phased implementation, many on the sales and product teams were not comfortable with the changes initially. Some actively resisted the changes. Some even left the firm. But those that embraced it started turning in great numbers in year 2 and spectacularly better numbers in year 3. Overall, Susan's team grew revenues by 1 percent in year 1, 2.5 percent in year 2, and 5. percent in year 3. Best of all there was no sign of flattening as there were many more segments of the market left to target and grow.

Chapter 5

Second Principle: Use Propensity-Based Segmentation

Susan Gomez's decision to use a novel segmentation scheme at EnServ was one of the key decisions that led to a threefold increase in the probability of a sale. Although these standout results surprised her veteran team, these experienced salespeople understood that talking to customers early in the decision-making process was a good thing. They never acted on this knowledge, though, because they also knew that randomly calling on customers in their territories would be a waste of time and would dramatically lower their chances of making their sales quota. EnServ's new segmentation scheme turned that around, providing the salesforce with a practical way to *identify* customers most likely to consult with them early in the buying process and then purchase from them.

EnServ had previously grouped customers according to industry vertical and size, which the sales team viewed as a practical guide. But despite good products and a growing market, EnServ's conventional segmentation, which focused on taking industry-related offers to bigger customers, had not helped the company grow during the past five years.

The segmentation developed by Susan and her team was equally practical, but much more growth-oriented. The EnServ story illustrates the second *Playbook* principle: *use propensity-based segmentation* to map and target customers. Susan's team identified customer characteristics that the sales team could observe just as readily as size or industry vertical. The difference was that these customer characteristics allowed the salesforce to efficiently target those prospects who were interested in building an information-based relationship with EnServ. This helped them zero in on the segment of energy-savvy facilities managers with responsibility for multiple, large buildings in states with stricter building codes who were much more likely to consult with and buy from a vendor like EnServ that had its salesforce call on them regularly.

The new segmentation enabled Susan's team to restart growth at their company. In fact, EnServ was able to outsell its competitors over the next three years because it could find and build relationships with the best potential customers quickly and efficiently. EnServ's sales team was empowered with the information they needed to target facilities managers with an inherent propensity to engage in early consultation. The salesforce could then provide those facilities managers with a behavior change value proposition focused on their identified needs: easy, low risk, and high return on investment offers that could be efficiently integrated into their planning process. Over time, the EnServ salespeople became their customers' go to source for advice and ideas. EnServ was consulted on nearly every potential project undertaken by their growing community of facilities managers. In turn, this led to EnServ's ideas being written into customers' RFPs, ensuring a much higher win rate than before. In just a year, Susan could report a growth rate of 1 percent— up from essentially zero. In years two, three, and four, she delivered growth rates double or more than the industry average. Given that she did this with essentially the same team and budget as before, the acceleration in revenue growth produced an even more favorable boost in profit.

This story reaffirms why textbooks and business schools are right to advocate so strongly that every business should segment its market. Doing and using segmentation properly is clearly a critical enabler of growth. The story also highlights the importance of *how* the segmentation is done. To grow, it's not enough to simply segment your market using commonly accepted approaches. Like EnServ before Susan's resegmentation, companies can have good needs-based, behavior-based, or demographic-based segmentation and still not be able to drive organic growth. In our experience, growing organically means doing segmentation in a way that gets to the heart of the growth challenge. Quite simply, with respect to segmentation, it means doing segmentation in a way that reveals customers' propensity to engage in a high-yield behavior.

Conventional wisdom

Segmentation is a basic pillar of marketing. Mapping customer differences, grouping customers into distinct categories, and tailoring product development, marketing, sales, and service activities to the requirements of different types of customers is the essence of a good business plan.[26] Every business uses some type of segmentation—either explicit or implicit—to help shape and prioritize its actions.

Business schools and textbooks are less prescriptive, however, about exactly what kind of segmentation businesses should use. Over the years, practitioners and academics have conceived and developed at least four schools of segmentation: demographic/geographic, needs, psychographic, and behavioral. Each school zeroes in on some subset of customer attributes as the basis for grouping them into segments. The underlying logic is that each segment exhibits similar attitudes or characteristics and differences across segments. Academics refer to this as *homogeneity within segments* and *heterogeneity across segments*.

The earliest type of segmentation—demographic/geographic—divided customers into groups based on who and where they were. Customers were sorted by characteristics like their age, gender, education, income, ethnicity, and home location. In our wine example in Chapter 3, a demographic/geographic segmentation of the market might sort consumers as over or under age thirty, making an annual salary over or under $100,000, and living in a big city or a suburb. In EnServ's case, their original segmentation was what B2B firms often call *firmographic segmentation*. Think of it as the demographics of the firm—it could include segmentation by industry sector, business size, or geographic location.

Demographic/geographic segmentations appeal to businesses because they usually make it easy to find groups of customers and target marketing or sales campaigns toward those groups. This segmentation has additional appeal because it seems obvious: customers with a higher income or more customers are clearly better targets than those with less income or fewer customers. Unfortunately, this type of segmentation provides a poor foundation for growth plans because the customers in each segment are only superficially homogenous. The reality is that within each demographic segment customers typically vary greatly in how they think and act. A segment defined as older and richer wine purchasers, for example, may be an attractive target and relatively easy to find, but the consumers within this segment are unlikely to want the same type of wine or purchase that wine through the same sales channels. The intrinsic flaw in demographic/geographic segmentation is that it provides businesses with no reliable insight into what to say or do in addressing those segments. This is one of the reasons why researchers have shifted their focus to the psychology of customers, developing a type of needs-based and/or psychographic-based approach to segmentation

Needs-based and psychographic segmentations divide customers into groups based on what they think.[27] A needs-based segmentation looks at customers by the number, nature, and strength of their stated interest in the attributes of a product and/or service. This approach splits consumers into groups according to the strength of their needs or wants. For example, in the wine market, segmentation would be based on the type of wine the customer likes (red versus white), the preferred alcohol content (high versus low), and the customer's preferred flavor profile (full bodied versus light). Psychographic segmentation looks beyond the product to broader aspects of consumer psychology. A psychographic approach to the wine market would divide consumers based on their attitudes toward alcoholic drinks overall, their psychological traits (integrity, imagination, novelty seeking, and so on), and/or their overall values (belief in religion, freedom, justice, and so on). In general, these approaches appeal to businesses because they seem to offer a lot of insight into what might appeal or not appeal to consumers. This informs marketing teams as to what should be said or not said in a campaign aimed at a particular segment. The problem with these two types of segmentation is that they're typically much more difficult and expensive to identify and target. Consumers who share a need for a full-bodied, high-alcohol, French-grown wine are likely scattered across a variety of demographic and psychological categories. Therefore it's more challenging, time consuming, and expensive to reach them through one or two types of media or channels.

As a result of frustration with the actionability of the psychological approaches, businesses have increasingly looked to use past purchase behavior to segment customers. Purchase-based behavior segmentation sorts customers by their loyalty to a product. For example, returning to our wine consumer, a purchase-based segmentation would look at the percentage of a consumer's purchases of champagne versus white wine, or a California vineyard versus a French vineyard. This approach might also segment consumers by their purchase and consumption patterns: whether they drink wine every day or only occasionally, or whether they typically drink wine at home or while traveling. Somewhat ironically, these purchase-based segmentations appeal to businesses for many of the same reasons as demographic/geographic segmentations. But they also tend to suffer from the same flaws. On the positive side, purchase-based segmentation seems to automatically highlight attractive customers. And, in an age where marketers can track a good percentage of purchase behaviors online, this approach can be cost effective for finding customers and targeting campaigns based on past purchases, like emailing ads with lower prices on French wines to people who have repeatedly bought French wines before. On the negative side, this type of segmentation doesn't provide significant insights for growth. In particular, this approach doesn't provide insights into whether customers are likely to change their buying behaviors, nor what messages or offers might convince a consumer to change their purchase patterns. In fact, purchase-based behavior segmentation creates a rearview mirror marketing approach by continually giving consumers exactly what they've bought in the past. This is fine as long as the road ahead is exactly like the road behind. This is rarely the case, and may lead to trouble when conditions change.

In our view, none of the traditional segmentation approaches provide businesses with a solid foundation for growth planning. Beyond their specific limitations, all four approaches are problematic with regard to growth in two fundamental ways: first, they force businesses into a trade-off between actionability and growth insights, and second, they don't provide teams with direct insights about target customers' growth behaviors.

Let's take a closer look at these two fundamental flaws. The demographic and purchase behavior-based approaches, for example, tend to provide relatively actionable segmentation frames, making it easy for businesses to uncover different segments, but they don't offer insights into how to activate those identified segments. Conversely, with the needs and psychographic-based approach, a convenience-seeking segment might be identified, but the research provides no guidance about how a company might cost-effectively find consumers in that segment or target their behavior. What's needed is an approach that defines each segment in a way that makes it easy to target and highlights the steps necessary to convince customers in that segment to change their behavior in a favorable way.

Conventional approaches to segmentation don't provide direct insight into how to target customers' growth behaviors. Instead they address whether, why, and how much customers perceive a product to be differentiated. Supporters of conventional segmentation believe that their approach drives growth because it helps teams strengthen the positioning of their product in the minds of customers, which in turn leads customers to buy more of their product. Unfortunately, only the first part of this belief system is completely true. Knowledge of customer needs or psychographics can help you develop a stronger product positioning. The second part of the argument is only partially true. As we've seen, while people don't buy products they dislike, they often don't buy the product they claim to like best or judge to be most differentiated. Instead, they're influenced by something they do or see during the purchase process. When this happens, they buy a product from another company because the buying process revealed something about the other product that wasn't noticed or attended to before. This is what we meant in Chapter 1 when we said that needs-based segmentation is necessary but not sufficient to drive growth. Every business must articulate a compelling case for its product relative to its competitors' products. Conventional segmentation (especially needs-based) can be helpful in developing product positioning. But knowing that there may be several segments that see a product as differentiated—which is all that such segmentations can reveal—is a long way from knowing how to convince customers in that segment to act on their feelings about a product and ultimately buy it.

The *Playbook* approach: Propensity-based segmentation

The core argument of the *Playbook*, as we've indicated earlier, is that the focus of commercial plans should be on the actions and messages that will convince customers to change targeted high-yield buying process behaviors in a favorable way. Customers, of course, vary in the frequency with which they engage in any high-yield behavior. Some naturally do it a lot and others less so. They also have different reasons for behaving as they do, which has implications for how easy or hard it may be to change the way or the frequency with which they act. This variation means that no single commercial approach will work well across a whole market. Instead, in our view, firms should segment their market to identify customers with different propensities and rationales for engaging in high-yield behaviors and tailor their approach accordingly.

Propensity-based segmentation, as we term it, is conceptually straightforward: it involves identifying groups of customers with similar propensities and rationales for engaging in a high-yield behavior that also share observable characteristics. Put the other way round, it is about finding segmentation variables—customer characteristics—that are strongly correlated with customers' behavioral propensities and using these variables to define groups of customers with similar propensities. The members of each group will exhibit similar patterns of behavior that are, however, distinct from the behavior patterns of other segments.

In Chapter 1, we noted that Amazon Prime customers purchase six times more than non-Prime customers, so getting non-Prime customers to sign up for Prime is clearly a high-yield behavior that Amazon would like to stimulate. But customers vary in their propensity to sign up—so which customers are most likely to sign up for Prime? Is it more affluent customers? Customers that live in densely populated urban areas? Consumers with small children who cannot get to stores as easily as those with no children? In the best of all worlds, Amazon would find that there is just one customer characteristic that predicts all the variance in customers' likelihood to sign up. Unfortunately, that is rarely the case. In fact, we've learned over time that differences in behavioral propensities are usually best explained by a combination of variables that include both demographic/firmographic and situational factors.[28]

The logic of propensity-based segmentation is most readily grasped by examining both its output and the process for getting there. As shown in Figure 5-1, the output of this approach is a segmentation frame that identifies distinct groups of customers. Each cell in the frame is defined by the intersection of carefully selected and nested customer characteristics. Each segment in the frame is, by definition, a group of customers—comprising one or more cells of the grid—with a particular, distinct propensity and rationale for engaging in the targeted high-yield behavior. The customers in Segment B, for example, engage in the high-yield behavior 75 percent of the time, while those in Segment E do it only 52 percent of the time. Each segment is *also* a group of customers with a particular combination of observable characteristics—for example, customer age, sex, and education, or customer size, industry, and so on—shown on the segmentation frame. The segmentation frame and the propensity-defined segments are connected because the observable customer characteristics—the segmentation variables—are strongly correlated with customers' propensities to do the high-yield behavior.

What the segmentation map shows, then, is that customers with certain characteristics are more likely to do the high-yield behavior than are others. From the Terrafix story we know, for instance, that an older, college educated woman who has not previously been assessed for ASD will have a much higher propensity to engage in the high-yield behavior (asking for the diagnostic test) than a younger woman with only a high school education. From the EnServ story, we know that facilities managers with experience in energy management projects who regularly track energy use in their portfolio of multiple, larger buildings will engage in the high-yield behavior (consulting with a vendor early on) about 90 percent of the time, while those running just one smaller building who do not check energy use regularly do this behavior only around 40 percent of the time.

FIGURE 5-1

A Generic Propensity-Based Segmentation

The "Frame" is constructed based on situation and firmographic variables

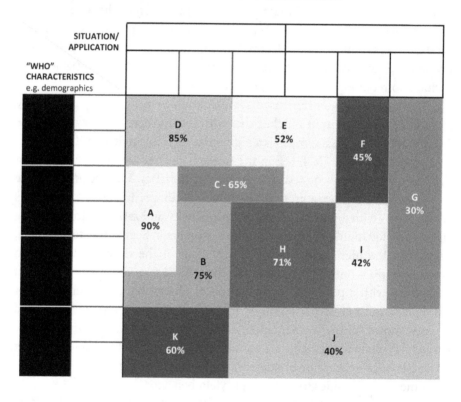

There are three major steps to creating a propensity-based segmentation map. The first is to identify a robust set of segmentation variables. The second is to construct a segmentation frame and populate it to create a buying propensity heat map. And the third step is to define the segments. While this process may appear to resemble the approach teams typically take in generating any other type of segmentation, the actual activities and analysis involved are quite different. We describe the method and the reasons behind it in detail in the next section. We have taken pains to create an approach to segmentation that avoids the common dilemmas and drawbacks that plague the traditional approaches. There are, in particular, three features of propensity-based segmentations that make them superior to other segmentation schemes.

First, propensity-based segmentation maps are valuable because they are both actionable and meaningful. Each segment is clearly identifiable and can be easily targeted by all relevant functions (for example, product development, marketing, supply chain, sales). This is because all of these functions will have participated in a process of choosing customer characteristics that are readily observable to all of them. Each segment is also meaningful in the sense of providing valuable, proprietary insight into why customers behave as they do. By definition, each propensity-based segment has a distinctive pattern and rationale for its behavior. Propensity-based segmentations thus avoid the dilemma that is the downfall of most traditional approaches. Most market segmentations suffer from being easy to implement but not particularly insightful—this is the Achilles heel of segmentations based solely on demographic/firmographic attributes or purchasing intensity—or they are insightful but not actionable—as with many needs-based and psychographic segmentations. The process we describe also eliminates the waste and confusion that occurs when different functions within a company develop and act upon their own functionally focused segmentation schemes, as very often happens.

Second, propensity-based segmentation maps are valuable because they point businesses toward the easiest sources of growth (and away from the toughest). Propensity-based segmentation naturally reveals both hot and cold spots within a market. In Figure 5-1, for example, a hot spot is identified in Segment A (with 90 percent propensity), while a cold spot is discovered in Segment J (with 40 percent propensity). Customers in high-propensity segments are already predisposed to the behavior and may only need a reminder to further increase the frequency or intensity of the behavior. Segments made up of customers who rarely engage in the high-yield behavior—cold spots—may have good reasons as to why they don't. It usually requires much more effort to convince these customers to make a change. These two attributes of propensity-based segmentation frames—the precision with which segments can be targeted and the clarity about which segments are easier to activate—are critical enablers of the extraordinarily high effectiveness of behavior-focused growth strategies. Recall that the Terrafix team dramatically increased sales by targeting and boosting the frequency of patients' asking for the test in just a few of the higher-propensity segments. As that buying process showed, a one percent increase in the rate of asking for the test translated into a three percent increase in sales.

The third valuable attribute of propensity-based segmentation is that it is intrinsically proprietary, providing a significant competitive advantage to businesses that create and use this type of segmentation. It's an unspoken truth that almost all companies in any given industry use virtually identical segmentation schemes. Nearly every pharmaceutical firm's segmentation, for example, is built off of the same segmentation variables—high versus low prescribing doctors, or primary care physician versus specialist. The same is true of the energy services industry, where customer size and industry vertical are the basis for marketing and sales plans. Most credit card companies target young, higher-income, urban adults. Because most companies see customers and evaluate them in a similar way, they end up targeting the same segments and having the same insights about those segments. They all then create astonishingly similar marketing and sales campaigns (not to mention products). The results of traditional segmentation are much like those of the trench warfare of World War I, involving huge costs for small territorial gains that are often retaken in the next battle.

Propensity-based segmentations, however, enable companies to see and target the market in a way that competitors can't easily understand or counteract. As noted in Chapter 3, the behavioral objectives that are the focus of a propensity-based segmentation are unique to each business.[29] Only Terrafix, for instance, benefitted from having patients ask their doctors for a specific test. In turn, Terrafix's segmentation frame was unique to its team's behavioral objectives. Terrafix's segmentation variables were not at all the same as those used by its competitors. The customer characteristics that were most correlated with Terrafix's behavioral objective of asking for an objective test were not the customer characteristics most likely to correlate with a different behavioral objective, such as visiting a specialist. A firm using propensity-based segmentation will see the market differently than its rivals. Thus, it will prioritize and invest in unique ways and use different tactics than its competitors. This approach usually befuddles a company's competitors whose traditional segmentation methods can't make sense of what a Terrafix or EnServ is doing. This in turn dramatically reduces competitors' ability to mount effective counterattacks. For example, when EnServ began targeting its segments 3 and 4, its rivals could see no pattern in EnServ's behavior. These segments were scattered—more or less randomly—across the size-based and industry-based segments that were being tracked by its rivals.

A propensity-based approach achieves these advantages by combining the strengths of other types of segmentation (see Conventional vs. Playbook Approach to Segmentation) and avoiding the inherent limitations of these approaches. A propensity-based segmentation is built specifically around the high-yield behaviors that the firm needs to activate to drive organic growth. Furthermore, this approach will be specific and proprietary to an individual company. In the next section, we explore in detail the process for building propensity-based segmentation frames.

Conventional vs. Playbook Approach to Segmentation

Conventional Approach	Playbook Approach
• Demographic/geographic: groups customers based on *who they are* • Needs-based: groups customers based on *what they want* from a product/offering • Psychographic: groups customers based on *attitudes, values, and beliefs* • Behavioral: groups customers based on *what they buy* currently	• Propensity-based: groups customers based on their *propensity to engage in high-yield behaviors* in the buying process

The second principle explained

As mentioned above, propensity-based segmentation has a specific format and has to be created in a particular way. The format is a two-axis grid with the grid's cells grouped into mutually exclusive, behaviorally defined segments. The two axes form the *segmentation frame*. Each axis is comprised of a small number of segmentation variables, carefully arranged and nested, that are both actionable (readily observable) and that are individually and collectively correlated with the chosen behavioral objective. Each segment consists of a group of customers who share a similar propensity for that behavioral objective and who have similar reasons for doing it.

Propensity-based segmentation maps should be built by senior level cross-functional teams following a three-part process. The first part of the process involves identifying a small number of customer characteristics (usually six to eight characteristics), which will be the candidates for the variables used to create the segmentation frame. Identifying segmentation variables is both critical and challenging to do well. The variables must be ones that each of the functions represented on the team can observe or find readily—that is, they must be actionable. The variables—or, more precisely, the specific value ranges for each variable—also have to be meaningfully correlated with the actual variance in customers' propensity to do the targeted behaviors so that the map accurately displays the market's variability.

The second part of the process is to construct the segmentation frame and behavior propensity heat map. Both science and judgment are used in this phase to figure out which combination of the candidate segmentation variables provides the most useful representation of customer behavior that is easiest to see and understand. The most powerful frames tend to be built around four to six customer characteristics with a few of those characteristics being descriptive of who the customers are (demographic/firmographic variables) and the rest being descriptive of what customers are doing or facing (variables describing the situation or occasion they are in, or what they are doing in that situation). Once the segmentation frame is constructed, data on customer behavior is used to populate each cell, thus creating a heat map of customer behavior across the whole market.

Science and judgment also play an important role in the third and final part of the process, which is to group the individual cells of the propensity heat map into distinct, coherent customer segments. Each should be composed of customers with roughly the same behavioral propensities and similar reasons for their behavior. Teams typically end up with 6-12 segments.

Both the format and the process for developing a propensity-based segmentation may strike management teams as overly prescriptive, exacting,

FIGURE 5-2

Propensity-Based Segmentation Process

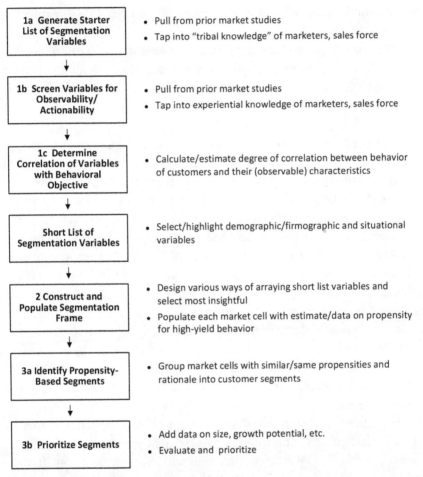

1a Generate Starter List of Segmentation Variables	• Pull from prior market studies • Tap into "tribal knowledge" of marketers, sales force
1b Screen Variables for Observability/ Actionability	• Pull from prior market studies • Tap into experiential knowledge of marketers, sales force
1c Determine Correlation of Variables with Behavioral Objective	• Calculate/estimate degree of correlation between behavior of customers and their (observable) characteristics
Short List of Segmentation Variables	• Select/highlight demographic/firmographic and situational variables
2 Construct and Populate Segmentation Frame	• Design various ways of arraying short list variables and select most insightful • Populate each market cell with estimate/data on propensity for high-yield behavior
3a Identify Propensity-Based Segments	• Group market cells with similar/same propensities and rationale into customer segments
3b Prioritize Segments	• Add data on size, growth potential, etc. • Evaluate and prioritize

and even finicky. Why does the map have to be a grid? Why use four to six segmentation variables? Why mix demographic/firmographic and situational variables? And why, above all, should it require a high ranking cross-functional team to build it? Our response is that this format and the process have proven to be the best way to create a high quality segmentation that will enable firms to grow. In order to unlock faster growth, a segmentation must satisfy four criteria—summarized by the acronym VAMPA. The segmentation should:

- Accurately reflect the intrinsic **variability** of a market (with respect to behaviors and thinking).
- Be both **actionable** for the business and provide **meaningful** insights to it.
- Be **proprietary** and therefore hard for competitors to see or respond to
- Ensure **alignment** (and hence effective action) of all the market facing functions, including product development, marketing, supply chain, and sales.

As we watched companies apply the traditional segmenting-targeting-positioning formula, we realized that there were a number of pitfalls that usually led to failed growth initiatives. Growth plans based on a segmentation map whose topography did not accurately reflect the variations in customer behavior in a granular way tended to fall flat. Segmentation schemes that made it hard for the functions to find and target customers or didn't highlight really useful information about customers similarly failed to produce growth. And firms whose market maps were identical twins to those used by every other firm in their category or industry also struggled to achieve growth. The VAMPA criteria set out the positive attributes that a segmentation must have in order to help teams identify and target real growth opportunities.

The VAMPA criteria are, in effect, the design criteria for the propensity-based segmentation process. Before describing the process in detail, it's worth delving a bit more deeply into the issues behind them so that the logic of the process will be clear.

Perhaps the most pernicious issue related to segmentation is that of functional misalignment. This trouble arises from the pervasive use of different segmentation schemes by different functions within an organization. Though this phenomenon has received relatively little attention or study, we've found that virtually every company we've worked with over the years had two or three segmentation schemes in active, simultaneous use. Marketing had one, of course. But sales was usually using a different one. Product development often had a segmentation of its own—and often enough, supply chain did as well. These dueling segmentations are trouble because of the high likelihood that each functional team will treat customers differently. Sales may have determined that a particular type of customer warrants a lot of attention and customization, while supply chain might put that type of customer into a low-priority or undesirable category and treat them poorly. At best, the inconsistent treatment confuses and annoys customers. At worst, it can chase them away. The functional alignment issue can be resolved through some specific organizational and management actions that we will describe later.

Dueling Segmentations

What seems to happen is that each key customer-facing functional team decides at some point that they can do their jobs better if they have a segmentation specifically suited to their purpose and practices. To an extent, this is understandable: as the marketing group is typically given formal responsibility for segmenting customers, they naturally select segmentation approaches and variables that will support the tasks of communications and brand building. The sales group usually creates its own segmentations. Almost always, these involve slicing customers into segments defined by the size of actual or potential purchases. Companies don't typically call their large and medium-sized customer segments by those plain names. Usually, large customers are called national, key, corporate, or global accounts, while mid-sized customers are called commercial or regional accounts. Whatever the name, sales potential is the dominant segmentation criterion.[30] Often, product engineering and research and development teams create yet another segmentation, typically sorting customers by their technology, applications, substitutes they consider, and so forth.

These additional function-specific segmentations crop up because, by and large, they're more helpful to those specific teams than the official segmentation. Sales management finds its segmentation more helpful in allocating expensive sales resources (bigger accounts should get more attention) and in designing customer interactions (small customers should be served online) than the segmentation proposed by marketing. Marketing management, for its part, rarely finds the sales segmentation approach helpful in allocating communications spend or in targeting messages because customers of similar size usually vary widely in their media habits, attitudes, and needs. Research & development and product design teams opt out for similar reasons: customer size doesn't tell them much about product needs (at least not consistently), and marketing's marcom-focused approach is too off point to be of much use.

A second challenge that our approach is designed to address is one that, like dueling segmentations, hides in plain sight. As discussed above, most segmentation schemes tend to be generic to an industry or category and therefore provide little competitive advantage to a firm. Any approach using segmentation variables that merely describe widely observable customer features is likely to fall into this trap. A propensity-based segmentation, on the other hand, is proprietary to a given firm because it is built around a set of behaviors in the buying process that are uniquely positioned to drive growth for that firm alone. Different leverage points and behavioral objectives will lead to different segmentations that are hard for others to understand or counteract, as we saw in the case of Terrafix.

The challenge of accurately representing the market topography in a way that is both actionable and meaningful requires considerable discipline and some different approaches. The challenge arises because businesses want their segmentation maps to tell them *where to target* in a way that doesn't exceed the sensing and targeting capabilities of their go-to-market system and they want it to provide intuitive guidance on *what to do* with the customers being targeted. On one hand, if a company's market facing groups can't readily see the customer characteristics used to define the segments, they can't target them. However clever the segmentation map might be, if it is not actionable by the company then they will struggle to grow. For example, a mid-sized firm working through unsophisticated dealers and without access to big databases or the talent to crunch the data might find it impossible to implement a nifty, highly granular psychographic segmentation that identifies segments by multiple variants of location, political affiliation, investable wealth, number of children in college, and type of car driven. On the other hand, companies also don't want easy to understand but meaningless maps. Building a strategy around groups of customers with nothing in common except being easy to find won't help drive growth. Simply put, companies need a way of sorting customers using factors that are both readily observable and that produce distinctive insight. In our experience, there just aren't many options apart from a propensity-based approach that reliably deliver these things.

We've noted several times that building a proprietary segmentation that provides an accurate, actionable, and meaningful representation of a market requires teams to design and run the process in a particular way. Putting in place the right process conditions—who is involved in the work, what their responsibilities are, and how the work gets done—is key to the success of the effort. Segmentation is often viewed as a technical task that is usually delegated to a working team comprised of subject matter experts, including market researchers, junior marketers, and consultants. It should not be. Rather the core *working team* should consist of the relevant general manager and senior leaders of the key go-to-market functions, such as marketing, sales, product development, and supply chain. These individuals might normally be part of the steering team overseeing a new growth strategy and spend a few hours over several months reviewing the work of the technical experts. We don't mean that. We believe these senior managers need to spend the time and do the work of debating which customer characteristics are actionable, proposing and defending potential segmentation frames, and so forth. Of course, the working team would also include marketers and market researchers. But the critical active members must be the senior leaders. This is exactly how the Terrafix and EnServ segmentation maps were developed, with deep personal involvement by Sam and Susan.

Why should senior business leaders spend their precious time this way? Because their deep engagement will produce a better segmentation and will go a long way toward ensuring alignment and suppressing dueling segmentations. For one thing, devising a good way of seeing a market requires business judgment. These senior leaders are often the ones best qualified to assess the capabilities their companies have to detect customer characteristics at different degrees of granularity and thus to determine the real actionability of potential segmentation variables. More broadly, agreeing on a common and effective way of seeing a market is a fundamental act of management alignment. Having the senior leaders of the various functions debate and declare which customer characteristics would be actionable and useful to their function—and ultimately agree and commit publicly to a segmentation frame—makes it much less likely that different functions will continue to develop and use function-specific segmentations. Being on the working team ensures these leaders build alignment around a single view and approach to the market. That alignment alone is worth the effort and investment of time.

Part 1: Identify actionable and meaningful segmentation variables

Identifying a small number of high quality segmentation variables is the first and most essential task of the working team. And it is not simple to do. In fact, the working team needs to undertake three distinct activities to get to a good list of variables for segmentation.

The first activity is to assemble as broad a set of potential segmentation variables as possible—everything that anyone on the team thinks is relevant. Our experience suggests that this starter list always includes a broad range of customer demographic or firmographic variables. Teams also almost always include various potential attitudes, values, and even potential needs of customers (fashion conscious/utilitarian for B2C businesses; innovation leader/fast follower or price sensitive for B2B). Typically, teams have to be nudged to generate and incorporate variables that describe the customer's circumstances, for example, variables describing how much or what kinds of pressures they face or variables describing the different occasions or applications for which the product is used. These situational variables are less top of mind for most teams. Yet they often turn out to be critically important in most propensity-based segmentations.

The team's second activity is to evaluate each variable on the starter list for its actionability. If a variable isn't actionable, it should be discarded at this stage. This decision involves determining whether or not the business is able to easily and accurately detect an attribute through examination of readily obtainable databases or published materials, or through customer interactions using simple, noninvasive questions or observation. The actionability of a characteristic will vary from firm to firm, depending on resources and sophistication. A small firm without serious data management or infrastructure capabilities will find it difficult to use variables like seasonal purchasing patterns to sort customers because it can't purchase, integrate, and analyze the necessary big databases that contain that information. Large, tech-savvy firms, on the other hand, might find this variable quite actionable.

Choosing Actionable Variables

The most common standard for actionability is that the segmentation variables must be knowable from the outside—in other words, observable. Naturally, you'd like your salespeople or customer service representatives to be able to tell what segment a customer falls in before interacting with them. But they can do this only if the characteristics and attributes used to segment customers can be determined by examining readily available databases, or through direct, inexpensive observation of individual customer communications or activities. For example, geographic location is easy to obtain and observe. A consumer's convenience-seeking behavior, however, isn't so easily observable. In markets with a modest number of customers, you might relax the observability standard and incorporate segmentation variables that require information directly from customers—but only if the information can be gleaned through simple, non-challenging questions that are likely to be answered truthfully.

In general, teams discard many variables when they screen them for actionability, usually ending up with a list of ten to fifteen customer characteristics that they believe their go-to-market system can identify and target. The EnServ team, for instance, found they had thirteen. Potential variables that represent customer attitudes, values, and needs almost never make the cut. As a rule, they're not observable, nor can they be accurately identified through self-reporting.[31] On the other hand, the actionable list almost always includes some demographic or firmographic variables. They're the easiest to observe for any firm. Application and situational segmentation variables typically make the cut because they're relatively easy to see or to determine through noninvasive questioning, and they often turn out to be strongly correlated with customers' behavioral propensities.

The purpose of the third activity is to screen the list of acceptably actionable customer characteristics for the strength of their correlation with customers' propensity to do the high-yield behavior(s) the company wants to target. This produces a final list of segmentation variables that are both actionable and meaningful, any of which may be used to form the segmentation frame. This correlation analysis is best performed quantitatively, though it can be done qualitatively, and done well, when it is not possible to gather data on a large, statistically significant scale.

The EnServ and Terrafix teams performed this screen quantitatively.

They surveyed large numbers of customers to quantify their behavior at each stage of the buying process. In particular, they determined how many times customers with certain characteristics engaged in high-value activities and what activities and outcomes then followed (for example, how often customers consulted with a vendor and how often those that did then put out a formal RFP). This data permitted them to calculate the correlation between customer behaviors and customer characteristics—the segmentation variables. This is how EnServ determined, for instance, that the number of buildings in a facilities manager's portfolio provided useful insight regarding differences in customer behaviors. To operationalize this variable, the team had to identify different value ranges (in this case, the number of buildings in the portfolio) that correlated with differences in behaviors. The analysis showed that the probability of the facilities manager consulting with a vendor (the chosen behavioral objective) rose 14 percent when the size of the facilities manager's portfolio went from just one or two buildings to three to five buildings. It then rose an additional 18 percent if their portfolio contained six or more buildings. In fact, this was one of the strongest correlations among the group of variables being evaluated. The data also permitted the team to calculate the overall correlation between a subset of actionable variables taken in combination and customers' behavioral propensities. So, they were able to compare the degree to which one combination of segmentation variables—say, the number of buildings in the portfolio, the size of buildings, the strictness of state building codes, and energy tracking—correlated to customers' behavioral propensities relative to another combination—say, industry vertical, size of buildings, public/private ownership, and energy tracking. The actionable variables with the highest collective correlation with the behavioral objective are typically the ones most suitable for segmenting the market.[32]

A final note on this third activity for B2B firms. Many B2B companies have a very small number of significant customers. There can also be a lot of complexity and variability within those customers (for example, each plant seems to operate a bit differently, the divisions seem to have different procurement policies). In these cases, it may not be possible to perform a straightforward, quantitative correlation analysis. Firms can, however, use alternative techniques, such as depth interviews with clients, direct observation, and a careful analysis of the stakeholder influence at each stage of the buying process to understand how customer characteristics are linked with behavioral propensities. Using multiple interviewers to triangulate findings often leads to novel, unexpected insights related to customer characteristics.

Part 2: Construct the segmentation frame and propensity heat map

The working team has two major tasks during this part of the process: first, to construct and publish a segmentation frame, and second, to populate the segmentation frame with data on customers' propensity to do target high-yield behavior(s), which yields a propensity heat map. The segmentation frame is a critical output in its own right as, done properly, it will reveal much of the underlying logic of the variation in customer behavior in the market. The heat map, for its part, is an intuitive representation of the propensity topography of the market and is the critical input to the final part of the process, defining propensity-based segments.

Technically, the work of constructing a segmentation frame is straightforward: it is to identify the most powerful combination of the candidate segmentation variables and arrange them on the axes of the frame in a way that best reveals the logic underlying the variation in customer behavior across the market. In practice, this work usually takes considerable time and effort as teams nearly always iterate through alternate answers and the debate itself can be very productive (building further alignment, among other things).

Identifying the most powerful *combination* of candidate variables may or may not require any work beyond that done in Part 1 of the process. If only a few customer characteristics (fewer than four) made it onto the working team's list of actionable and highly correlated segmentation variables, then these will form the final set. In cases where there are six or more such customer characteristics—each with a meaningful individual correlation with customer propensities—then it is necessary for the team to do additional analysis and thinking. In particular, they will need to compare the degree to which a particular combination of segmentation variables correlates to customers' behavioral propensities relative to another combination of potential variables. In general, teams should strive to find the four to six variables with the *highest collective correlation* with the behavioral objective to use in creating the segmentation frame.

Before closing the list, the team should check to ensure that the range of values used to describe each variable has been appropriately chosen to maximize the correlation with behaviors. In some cases, the choice of values for a given variable will be straightforward (for example, male versus female). In others, it may involve further analysis to understand the meaningful break points within a range. For example, if customer size is one of the variables, the team will need to have an operational definition of size (for example, annual revenue) and determine if behavioral correlation changes as revenue changes. They will also need to determine whether this variable is best represented using two values (for example, less than X dollars in annual revenue or greater than X dollars), or whether a more fine-grained division better correlates with differences in behavior. Likewise, if channel choice is a significant variable, the team will need to determine which channels are associated with significant changes in customer propensity. It is these specific values (rather than the general variable they define) that should be positioned on the segmentation frame to create the grid, as shown in Figure 5-3.

FIGURE 5-3

The Segmentation Frame of a Propensity-Based Segmentation

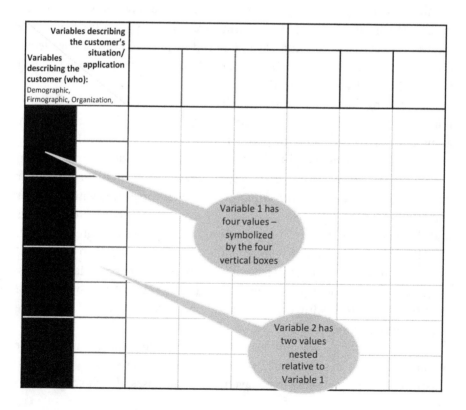

What we've found over time is that the subset of actionable variables with the highest behavioral correlation nearly always turns out to be a combination of demographic/firmographic and situational/application variables. The Terrafix team's segmentation frame, for example, had three demographic variables (gender, age, and education level) along with two situational variables (whether the patient had ever been assessed for the disease and their risk factors for having the disease). The EnServ team's frame contained more situational variables (strictness of building codes in the customer's state, number of times they'd done energy projects, and capability of tracking energy use frequently) than firmographic variables (size of buildings and number of buildings in the facilities manager's portfolio), but it was still composed of those two types of variables.[33]

With the list in place, the team can move on to constructing the segmentation frame. As mentioned before, the frame is simply a nested arrangement of the short list of actionable, highly correlated variables. *Any* arrangement of that list of variables, and there are multiple possibilities, is *technically* correct. Both the Terrafix and EnServ teams had several dozen possible arrangements of the variables on their frames. Figure 5-4 shows a number of the arrangements the EnServ team considered.

However, it is almost always the case that some arrangements are more understandable than others and do a better job of revealing the underlying logic of the variation in customer behavior, that is, *why* the customers' propensity is higher or lower. So for example, in EnServ's case, when they nested the values describing the portfolio size and the building size variables together, the team could see at a glance what kind of role the facilities manager had and how important and demanding the job was likely to be. This framing provided an intuitive window into the kinds of pressures and likely behaviors of customers in different parts of the matrix. In fact, a well-arranged frame should anticipate some of the significant dimensions of the customer narrative (described in detail in Chapter 7) from which teams infer the key drivers and barriers to changing behavioral propensities.

FIGURE 5-4

Constructing a Segmentation Frame

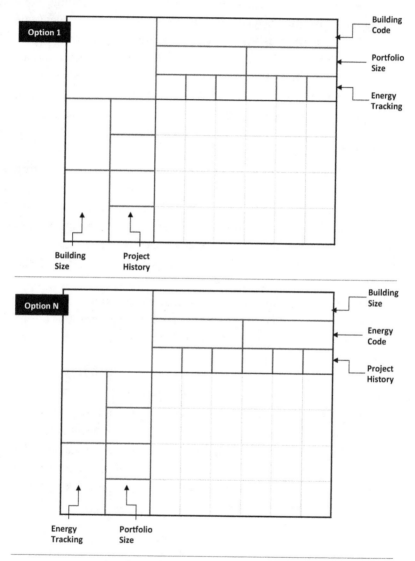

In general, the best segmentation frames tend to include demographic/ firmographic variables on one axis (the *who* axis), and the variables that describe what customers are doing or the situation they're in along the other axis (*environment or situation* axis). This is shown in Figure 5-5. A quick glance back at Figure 4-7 shows that the EnServ team put two firmographic variables from its short list—number of buildings in a facilities manager's portfolio and size of the buildings in the portfolio—on the vertical axis, while it put the situational or usage-related variables—stringency of building codes, energy tracking, and number of prior energy projects—on the other axis.

FIGURE 5-5

Logic of a Segmentation Frame

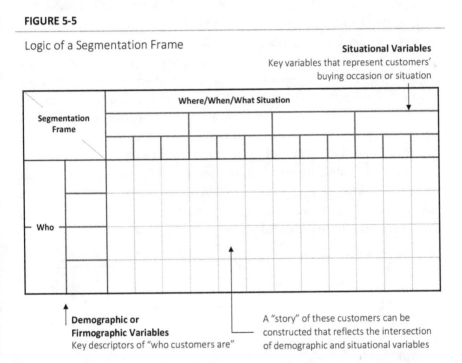

The second major activity in this part of the process is transforming the segmentation frame into a heat map that accurately describes the topography of customers' varying tendencies to do the target behaviors. As noted earlier, customers simply don't have the same propensity to do *any* activity in a buying process, much less a target high-yield behavior. Typically, a small percentage of customers will 'ask for the test' or 'consult a vendor' nearly every time they buy while others nearly never do. Most customers will do the high-yield behavior some of the time, and it is this propensity to engage in the behavior that the heat map is designed to record for each cell in the segmentation grid.

The reasons why customers do or don't engage in the selected high-yield behavior also vary, as we'll explore in detail in Chapter 7.

A typical heat map is shown in Figure 5-6. Each of the cells formed by the intersection or combination of the frame's variables is a distinctly defined group of customers (indeed, is a potential segment) that will have a distinct average propensity to do the target behavior (or any other behavior). Ideally, these estimates are quantitative, derived from the kind of quantitative survey work done by the Terrafix and EnServ teams. When statistically reliable data is unavailable or hard to obtain—as is often the case in markets with few, highly concentrated buyers—teams must draw on their understanding of the buying process for clues to the frequency with which customers in different cells do different buying process behaviors. In effect, the team conducts thought experiments in which they ask themselves: is a customer with this combination of characteristics (for example, the manager of many, large buildings, who regularly tracks energy usage) very likely to consult a vendor early on or more likely to never consult with vendors early on. In the absence of specific quantitative data, teams can assign a qualitative ranking of high, medium, or low propensity for each cell. They can then refine and calibrate these estimates by comparing the strength of the logic and story for one cell relative to other cells to get a final picture.

FIGURE 5-6

A Propensity Heat Map Before Grouping Cells

			72%	70%	62%	60%	63%	55%
			69%	72%	74%	65%	51%	52%
			88%	83%	79%	43%	48%	49%
			91%	43%	40%	34%	28%	31%

Creating and viewing the heat map of the segmentation frame is typically a watershed moment for a team. Both Sam Wilcox and Susan Gomez acknowledged this was the first time they could see at a glance the full range of behavior across their market as well as which types of customers formed their market's hot and cold spots. The differences across the market are usually quite wide. In the EnServ heat map analysis, the spread between cells with the highest and lowest propensities to consult a vendor was 95 percent and 42 percent respectively (see Figure 4-7). Moreover, there are usually many propensity clusters between these outer parameters. These result from systematic differences in the way customers in each cell think about and approach the buying process. As both Sam and Susan noted, the simple act of seeing the variation in behavior of different types of customers across the heat map got their teams excited and productively engaged. Vigorous debate and discussion broke out as team members immediately began to draw conclusions from the heat map. Some pointed out areas where they'd wasted money on customers who turned out to have low propensities. Others jumped in to express surprise or skepticism about areas where the heat map identified customers with higher propensities.

Part 3: Define propensity-based segments

Debate is quite typical, and desirable, because the heat map is the canvas for the last step of the process in which the team defines and prioritizes customer segments. In theory, a business can simply adopt the heat map as its segmentation frame. After all, each cell of the heat map represents a well-defined set of customers who share a certain propensity to do a high-yield behavior. But many businesses find the notion of separately targeting the heat map's twenty to fifty cells daunting. Moreover, teams typically notice that multiple cells may have the same or similar propensities toward (and rationale for) the high-yield behavior and can be combined into a smaller number of segments. For example, the EnServ team found twelve segments within the twenty-four cells of its segmentation frame. Identifying segments this way greatly eases the burden of targeting at a minimal loss in precision and effectiveness.

Getting from the frame to a smaller number of segments is usually an iterative, part art, part science exercise. The stylized heat map in Figure 5-6 shows the propensities to engage in the targeted behavior, ranging from a low of 28 percent to a high of 91 percent. Typically, four or five distinct sets of cells can be defined as segments right away. (Figure 5-7 shows an example of how the Figure 5-6 heat map was condensed into a smaller set of segments.) There will be a set of cells whose individual propensities are all at the high end of the range and within a few percentage points of each other, and another set at the low end. Usually, several other clusters of numerically tight cells will stand out as well.[34] Using these cells as anchors, you can postulate and test for the existence of other segments among the remaining cells. Both quantitative techniques and qualitative evaluation of the possible similarities and differences of the various cells' back stories are used to draw conclusions about whether or not to group these cells into a segment, or simply have each cell remain as its own segment. This iterative process usually resolves itself into a segmentation frame that contains eight to twelve well-defined segments.

FIGURE 5-7

Identifying Customer Segments Based on Similar Propensities to Do High Leverage Behavior

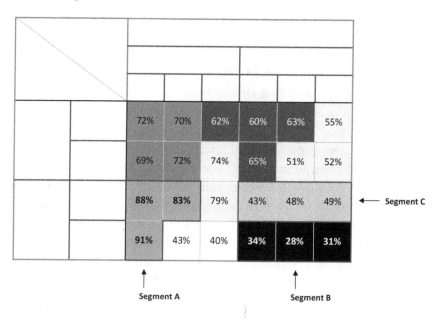

Running throughout the discussion of which cells might form a segment, and often muddying it, is a parallel conversation about which cells/segments should be prioritized. This is a distinct exercise that should be performed

after the segments have been clearly defined. Prioritization, of course, is a matter of assessing both the likely benefits and costs of successfully pursuing business in a segment or segments. Those that should be targeted first or most aggressively are those that promise the greatest net return. In making this assessment, the most important piece of data—the segment's propensities to adopt a high-yield behavior—is built into the segmentation itself. Segments with relatively high behavioral propensities are intrinsically attractive. However, the high propensity segments may be poor financial targets due to relatively small volume, slow growth, or low margins. These and other relevant economic considerations must be taken into account. They can, and often do, significantly alter a straightforward propensity-based ranking.

Conclusion

Following the process described above leads to a highly efficient and effective segmentation that overcomes two major challenges businesses face in segmenting markets: an inability to cost-effectively find, reach, and activate key segments, and the tendency for organizations to develop multiple, conflicting segmentation schemes. Our approach addresses the issue of developing highly actionable segmentations by relentlessly excluding customer characteristics that aren't observable. By focusing on characteristics that are strongly correlated with variations in customer behavior, this approach also produces a highly meaningful segmentation that identifies distinct groups of customers who behave differently from other groups.

Equally important is the impact that this well-defined process can have on fostering and maintaining alignment among different functions. A cross-functional effort to identify and select actionable segmentation variables and define customer segments results in a map of the market that is equally useful for all users in the company. This process can help avoid the waste and misalignment that arises when different parts of the organization employ different segmentation schemes.

The ultimate value of a propensity-based segmentation lies in the way it maximizes the effectiveness of marketplace activities. A propensity-based segmentation focuses attention on finding ways to increase the rate at which customers perform high-yield behaviors, which will lead to even larger increase in purchases. In practical terms, this means that regardless of the segments chosen, it is possible to generate a high return on investment. With the help of her propensity-based segmentation, Susan Gomez was able to quickly and inexpensively create customer call lists for her salesforce. Knowing her targets, she was able to tailor EnServ's products, offers, and messages into campaigns that were compelling to the customer segments targeted in the initial phases of the campaign.

Of course, segments vary considerably in their propensity toward a given high-yield behavior, as does the difficulty of inducing customers to perform that activity more often. In general, it's easier to convince customers who are already prone to a behavior to do more of it than it is to convince those with a lower propensity. The EnServ team found, for example, that they were able to generate nearly four dollars in incremental sales for every one dollar spent on campaigns focused on the high-propensity segments (Segments 3 and 4) where they chose to focus first. Once they turned their attention to other segments, however, they found that they were still able to produce nearly two dollars in incremental sales for every one dollar invested in a campaign aimed at changing the consulting behaviors of Segments 8 and 12 (see Figure 4-7), where the propensity to consult was a market low of around 40 percent.

A well-run propensity-based segmentation process therefore accomplishes many difficult things at once. It breaks through the dilemma that companies often face between having actionable segmentations based on easily observable customer attributes that are, however, not very insightful, and the opposite problem of designing highly meaningful segmentations that are impossible to implement. It also ensures that the resulting segmentation will be proprietary and highly differentiated from the map that the rest of the industry is using. Finally, because the segmentation is built around the specific drivers in the buying process that are likely to drive organic growth for the firm, a propensity-based segmentation enables teams to tailor highly customized, segment-specific campaigns aimed at influencing those specific high-yield behaviors.

Chapter 6

Sparkle Cosmetics: Winning at the Wall

Maya Stone, head of marketing for Helena Styx Cosmetics, glanced apprehensively at the time. A meeting with marketing managers from the company's two cosmetics lines was scheduled in less than an hour and Maya was braced for a heated debate about how to kick-start the group's flagging growth.

Helena Styx Cosmetics was a division of a multibillion dollar packaged goods company. The company's flagship Sparkle cosmetics brand had long been a leader in the United States and was one of the most recognized names on the market. The brand appealed primarily to younger women (teens to thirties) and offered a complete range of products, including foundation and color cosmetics (lipstick, nail polish, blush, eye shadow, and so on). Sparkle was widely distributed through mass retail channels, including drugstores and large grocery chains. At the time of the meeting, the company's Jean Drou brand, sold largely in department stores, was positioned as the professional's choice, targeting sophisticated consumers of any age. Despite the strong heritage of these brands, sales had slowed while the industry as a whole was experiencing moderate growth. The compound annual growth rate (CAGR) for Sparkle had fallen to 1 percent per year for the previous three to four years, while Jean Drou sales had been stalled for so long that the brand's viability was in question. Perception studies found that the identities for these brands had become blurred as consumers increasingly lumped them together with other brands. The challenge facing Maya was to reignite growth for the Sparkle brand and determine whether Jean Drou could be put back on a path to profitable growth.

Point-of-entry customers—teenage girls buying cosmetics for the first time—were of particular concern. Attracting these new users as they entered the category was critical. The company believed that brand preferences, once established, continued to influence purchase behaviors for years to come. A number of efforts had been made to boost sales of both brands with varied success. Some initiatives appeared to work for a while before falling off, while others failed to move the needle at all. Frustration within the team boiled over into a major row about the best way to revitalize the brands and recapture share within the all-important point-of-entry segment. The meeting that Maya was about to walk into was intended as a kind of summit to bring together the team members who were split into two opposing camps.

The first group advocated redoubling the traditional approach based heavily on print and video advertisement. Like other cosmetics makers, Helena Styx viewed makeup as a fashion product subject to changing trends. Customer segments were thus defined according to age and psychographic factors such as attitudes toward wearing makeup, color preferences, and fashion sense (for example, being fashion-forward). The Sparkle brand had long been positioned as an aspirational product for young women with media campaigns centered on highly recognizable young celebrities. While the look and profiles of the celebrities had evolved over time—recent campaigns featured pop stars rather than models—the goal was to position Sparkle as the face of youthful glamour, fresh and of the moment. This positioning had worked well for Sparkle in the past. About half of the group argued that this positioning could reinvigorate the brand if additional resources, fresh ideas, and great creative work were added to the mix.

The second camp emphasized the role of social media, pointing out that new media and devices consumed a much larger share of time and attention in young women's daily lives. These marketers argued for the growing importance of bloggers, Facebook, Instagram, and YouTube personalities seen as peer role models who often dispensed advice on cosmetics. Rather than focus on traditional celebrities, this group maintained that the priority should be to place the brand and influence messages received through social media. While Helena Styx had dabbled in these channels, the marketers argued for suspending much of the traditional activity and redirecting Sparkle's spend heavily toward online platforms that catered to teens in a bid to regain relevance with point-of-entry customers. The number of voices on each side was evenly matched, with each group marshaling evidence to support its case.

Maya knew that any decision had to be based on solid evidence, since the losing side would likely challenge the methodology and findings. The burden of proof was thus high, as were the stakes. "It felt like an existential moment for us. We needed to be bold, but most of all we needed to be right," she recalled. As she reviewed the two sides of the argument, she noted some of the underlying assumptions on which they were based. Both proposals were rooted in a strong belief in the importance of brand—a conviction that women went to the store looking for their preferred brands and then bought them if available. The essence of the disagreement was about which types of aspirational figures and which type of media would be most effective in attracting young women to the Sparkle brand. While these assumptions were widely held throughout the industry, Maya hesitated. Did they truly understand the factors that motivated customer behavior?

As people gathered in the conference room, Maya stepped to the white board and began writing some of the fundamental questions she'd been pondering before the meeting: How do women choose which brand they wear? Why do they switch brands? What makes them buy the products they do? The room grew quiet as the team read the board. "At that point it became clear to everyone that it's not enough that we believe certain things about the market. We have to *know* it." Only then could they build agreement and get buy-in on which approach to pursue.

The buying process and high-yield behavior change

Over the next couple of months, Maya's team undertook a study to examine the end-to-end buying process for cosmetics. They received about 4,000 completed responses to more than 7,000 surveys asking customers how they selected and purchased cosmetics in different categories. As the results were compiled, a few key themes emerged. The data confirmed and elaborated on some widely held beliefs within the industry, including the role of influencers in providing information on and shaping preferences for certain brands. This was particularly true with respect to teenagers, who were strongly influenced by the opinions of their mothers, sisters, and friends. However, the survey data upended at least two of the team's (and the industry's) most important assumptions about how women purchased cosmetics. One of the most striking findings was that customers were much less concerned about brand than they were about finding the right color: "Finding colors that look good on me" was the single biggest factor in their decision to buy a product. This insight was the exact opposite of what Maya's team had believed. "We never articulated it this way," said Maya, "but if you'd asked how women chose which products to buy, most people in the industry would have told you they shopped for the brand first and bought the best color for them within that brand. What the data showed is that they actually shop for the right color among a group of acceptable brands. It's a world of difference."

The other big finding was the huge impact of in-channel evaluation. The data showed that most women judged color suitability "at the wall" in the store—by trying things on where they could—for example, in cosmetic-counter makeovers, or, most often, by scrutinizing and comparing the colors shown on the packages. In fact, as the excerpt from the buying process shown in Figure 6-1 indicates, only 20 percent of women went to the store looking for a single, preferred brand, and just one in twenty of those women looked for and bought Sparkle. The other 80 percent of women searched for the right color and considered several different brands when they shopped. Remarkably, women purchased Sparkle at a higher rate when they browsed multiple brands at the store. About one in five women who compared and chose products by looking at the color swatches on packages purchased Sparkle. The rate was even higher among those who actually tried on color cosmetics at the store—with nearly one in two choosing Sparkle.

"The big shock for us was that, for color cosmetics, brand considerations didn't actually drive purchasing behavior the way we believed," said Maya. "The leverage point is at a later stage in the process during in-channel evaluation. When you see the data like that, it just makes you question how much of what we've been doing to promote brand preference really works."

Finally, the data reshaped the team's thinking about how loyal their customers were over time. The team's belief was that brand preference, while strongest early in a woman's life (just after she'd been won over to the brand), remained stable for most women. What the data showed was a much more complicated reality in which women went in and out of brands over time. They might purchase one brand steadily for a number of years, abandon it for many more, and then return to it—sometimes just briefly, but often for the long term.

All in all, the buying process work both puzzled and galvanized Maya's team, leading them to come together to rethink their whole approach to marketing Sparkle. (They set aside work on Jean Drou until they could get a handle on what to do for their key brand.) They decided to rebuild their approach around influencing the in-channel behaviors that emerged as the

FIGURE 6-1

Excerpt from Color Cosmetics Buying Process

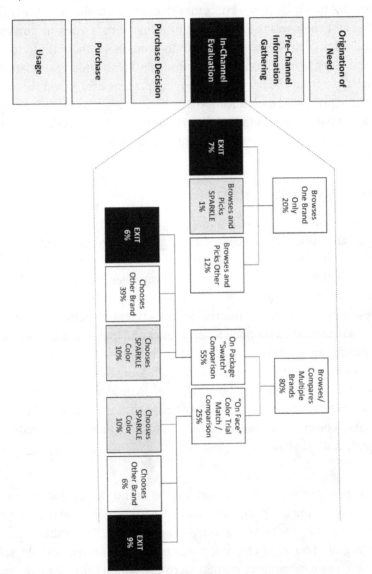

critical step in the buying process. Specifically, they identified two primary high-yield behaviors. The first, which applied to all age groups, was to get women to test whether Sparkle's colors looked good on them. Trying Sparkle colors at the point of purchase was thus an important leverage point. This was a significant shift for the team and challenged assumptions that held sway across the industry—namely, that women looked for the specific brands of color cosmetics to which they were committed. The data showed clearly that finding the right color was the biggest factor influencing a woman's purchase. The second high-yield behavior applied to women in their mid- to late twenties and older who had once been Sparkle and Jean Drou customers, but had moved away from the brands. The buying process data found that these women, who represented a significant share of the market, were more likely to come back to their former brands if they tried them again. The desired high-yield behavior was thus to get women to reengage with the brands they loved when they were younger.

Rethinking segmentation

The team then turned to the task of remapping their view of the market around these target behaviors. They developed a new, propensity-based segmentation around factors that best predicted customer behavior with regard to the two behavioral objectives. The team found four variables that correlated most strongly with these behaviors.

The resulting segmentation frame (Figure 6-2) reflected choices about the channels in which women shopped for cosmetics and their life situation—age, working status, and whether they had young children at home. The analysis revealed a fascinating interaction between where women shopped, their stage in life, and what cosmetics they bought. When considered in isolation, the variables were just moderately indicative of brand choice and buying behavior. When taken in combination, however, they turned out to be strong predictors of brand purchasing behavior.

Given the urgency of reaching and shaping the brand-buying habits of new customers entering the category, the team chose to focus first on growing the flagship Sparkle brand with young teens (Segment A). While this segment wasn't the largest in terms of revenue, it was one of the top segments by sales volume. These point-of-entry customers were also a high priority for Sparkle, since the research showed that many women tended to come back to their early brand choices later in life. Putting aside the debate about whether to try

FIGURE 6-2

Propensity-Based Segmentation for Women Purchasing Color Cosmetics

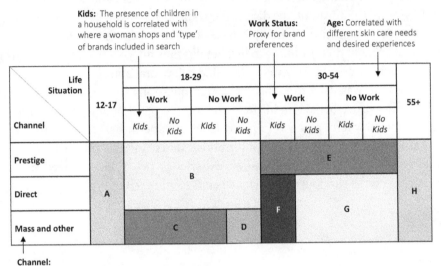

Kids: The presence of children in a household is correlated with where a woman shops and 'type' of brands included in search

Work Status: Proxy for brand preferences

Age: Correlated with different skin care needs and desired experiences

Channel: Correlated with which brands are available for purchase

to reach these young women through traditional advertising or social media, the team took a deeper look at the factors that motivated behaviors and purchase decisions for this segment.

Drivers and barriers to behavior change

Having identified and prioritized Segment A, the team turned its focus to understanding the buying behaviors of these point-of-entry customers. The data made clear that the average age at which girls started using makeup was younger than previously thought, beginning in the late preteen years. It also suggested that, as a group, teens were a high-trial segment and typically bought many different brands in a range of colors. They also switched brands frequently, often abandoning recently purchased products. Teens typically shopped for makeup in pharmacies and discount stores. The average amount they spent on each shopping trip was fairly low—about $11 per store visit. However, they tended to shop frequently for cosmetics.

The challenge for Maya and her team was to explain these distinctive buying behaviors and what motivated them. The team followed a three-stage process to develop a data-rich understanding of this segment. First, they designed and conducted additional research on point-of-entry customers following the guiding questions laid out by the customer behavior framework (CBF). Next, they drew on the data and insights from this analysis to construct an integrated narrative about why these customers behaved as they did in a way that brought their thinking to life. Finally, they inferred from the narrative a list of drivers and barriers to the targeted behavioral objectives.

The CBF was used to identify research questions and organize findings about what drove behaviors in this segment: the physical and social context (how, when, where, and with whom teens shopped), beliefs and attitudes (what teens thought and felt about brands, colors, and channels where they shopped for cosmetics), and desired experience (what teens looked for in makeup and the shopping experience itself) (Figure 6-3).

FIGURE 6-3

Customer Behavior Framework

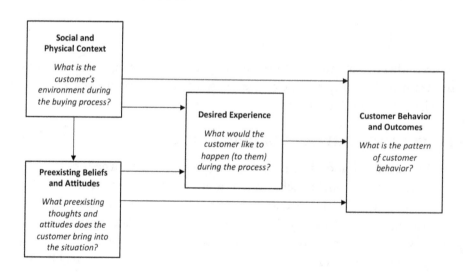

The findings from this research helped elucidate the particular factors and motivations of teens buying makeup and revealed some key themes. For example, social interactions and fitting in played a role in how these young women shopped for and purchased cosmetics (Figure 6-4).

FIGURE 6-4

Customer Behavior Data for Segment A (Point-of-Entry Customers)

Social and Physical Context

- Shops with mom and / or with friends (not alone)
- Shopping with Mom
  - *First purchase typically with Mom*
  - *Initial information she receives is mainly from Mom; she then gathers information from magazine ads, TV ads, good friends*
  - *Mom often supports / facilitates makeup purchase as long as daughters don't choose "unacceptable" colors*
- Shopping with Friends
  - *Purchases with friends usually occur after she has entered the category*
  - *Shopping with friends is fun, recreational*
- Has time to shop for makeup and enjoys spending the time looking at products; makeup is generally not a destination purchase; spends a lot of time in malls
- Generally does not have a lot of money to spend; gets money from others (e.g., allowance, gifts); makeup is something she chooses to spend her money on
- Sources of influence: Mom, friends, magazine ads, TV ads and models influence products / brands she buys. She is also influenced at POS by sales and color displays

Beliefs and Attitudes

- Believes shopping for makeup is fun; shopping with friends can help build friendships
- Favorite things about shopping experience are trying new things, looking at colors, looking at new brands, trying samples
- Favorite places to shop for makeup are mall and drug stores, where she perceives wide variety, accessibility (close, goes there a lot), and lower prices
- Attracted to color displays and clear signage around new colors and products
- Believes testers are unsanitary and unappealing, yet wants to sample products and experiment in-store (she believes this is the most fun part about the in-store experience)
- Believes she can trust her Mom to choose the right products and brands for her (not yet fully confident in own ability to choose)

Desired Experience

- She wants a fun, recreational shopping experience in which she can experiment and play with new products and colors; she also wants new products / colors to be easy to find (e.g., indicated through signs), information on how to select products and colors and lower prices or sales, teen-friendly store atmosphere
- She likes shopping with both Mom and friends but for different reasons
  - *Likes shopping with Mom since she often pays; Mom provides approval*
  - *Enjoys shopping with friends because it's fun, social; friends provide advice / acceptance*
- Likes least about shopping: hard to choose / find right colors, takes long time, paying for it
- Main reasons she bought first brand are colors or styles, Mom buys or uses it, price, friend uses it
  - *Color is a key influencer of both product and brand choice*
  - *She is willing to pay more for colors she likes or higher quality products (i.e., last longer, won't give pimples, e.g., she may switch to Brand X from Brand M)*

Customer Behavior and Outcomes

- Typically first bought products / brands Mom had or recommended
- First brands bought are Brand X, Brand M, and Brand C; also buys products from specialty retail outlets (e.g., Claire's)
- 93% still buy first brands bought, but have added others to their brand set
- She and/or Mom pays; may ask Mom to buy her makeup at the point of sale
- Shops primarily at discount and drug stores; also shops for makeup in malls (drug and specialty retail stores)
- Looks at makeup whenever in drug / discount store with Mom, or when shopping at mall with friends / Mom

The CBF research provided copious qualitative and quantitative data for the team but initially appeared to be a list of key insights. So, the team chose to synthesize these data into a story about the customer that emphasized key themes. While focused around cosmetics, this story also explored the larger picture of what this customer wanted and cared about. "It's sort of like telling a fairy tale," remarked Maya. "Like, 'Once upon a time there was a customer...' and they're on a sort of quest, with triumphs and struggles along the way. When you get a good customer narrative, the reaction should be, 'Hey, I know that person.' It turns the data into a human being."

The final step for Maya's team was to distill these themes and data into a set of drivers and barriers that became pivotal guidelines for the redesign of Sparkle's marketing campaign. Drivers are factors that motivate customers to engage in specific high-yield behaviors. Barriers, by contrast, include the emotional, psychological, and physical impediments customers experience with regard to these behaviors. Enhancing drivers while eliminating or mitigating barriers is core to an effective activation strategy.

Among the insights that stood out clearly from this analysis was the importance of buying makeup as a *social experience* for young teens. One critical aspect was the way they interacted with friends, sisters, and mothers while shopping for, and applying, cosmetics, which contributed to the fun and excitement of trying cosmetics. Another aspect was the sense of wearing makeup as a rite of passage into early adulthood. Mothers played a key role in the experience, both as influencers and gatekeepers. Teens' first cosmetics purchases were typically made with their mothers and were strongly influenced by her views on products and brands. Input received from these important influencers could be an important driver or barrier to try and purchase Sparkle cosmetics.

Another important theme was teens' desire to fit in with a social peer group. Part of fitting in for this customer involved wearing makeup and colors that looked good on her and were appropriate and consistent with what others were doing. Teens were especially likely to experiment with a range of colors as they figured out their own personal style. They therefore wanted to try fun and unusual shades in addition to more conservative choices. Having a range of colors to try was thus an important sales driver for this group.

FIGURE 6-5

Customer Narrative for Segment A (Point-of-Entry Customers)

A Rite of Passage	The "Point-of-Entry" customer (age 12) is in the midst of the transition from girl to teenager. Wearing makeup is one of the rites of passage in becoming a woman. This rite often involves her mother, sisters and friends. She has prepared for this transition from an early age by watching her mother apply and wear makeup and by playing "dress up." Using makeup "for real" and having makeup of her own is a big step up for her.
Everybody's Wearing Makeup	Her desire to wear makeup comes primarily from noticing peers or aspirational others (e.g., older girls, sisters) wearing makeup. Fitting in is very important to her, which she believes she accomplishes in part by wearing makeup.
She Wants Mom's O.K.	Her mother is the gatekeeper. Once she has her mother's approval to wear makeup, her mother shepherds her through this transition. She likes to have her Mom's input and she trusts Mom's judgment and experience.
She Needs to Fit in and Be Appropriate . . .	As she begins to wear makeup, she tries to manage the tension between wanting to signal that she is wearing makeup and wanting to be appropriate. The first makeup products she wears are color products (lipstick and nail polish) because they signal that she is wearing makeup. She believes wearing makeup helps her fit in; but she also believes that a misstep, such as wearing too much makeup, has serious social consequences. She believes that getting it right will make her more attractive, which will enhance her popularity. Experimenting and noticing what others are doing help her learn more about makeup and become better able to manage the tension between signaling usage and being appropriate. In addition to the information she gets from Mom and from her friends, she also seeks information from magazine and TV advertisements.
. . . And She Also Wants to Have Fun	Buying and wearing makeup "for real" are an extension of "play" for her; they're fun. Another reason she starts with color is because she finds color products fun to buy and wear. She's interested in having the latest products, for example body glitter, hair mascara and especially the latest, fun colors.
Mom Influences Her Brand Choice	When buying makeup, she often chooses Mom's brands because they have Mom's approval and because she has had the opportunity to try them. They are also more accessible to her (e.g., if Mom uses Brand C, she can easily order products when Mom orders; she often accompanies Mom on shopping trips to the drug store).
Brands She Considers . . .	She is attracted to teen-oriented brands in part because she likes the colors, and in part because she thinks the brand is appropriate for teens (e.g., by advertising in teen magazines). She also chooses brands which she can afford, since she has a limited budget, doesn't work, and largely depends on others for spending money. Given these factors, brands in her consideration set include Brand X, Brand C, Brand M, Brand F, and specialty retail brands.
Shopping Is Fun!	She enjoys shopping for and experimenting with makeup, which can be a source of bonding with her friends, and she has time to shop and linger at the display. When shopping, she is attracted to makeup products / brands by color displays, new products / colors and sales.

The shopping experience itself was also important. These young women felt most comfortable in a teen-friendly store atmosphere that made it easy to find and try products that were within their limited budgets. Teens often

FIGURE 6-6

Drivers and Barriers for Segment A (Point-of-Entry Customers)

Drivers	Barriers
• Mother (or older sister) wears and/or recommends the brand • 'Expert' assistance in selecting, applying the brand • Friends, "aspirational peers" wear the brand • Wide range of colors – both 'fun/push-the-limits' and 'normal' • Able to see actual color on self with intended clothes/outfits	• High (absolute) price • Color doesn't look good on them (i.e., with respect to complexion, hair color, clothes color palette) • Friends, "aspirational peers" denigrate the brand (e.g., as "cheap," "for kids," etc.) • Not available in nearby stores or online • Hard/impossible to try on before purchase (closed package, no mirror)

worried about choosing the wrong colors, brands, or overall look, so being able to try out products was especially important for these first-time cosmetics buyers. Not being able to find or experiment with Sparkle brands in the stores where they preferred to shop constituted a significant barrier.

A number of other factors could also promote or inhibit in-channel trial. One key barrier to trying color cosmetics before buying was the way that the makeup was packaged and displayed, especially in the mass retail channels where Sparkle brand products were sold. Products were sealed in plastic packaging, making it impossible to try them in the store and complicating the task of finding appropriate colors. Furthermore, as with other fashion items, cosmetics makers were continually changing the colors available to reflect changing trends. Color products purchased in the past might thus be hard to find again. Users therefore switched products and brands fairly frequently.

As Maya recalled, the discussion of this barrier prompted one brand manager to exclaim, "Now I understand why women have so many barely used cosmetics in their cabinets at home!" Because it was often difficult to determine the true color of packaged products in the store, women ended up making guesses about the colors that would suit them and often found that they didn't like those colors once they got home and were able to try them. While Sparkle managers had long observed this phenomenon in consumer research, the current analysis made clear what was driving this behavior.

These insights caused Maya and her team to reassess the alternative marketing campaigns over which they had stood bitterly divided only a few months before. "With the understanding we had from the analysis, it was a different kind of conversation," said Maya. "It wasn't about which pop singer or which teen blogger we want. It was all about how we influence the behaviors that lead to purchase standing at the wall—usually with mom looking over her shoulder!"

Behavior change value proposition

The new Sparkle brand campaign broke dramatically from past approaches, which relied heavily on print and TV. It included significant changes along three dimensions: the *product*, the *presentation*, and the *context* for teens buying cosmetics.

The first element of the campaign to encourage teens to try Sparkle centered on the product itself. As the customer narrative revealed, wanting to fit in and be appropriate were important motivators for these customers. An important element of this was color choice. In addition to traditional shades and styles, young women were attracted to bright, fun colors appropriate to their age. As they tried to figure out their own style, they wanted to experiment with a wide range of colors while avoiding styles that were either too grown up or uncool. The Sparkle team responded by increasing the range of bright colors favored by teens and giving them greater prominence on store shelves. Because teens tended to make frequent, small purchases, products were priced to fit within the $11 per visit budget that was typical for this segment.

The second big shift in strategy was to reimagine the presentation of Sparkle products at the wall in the discount and mass merchandise stores where teens shopped most often. The key was to redesign displays to improve the odds that teens would find a good color match. The team did this in multiple ways. It redesigned Sparkle's packaging using higher-quality color printing and better visibility of the product to show the actual colors in a way that was more true to life. Product guides and inserts explained how the colors could be used to create desired looks that appealed to teens. The team also created informational cards at the point of display that identified color options based on skin type and allowed young women to better match the colors that looked good on them.

The team went further, working with a few especially open-minded retailers to allow real in-store trial. Point-of-sale displays in these mass merchandise stores were redesigned to include large, attractive displays with mirrors that were big enough for two or three people to use at the same time, enabling the social aspect of trying makeup with friends. The displays showed photos of young women with different complexions so that teens could appropriately match themselves with what these aspirational peers were wearing. In some retail locations, the Sparkle displays included small, single-use product samples that enabled teens to test how the colors actually looked on them. Finally, understanding the important role that technology—particularly cell phones—played for teen customers, the Sparkle team developed a downloadable app for in-store use. Customers could use the app to scan product bar codes on the shelf and see those exact colors and styles applied to a selfie on their phones.

The third dimension of the revamped marketing campaign focused on engaging with key influencers. These influencers included teens' immediate social group, sisters, and mothers as well as aspirational peers. In addition to creating fun and inviting displays that encouraged the social aspect of shopping for makeup with friends, the company tapped the potential of social media to enable teens to connect with a broader group of peers. Using a proprietary app, teens could instantly share photos and information about the products they were trying with others whom they could ask to "rate my look." Importantly, this use of social technology wasn't about getting endorsements from social media celebrities, but rather from customers' wider peer group.

Recognizing the importance of mothers as role models and the gatekeepers who often financed teens' initial makeup purchases, Sparkle developed tools for moms to use in talking to their daughters about selecting and using makeup. The marketing team also organized special events such as mother-daughter makeovers in some of the largest mass retail stores where these mothers and daughters tended to shop. Often these events were timed for the back-to-school season at the end of summer.

As Maya commented, "In retrospect, some of the things we did seem almost obvious. But there's no way we would have gotten there without the process and working through the process in a methodical way. We had people ready to go to the mat over print versus social media. We now realize we were missing an important piece of the picture. Once we started looking together at how we could change buying behaviors at the point of sale, the ideas and the collaboration just took off."

Disproportionate investment

In contrast to the traditional emphasis on building brand awareness through media, Sparkle moved aggressively to reinvent the in-channel shopping experience. As noted earlier, they focused first on changing behaviors in the point-of-entry segment of young teens (Segment A). For the first two years of the campaign, they reallocated a disproportionate amount (65 percent) of their marketing spend toward this segment.

As the new strategy began to deliver results, Maya and the team looked to apply the same lessons of organic growth across the rest of their portfolio. Starting in the third year, they expanded their activities with new campaigns to promote Sparkle and Jean Drou with Segments B and E. Again, a disproportionate share of the Jean Drou marketing spend was redirected away from advertisements to expanding the brand's footprint in channels where busy working women tended to shop, enabling them to rediscover the brand.

Epilogue

Maya's challenge to her team to understand the true drivers and barriers of customer buying behavior catalyzed a major turnaround in Helena Styx's fortunes. Redesigning the point of sale displays and experience helped the Sparkle brand regain both volume and share leadership in the category. Four years on, year over year growth continued to accelerate. During this initial period, the brand grew revenue by 25 percent (over $100 million) and share within the teen segment grew 15 percent. Market surveys named Sparkle one of the top five coolest brands for teens across all the brands they experienced.

FIGURE 6-7

Reigniting Organic Growth for Sparkle Brand

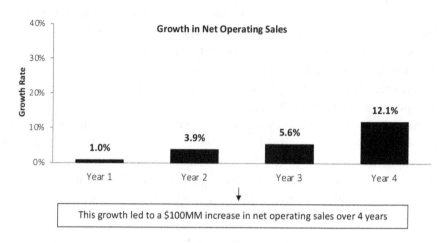

As mentioned above, the team used a similar process to revitalize the flagging Jean Drou brand, which was sold primarily through mid-tier department stores. The buying process analysis showed that usage of the brand dipped considerably among segments of working women with kids. This phenomenon was largely attributable to where these women shopped. Women who were busy with work and kids tended to shop less frequently in the channels where Jean Drou was being sold.

The company adopted a strategy of encouraging these women to come back to Jean Drou. Product displays were designed to remind them of the brands they had once worn and to try them again. Jean Drou also expanded into a limited number of upscale mass retailers, warehouse clubs, and independent pharmacies where these target customers shopped. These efforts helped stabilize Jean Drou, enabling it to regain its profitable niche positioning as a high-end choice for sophisticated consumers.

Chapter 7

Third Principle: Unearth the Critical Drivers and Barriers of Target Behaviors

The striking and pivotal part of the Sparkle story is how vital it was to unearth and do something about barriers to purchase. Maya Stone's team had been pursuing the right source of growth—brand choice—for years. They had recognized—more or less—what outcomes women sought from cosmetics all along. Moreover, they had been running well-funded and generally well-executed communications and promotional campaigns emphasizing the benefits and value of the Sparkle brand. Their hope, as it is for many product teams, was to make Sparkle's benefits so clear and compelling in women's minds that they'd put it on their shopping list and, looking neither right nor left, buy the brand and bring it home. But things rarely worked as well as hoped. Sales surged and ebbed in puzzling ways. Sometimes the ads and promotions worked, other times they didn't.

The insight that put Maya's business on a more sustained growth trajectory was that while consumers would happily acknowledge all the good things Sparkle said about its brand, they would not buy the brand unless their concerns about the products—especially how the colors would look on them—were allayed. The Sparkle team had been trying to build what marketers term a differentiated brand for years. But what was in the minds of consumers wasn't just the differentiation promoted by Sparkle, but a balanced view of both benefits and deficiencies rooted in their experience of Sparkle and other cosmetics brands. Women knew that the look of a cosmetic on the box, or on the model promoting it, wasn't how it would look on them. Until they were assured that it would look good on them, they would hesitate to buy. They made their choice to buy Sparkle based on an overall, balanced assessment of the cosmetic. It was only when the Sparkle team began to understand this that they realized they had to do something about this important barrier to purchase. Changing their go-to-market approach to remove or reduce barriers in addition to emphasizing benefits was the key to rapid and consistent growth.

Reducing or removing the key barriers to trial and brand choice wasn't an easy thing. Maya's team had to do a major redesign of Sparkle's go-to-market approach in order to provide consumers with convenient, low-cost ways of pretesting whether the Sparkle colors would suit their look and complexion. Packages had to be redesigned to make it easier to see the color of the actual product. Money had to be diverted from broadcast and print advertising and put into social media (the "see it on you" app) and in-store kiosks. They also made changes to the product itself (for example, expanded color variety). But altering Sparkle's value proposition to address both barriers and drivers in this way had huge benefits. As noted in the Sparkle story, the brand regained both volume and share leadership and grew 25 percent (over $100 million) in the three years after the redesign.

The Sparkle team found that identifying the full set of critical drivers and barriers provided the insights needed to fuel supercharged growth. How to unearth such drivers and barriers is the subject of this chapter. In a sentence, the key is gaining a deep, thorough, and *balanced* understanding of why customers behave as they do. Over the past two decades, we've refined a three-component approach to unearthing the drivers of, and barriers to, changing customer behavior. The first component is the customer behavior framework (CBF), through which we ask and answer a series of guiding questions about each segment organized around the major factors that underpin customer decision making. The second component, the customer narrative, weaves the insights gained through the CBF into an explanatory story about each segment. The third component is the distillation of each segment's drivers and barriers to the critical high-yield behaviors. These provide a subtle but critical pivot from simply understanding why customers in the segment exhibit certain behavioral propensities to what can be done to influence and change those propensities.

Conventional wisdom

While the type of customer research we're advocating may seem familiar to marketers, we're actually talking about something quite different from the approach that we see many firms take. In particular, there are three subtle but dangerous blind spots in the way marketers typically study and generate insights about customer behaviors. The usual approach is to compile data about product preferences, values, lifestyle, and demographics of the customers in each segment, often organized in the form of a segment profile or persona. Firms then mine that profile for insights about how to clarify product benefits in customers' minds.

The first, and most dangerous, blind spot in this approach is that the profiles are heavily product-centric, albeit with a customer identity wrapper. The product or category is the clear center of attention. The customer's life is described and analyzed only in relation to it. The second is that the profiles, and the insights drawn from them, are overwhelmingly focused on benefits— the positive things that happen when a product is purchased and used. The negatives—the challenges customers have in learning about, finding, buying, and using the product—receive little attention or are ignored entirely. The third blind spot is that these negatives, if and when they are acknowledged, are reframed and then effectively dismissed as issues related to being (or not being) easy to do business with.

Product centricity

Segment profiles typically provide a detailed picture of how people in a segment think about a category and the products or brands within it.[35] The data that receives the most attention in these traditional profiles is about when, where, and how often customers use the product and their attitudes towards it. Customers are often surveyed in great detail on the relative importance of specific elements of the product's functionality and features, as well as their assessment of how well a given product performs relative to competition or expectation. For example, we've seen automakers build exhaustive questionnaires to elicit customer attitudes about things like engine size, horsepower, number of seats, tire size, number of airbags, and communications systems. Likewise, we've seen mining equipment and machine tool manufacturers go to great lengths to document customers' ratings of the functionality and features of their bulldozers or computer controlled lathes.

Of course, conventional profiles usually do contain information about customers themselves. A high-quality traditional profile will provide a layer of descriptive information about the customers in the segment. In profiles for B2C markets, this customer wrapper will highlight the basic demographics of the segment (for example, age, sex, race, income) and may include information about values and lifestyle. For B2B market profiles, the customer wrapper provides information about company size, operating model, and other characteristics of the firms within the segment. Some go further and attempt to make them customer-centric by adding more information about core values and activities, often organized into the form of a story about a day in the life of a customer. But both the basic and the more sophisticated versions of the traditional customer profile are fundamentally product focused. The data they provide on customers is there largely to make clear *who* it is that has the product preferences and attitudes and describe how the product is used in their daily lives.

The issue, the blind spot, in this type of profile—regardless of how much data about customer identity it contains—is that it's too narrow and leads to a kind of tunnel vision. Finding out what people like or want in a product and showing them that your brand has those things is obviously important. But they provide only a part of the insight that's needed to unlock fast, consistent growth. You also need to understand the larger context and obstacles that might stand between what customers like and what they actually do during the buying process.

A bias for drivers

The second blind spot of the traditional approach is its extreme overemphasis on product benefits. The traditional profile or persona not only narrows your focus to products (ignoring other aspects of the buying process), but imparts a strong bias toward the positive. The data in the profile is set up in a way that compares customers' perceptions of the products in a category to help differentiate the benefits a product can offer relative to competitors. The fundamental problem is that customers actually hold a balanced, two-sided view of categories and products in their minds. Especially in long established, hotly contested markets, they see and remember the drawbacks and negatives of each product as clearly and as strongly as they do the advantages and benefits. Moreover, customers' broader experience of the benefits and negatives of the process of searching for and buying a product are also inextricably linked to their views of the product itself (see Ignoring the Negative Aspects of Buyer Behavior).

Ignoring the Negative Aspects of Buyer Behavior

The limitations of focusing only or primarily on positive benefits can be seen in the case of airline travel. Many airline campaigns focus on the quality of the inflight experience, rewards programs, the extent of their global partner network, or on-time departure metrics. For many travelers, however, the issue is one of pain mitigation throughout the entire planning and travel process. It's not the comforts of air travel but the potential hassles that occupy their attention—for example: Can I figure out how to buy a ticket on a company's website? Will security have long lines? Will my flight be delayed? Will I be able to store my bag in the overhead compartment? Airlines that focus only on the benefits of air travel and ignore the negatives will have trouble building effective growth plans.

Easy to do business with

Of course, neither management teams nor management academics entirely ignore the negative experiences that customer profiles reveal. In our view, however, the conventional approach doesn't fully credit and address the real importance of these findings. Findings about things that customers dislike about the product itself are typically (only) brought to the attention of the product development group. More often, however, companies frame customers' negative experiences as issues of being easy to do business with. In many cases, this trivializes the real insights about the true obstacles to growth.

There's a considerable thread of thinking and practice about being easy to do business with (E2DBW) whose focus is on helping businesses remove impediments for customers wanting to buy their product.[36] Answering the phone within three rings, having the full record of a customer's purchases at a sales person's fingertips or in a fast responding website, and being in stock are all common examples of ways to be E2DBW. These and other actions can indeed have an important impact on customers' perceptions and can go a long way to mitigating or reversing negative customer experiences.

The problem with the E2DBW approach is that the actions it suggests aren't specifically tailored to segments or to high-yield behaviors that drive growth. The literature typically frames being E2DBW as a matter of business hygiene. The presumption is that there are a set of policies, service levels, and actions that firms should offer every customer. There's no notion that special care should be taken around certain high-yield customer activities, and E2DBW policies rarely differentiate among the needs of different segments. Thus, while across the board efforts to mitigate negatives nearly always do some good, they still leave marketing teams exposed to the unexpected and puzzling caprices of customer behavior that can derail growth campaigns despite firms' best efforts to do all the right things.

Despite these limitations, the increasing attention on being E2DBW is a step in the right direction. Firms that have adopted these practices recognize that they need to do more than differentiate and promote positive product benefits. They also need to address obstacles in the customer journey. Our experience suggests that removing or reducing barriers to customers' engaging in *high-yield behaviors* is the surest and best way to unlock growth. Indeed, we've found that mitigating important barriers is the critical centerpiece of most successful growth plans. The *Playbook* approach extends the logic of E2DBW by focusing attention and resources on the drivers and barriers to desired customer behaviors that matter most.

The *Playbook* approach: Drivers and barriers of behavior change

Our approach differs from the conventional one in a number of ways. The conventional approach focuses on understanding what customers like or don't like about a category or a brand and mining those insights in developing a product positioning. Our approach leads teams to compile and analyze data about customers in order to explain why they engage in targeted high-yield buying behaviors with a particular frequency. These insights, distilled into key drivers and barriers, guide the design of integrated campaigns to increase how often customers in each segment do the high-yield behavior.

Our third principle is about the work of unearthing (and articulating) these drivers and barriers. As such, it marks a critical pivot in the *Playbook*. The *Playbook* begins by locating high potential where-to-play targets by identifying high-yield behaviors and segments with a high propensity to high-yield behaviors. The process then turns to making an integrated set of how-to-win choices, that is, about offers, messages, products, and marketing/sales mix for each target segment. The methods and tools that underpin the third principle provide the bridge between the where-to-play and the how-to-win choices. One pillar of this bridge is a deep, rich understanding of why customers behave as they do. This leads naturally to the next pillar, namely, the things that, if changed, would lead them to change their behavior favorably— what we term drivers and barriers.

FIGURE 7-1

Three-Phase Process

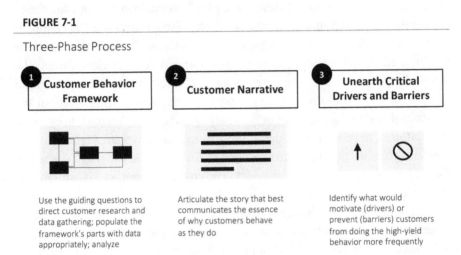

1 Customer Behavior Framework	2 Customer Narrative	3 Unearth Critical Drivers and Barriers
Use the guiding questions to direct customer research and data gathering; populate the framework's parts with data appropriately; analyze	Articulate the story that best communicates the essence of why customers behave as they do	Identify what would motivate (drivers) or prevent (barriers) customers from doing the high-yield behavior more frequently

Generating this kind of practical insight into the factors that shape customer's choices involves a three-step process, as shown in Figure 7-1. The first step is to gather and the full range of data needed to explain a segment's characteristic buying behavior and to organize and analyze it using the customer behavior framework (CBF). The second step is to synthesize these findings into a highly digestible and usable format as a customer narrative. The third and final step is to distill the insights from the CBF and customer narrative into a two-sided list of discrete, concrete factors that either strongly motivate key behaviors (drivers) or discourage them (barriers).

The analytical centerpiece of our approach is the CBF, and building it is the most time consuming and challenging step. The CBF is a schematic model of what the last twenty years' worth of research in consumer psychology, behavioral economics, and cognitive psychology has identified as the major influences on customer's choice making, and how those factors interact.[37] The framework names three factors—the customer's social and physical context, their preexisting beliefs and attitudes, and their desired experience during their buying process—that, taken together, explain the distinctive frequency with which customers in each segment do various buying process activities and purchase particular products.

The structure of the CBF roughly reflects how a customer's thinking happens as he or she moves into and through a buying process. It posits that particular aspects of the social and physical environment in which the customer finds themselves (while "shopping") act as mental cues for them, triggering two simultaneous mental processes. First, things like the character of the store or website or the corporate process through which they examine products affects what the customer recalls from similar past experiences. The physical context shapes what memories and associations are top of mind for the customer and thus which preexisting beliefs and attitudes about the goods and bads of an activity or product are triggered. Second, they cause the customer to project what they'd most like to have happen to them in that kind of situation, that is, to form a view of their desired experience when in the buying process or using a product. The customer then weighs and judges those memories and expectations in making their current choices. In reality, of course, it's a messy thought process. What's key from a growth strategy perspective is that each segment's characteristic patterns of behaviors and outcomes are the result of a thought process that is framed and driven by current context.[38] Context affects both what customers remember most about what products or buying process activities do for them and what they really want. Changing the context—for example, where and with whom a buying process takes place—will usually alter the customer's desired experience and purchasing behaviors. Change the context, and what the customer believes about the efficacy and value of a product or a buying process activity (or, more precisely, what they remember about the efficacy and value) changes.

The completed CBF can be a dense document, containing many discrete facts. To generate real insight requires a synthesis of why customers in a segment behave as they do. We've found that this is most powerfully and usefully done in a story format.[39] The customer narrative is a vivid, story-formatted reconstruction of the interplay among the three CBF factors in the customer's mind. It is particularly powerful in helping teams make sense of the often puzzling or contradictory behaviors sometimes observed in the customer research. It's how, for example, the Sparkle team came to understand that an older woman could be telling the truth about her strong affinity for the Sparkle brand while buying it infrequently. After writing the customer narrative for this segment, the team could finally see how those customers frequently found themselves in circumstances where buying Sparkle was impractical or would send the wrong social signal. The Sparkle team's experience is a common one, for the narrative conveys the insights in a format—an actual story—that is compelling to people. Ideas and conclusions delivered by story stick longer, stronger, and more clearly than ideas delivered by numbers and tables.

The third step in the process, developing the list of drivers and barriers, is an exercise in extraction and articulation of insights rather than their generation. Its purpose is to disaggregate the customer narrative's holistic explanation of segment behavior into a set of discrete, concrete, actionable requirements for changing segment behavior. Each barrier or driver should capture one (or, at most, two) meaningful threads of a customer's situation, beliefs, or expectations that must be addressed in the right way in order to shift customer behavior. For example, one barrier that the EnServ team picked out was whether an energy saving project would fit within the facilities manager's discretionary budget. One of the unexpected drivers they found was the degree to which doing an energy saving project could be positioned to enhance their reputation with their peers (see Five Types of Buyer Behavior Barriers).

Five Types of Buying Behavior Barriers

The literature of consumer psychology and behavioral economics, as well as our own experience, suggest that while almost anything can form a barrier to, or be a driver of, a buying process behavior and product purchase, the most prevalent ones seem can be logically sorted into five types. The simplest to understand and spot are *physical* barriers—things like the customer not being able to reach the channels where the product is sold, or the product being out of stock, in an unusable size, or lacking critical functionality. *Economic* barriers—the initial purchase price, lifecycle cost and so forth of a product, or the opportunity cost of time needed to engage in a particular step in a buying process—form a second group, ones that are also common and relatively easy to see. The nature, availability, and credibility of *information sources*, for example, the ease or difficulty of sampling a brand directly, or talking to an actual user of the brand, form a third group of drivers and barriers. These are somewhat subtler, and often harder to see. The fourth group of drivers and barriers that are harder to spot, but often exceptionally important, are *social/psychological* considerations. These include things such as the lack of adoption of the product by others that the customer admires and wants to impress or the desire to avoid conflict with a superior who favors a particular product or solution. Finally, there are *institutional* barriers and drivers. Some of this fifth type are external to a business, like regulations that compel firms to do certain kinds of testing, or cultural norms that prescribe what it means to do a good job when shopping. Other institutional barriers or drivers arise internally, from things like a business' organizational structure or incentive scheme, or from the size and composition of a household.

Collectively, drivers and barriers are the span of the bridge built by applying the third principle. As will be explained more thoroughly in Chapter 9, the list of drivers and barriers for a segment are, in effect, the initial version of the requirements document for a campaign to accelerate growth in that segment. Each driver or barrier describes something in the thinking (or the environment) of customers in a segment that, once changed or altered by some element of a growth campaign, would materially improve their propensity to do a high-yield behavior. A campaign that mitigated each barrier or boosted customers' experience of each driver would dramatically accelerate growth.

The third principle explained

The third principle directs teams' attention away from the choices they must make about what behavior and which segment to target toward the choices they must make about how to increase the frequency of high-yield behaviors. It is fundamentally an enabling principle, through which teams uncover and prioritize the insights about consumer behavior, that will act as sign posts and guardrails for later how-to-win choices about offers, messages, and go-to-market activation.

The third principle is all about what goes on the people's minds as they work through the buying process. Of course, this is territory that is still not thoroughly understood. Yet great progress has been made, enough to allow for accurate (albeit not precise) reconstruction of consumer decision-making. Doing so takes some new approaches and frameworks and a good deal of work. We begin by assembling, organizing, and analyzing data on why customers act the way they do. We then translate that understanding into something practical for managers to use.

Step 1: Complete the customer behavior framework

The CBF, as sketched above, is a multifactor explanatory model. It stands apart from other models of customer decision making that we have observed in practice in two key ways. The first and foremost of these is that its primary purpose is to explain customer behavior during the buying process, rather than to explain their product preferences (although these are incorporated in it). The second distinction is that it has a customer's immediate context—their social and physical environment—acting as a critical, perhaps *the* critical, factor in customers' decision making.

The CBF model isn't easy to explain (or build, for that matter). As with other multifactor models in which the factors frequently run both ways, it can be hard to understand how the whole model works without a thorough grasp of each of the constituent parts. Yet an understanding of how the whole works adds immeasurably to understanding the why and what of each individual part. In this section we'll start with the piece parts, discussing separately what each part is and how to build it before explaining how they all work together.

Figure 7-2 illustrates the four elements of the CBF and how they interact: the combination of *context*, preexisting *beliefs and attitudes*, and *desired experience* together explain the pattern of actual *buying process behaviors and purchasing outcomes* that is characteristic of each segment. The factors are broad in nature. As such each tries to capture or synthesize a rather wide range of customer activity or thought. There is, consequently, a set of guiding questions for each factor, questions that provide teams with rough but robust guidelines on what to research and study, and what to ignore.

Note that, while research on customer behavior can be conducted for the entire market, the CBF should be completed at the level of an individual segment. Each segment exhibits different purchasing behaviors and differing propensities toward the high-yield behaviors in the buying process. The goal is to understand the factors that explain these characteristic patterns of behavior for a particular segment. The final box in the framework, customer behaviors and outcomes, essentially constitutes the problem statement—it's the thing that the other boxes are trying to explain. We therefore begin our explication of the model at its end.

Step 1a: Document behaviors and outcomes

The focal point of a segment's CBF is a clear, quantified statement of what those customers actually do in the buying process. This pattern of behaviors and outcomes is what the rest of the CBF is intended to explain. The guiding questions for the behaviors and outcomes factor, illustrated in Figure 7-3, indicate the type of information that teams should strive to collect on how, when, and where customers purchase and use products.

FIGURE 7-2

Customer Behavior Framework

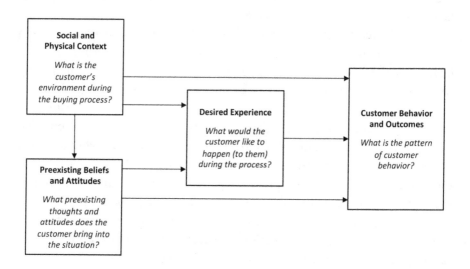

In general, the documentation of a segment's buying activities should identify the full range of media viewed, channels visited, and information sources consulted, as well as the frequency and intensity with which they were used. It should document the various sampling, testing, and analytical activities (for example, building and using a cost model) that occurred—and how often. It should document when and how often the participants in a buying process met to discuss possible purchases, and who was part of those discussions. And it should identify clearly where potential customers stopped looking and dropped out of the process—and how many did so and how often.

So, for example, the EnServ team's summary of behaviors and outcomes in Segment 3 noted that these customers consulted vendors early on 95 percent

FIGURE 7-3

Guiding Questions: Customer Behavior and Outcomes

Buying Process Behavior	Purchase Behavior

Buying Process Behavior

- What is the frequency of the different occasions and/or situations that trigger the buying process?
- How many customers participate in or exit from the buying process at each stage?
- Do customers iterate between stages? If so, which stages, and how frequently do these feedback loops occur?
- Of the multiple activities open to customers at each stage:
  - *How many customers do just one? Do two, three, etc.?*
  - *What is the frequency with which customers do the activities within a stage?*
  - *Of customers doing more than one activity per stage, is there a consistent order to them?*
- What is the inter-stage 'path dependency' of a particular buying process activity, i.e., what percentage of customers who engage in an activity occurring in one stage move on to the next stage? To the stage beyond that? To actually buying a product? To the purchase of a specific brand?
- From which sources do customers get their information – overall and by stage?
  - *How many sources?*
  - *Which sources are used for which type of information (i.e., are websites used for product and price information, but direct calls for assessment of quality)?*
- How frequently do customers use different sources of information?
- What/how many tests are used to evaluate or analyze product or service? Are the tests formal or informal? How often do they sample, and under what circumstances?
- Which tests are used in each stage?
- How many channels do customers typically use? How frequently do they use each? Do customers use certain channels more often given one type of triggering situation rather than another?

Purchase Behavior

Within Category

- What is the distribution of where and how products/brands are purchased, i.e., what percentage of volume, units, etc. is purchased via internet, in person, in stores of different types, direct or from distributors of different types etc.?
- What is the distribution of purchases across brands/products in the category?
- How often do they purchase the category? Specific brands or products?
- How many different brands or products (in the category) do they buy?
- When, and in what patterns over time, do purchases occur, i.e., daily, weekly, monthly, annually, etc.?
- How often do they switch companies and/or brands? What is the pattern of switching – over time, and between products/brands?
- What is the distribution of size of purchases at a given time, and over time – by volume, revenue, unit, etc.?
  - *Total per purchase*
  - *Format/package size per purchase*
- How many purchases were transactional? How many under contract? What percentage of total volume/units/revenue of purchases were made each way?
- What was the triggering event or situation for the purchase, and who is present when purchase occurs – on both buyer and seller side?

Across Substitutes

- What is the distribution of purchases (for a given trigger/purpose) across functional substitutes, i.e., across categories?
- How often do they purchase substitutes? How much?
- When, and with what patterns over time, do they purchase substitutes?
- How often do they switch between the category and substitutes?

of the time and that they did most of their exploratory research by reviewing white papers and articles from trade shows and trade magazines. They decided to move on to a real project 70 percent of the time but ran a formal RFP process with multiple bidders only 38 percent of the time. Seventy-five percent of the time they chose the vendor whom they initially consulted early in the process. What the team documented for customers in Segment 8 showed a different pattern. They consulted a vendor early on far less frequently (only 45 percent of the time), did most of their early exploratory research online (90 percent), moved on to a formal project 60 percent of the time but did a formal RFP process for nearly every one they decided to move ahead with. It's these different patterns of behaviors between segments that the CBF is designed to explain.

The documentation of actual purchases—outcomes—for each segment should be equally wide and deep. It should lay out which products were purchased, by whom, where and when, in what quantities, at which price, and note any particular circumstances of purchase or use, for example, promotions, presence of influencers, and so on.[40,41]

The patterns of purchase and use outcomes will be as distinctive across segments as the patterns of buying behavior. Each segment has a different, characteristic pattern of behaviors and outcomes that should be documented in full. The next step is to reconstruct the factors that lead to these distinctive behaviors.

Step 1b: Define the customer's desired experience

Working backward through the CBF, the first explanatory factors we encounter are customers' preexisting beliefs and attitudes and their *desired experience*. As we'll discuss later, these two factors operate together like blades of a scissors; both are essential to customer decision making. The notion of the customer's desired experience is, however, less familiar, and we'll discuss it first.

Unlike the narrowly product-centric notion of what customers' desire that underpins much of conventional thinking on this topic, we mean something much broader. One profound meta-result that emerges from research in behavioral economics and cognitive psychology is that customers don't think strictly or even primarily about products and their attributes in making purchasing decisions. Instead, what customers are thinking about is what they'd like to have happen to them during or as a result of being in that part of their buying process. [42] They consider what kind of experience they'd like to have at that time and place. In our shorthand, they define victory for themselves as the kind of experience they'd like. This desired experience might involve greater recognition, or inclusion in a group, or simply a feeling of self-worth. [43] The products they purchase at the end of the process may contribute to that experience positively or negatively, a lot or a little. That is, products are important only for their role in enabling the customer to reach for and achieve their desired experience.

Accordingly, the set of guiding questions for the desired experience part of the CBF (Figure 7-4) is quite broad and largely non-product oriented in nature. Most concern fundamental human, experiential outcomes that individuals desire from situations—advancement, increased respect, greater connection, and so forth. There are guiding questions about category and product, and some are of the classic "how much do you value this attribute relative to that attribute" kind. But mostly the product-related guiding questions are about the *role* the product might play for the customer in achieving their desired experience.

For instance, the Sparkle story revealed quite clearly that young women considering purchasing lipstick or nail polish weren't laddering up from the particular attributes of a product (for example, smoothness and completeness of application) to a belief that purchasing and using it would make them beautiful. What they wanted most was to look right, both as an individual (that is, the cosmetic would complement their hair color or complexion) and as a member of some group—their family (mother and sister) or friends or those they wanted to be friends with. What they wanted from the nail polish or lipstick was help in achieving the desired experience of fitting in—while shopping and elsewhere.

The notion of a situational desired experience being a key element in customer decision making is more readily understood and accepted in B2C markets. This idea is often described as "occasion-based marketing." But situationally derived desired experiences are a critical element in customer decision making throughout B2B markets as well. Even deep in a procurement-heavy buying processes where spreadsheet rationality is supposed to dominate, what critical decision-makers and influencers (for example, the procurement manager or the design engineer) want from that buying process isn't strictly related to the product. Rather, their definition of victory has to do with some combination of risk avoidance (that is, not making a recommendation that will get them in trouble, or worse yet, fired), hitting their numbers, earning the respect of their professional peers, or a desire for advancement. These are all the kind of fundamental human, experiential outcomes that consumers in B2B markets desire. What a design engineer wants when evaluating suppliers of materials or parts is a way to design something clever and useful and get recognition for doing so. The product is only important to the degree that it helps them get this recognition.

FIGURE 7-4

Guiding Questions: Desired Experience

Desired Experience

- What, in their minds, is the situation they find themselves in? (how do they describe it?)
- What, in their minds, is/are the jobs to be done given the situation or occasion that triggered the buying process, i.e., what is the real goal (beyond the purchase) of the work?
- How do they measure or define successful accomplishment of the job(s) to be done – qualitatively and/or quantitatively?
- What would they like to happen to (or for) them specifically during the buying process overall or particular activities, and/or as a result of the buying process or activity, e.g., change in status/reputation, change in role or position, acquisition of more freedom, minimization of risk/exposure? How do they define victory for themselves as they go through the various activities, and overall?

- In what ways does the particular category that is the focus of their buying process affect the overall 'job to be done?'
  - *Objectively and subjectively – does the category/product play an important or essential role? What is the nature of its role, i.e., what does that product/category contribute to doing the job or the outcome of the job?*
  - *Are there other categories/products needed to accomplish the job, and how important are they?*
- What aspects of the experience of doing a buying process stage/activity are most important, e.g., aesthetics, efficiency, effectiveness with which the activity can be performed? How do they judge those attributes?
- What aspects of the product/category are most important, i.e., what functional, aesthetic, emotional benefits do they expect to get, and which are most important?

It should be clear by now that there's a subtle but important distinction between our approach and traditional thinking on the topic of what customers want. In the traditional approach, customer decision making is brand focused and situation neutral. In ours, it's situation driven and brand neutral. The traditional approach assumes that what customers want are the features and functionality of particular brands or products. As exemplified by the benefit ladder framework, customers are assumed to reason up the ladder from discrete attributes of a product to some end state—beauty, wealth, and so on—that the product will create for them. In this product out view, the end states the product can create are always available, and always desirable.

Our approach, by contrast, works back from the customer and situation. We've learned that what customers want depends on what they're doing, with whom, under what conditions. In effect, when the customer's situation changes, so does their desired experience. Customers have an internal definition of victory for themselves (independent of product) in every situation and they want a product—any product—only to the extent that it helps them achieve that definition of victory. They don't ladder up from product attributes to outcomes. Instead, they define their desired outcome, then ask themselves whether a product or a buying process activity can play a helpful role in achieving it.

All of our client stories illustrate this change of focus. In the Terrafix story, for instance, the team learned that one of the most important things patients in the target segment wanted from their annual physical was affirmation that they were taking good care of themselves. They wanted to feel good about themselves by demonstrating they were good stewards of their own health.

Within the CBF, desired experience as well as preexisting beliefs and attitudes are indispensable parts of customer decision making. Both, as shown in Figure 7-2, directly influence customer behaviors and outcomes. But desired experience is a first among equals in the model because it's the mission that puts energy into the decision-making process.

Step 1c: Document preexisting beliefs and attitudes

The preexisting beliefs and attitudes portion of the CBF uncovers and documents the memories of the consequences of past activities or purchases that customers bring into a new, present day decision process. These memories are an essential part of their decision-making process. As we'll discuss more fully later, customers make choices by comparing and contrasting what they want in a new situation—their desired experience—with what their memories tell them they're likely to get from a given activity or product in that situation.

Modern research into how memories are created, maintained, and recalled reveals that memory is a more sophisticated and complex phenomenon than is commonly portrayed. [44] Historically, memory was likened to a miniaturized filing cabinet or storage device with billions of folders—each one holding a discrete fact, conclusion, or feeling about product performance, the usefulness of a buying process activity, moral values, and the like. This view of how memory works makes it perfectly sensible to ask customers to report about narrow slices of their experience with a product or a buying process activity, for example, to ask them to rate and rank their satisfaction with individual product attributes, or to recount which particular moral value is most important to them. However, this atomistic model of memory is incomplete and so misleading. Human memory is, in fact, profoundly *associative*. [45] When someone experiences or learns about an activity or a product, they actually take in and store a wide range of images, feelings, conclusions, and ideas about it and about everything in its neighborhood.

Metaphorically—and physically—people's memories are webs.[46] Each web contains and connects bits of data a person takes in about the situation surrounding the activity—the time, the place, the people, the noise level, the colors—with bits of data about the person's assessment of the results (good and bad) of doing the activity and of what (positive and negative) emotions were evoked. What will run through the mind of a young woman looking at a display of lipstick brands in a store, for instance, will be her recollection of who she was with when she last bought and used that brand, how tricky it was to apply it correctly, how greasy it felt, her friend's or mother's negative reaction to her new look, and her feelings about their reaction, along with her assessment of the prestige of the store she's in, the success (or failure) she's had in buying things there before, and many other things. The point is that when people bring the beliefs and attitudes they formed during past experiences into a new buying process, they're not in neatly separated buckets, for example, about product performance, values, and so on, that can be documented, understood, and ultimately addressed in a completely independent way. Indeed, it's this fundamentally connected nature of customers' beliefs and attitudes about things that led us to question the efficacy of marketing and sales' traditional commitment to communicate (only) the positive, and ultimately to the conviction that *both* drivers and barriers must be addressed before customers will change their minds and their behavior. After all, a customer thinking about going to a particular store, or considering a brand, instantly recalls all of the positives and the negatives they experienced or learned about. Communications that only point to positive things are thus perceived as inauthentic (at best) or untruthful.

Clearly, the associative nature of customers' memories affects not only what data needs to be collected about their preexisting beliefs and attitudes, but also how it should be gathered. Not surprisingly, a good portion of the guiding questions for preexisting beliefs and attitudes, illustrated in Figure 7-5, will look familiar: they concern customers' attitudes toward the category and the products and brands within it. There are also multiple guiding questions, however, digging into the role, efficacy, and value of various activities within the buying process, such as which sources they find most credible for different types of information, or which channels are easiest to find or most accommodating. Also critical, although often treated as just nice to have in conventional planning, are the guiding questions that are intended to get at what customers remember and feel about their context. Namely, about the nature and strength of their relationships with the people with them in the buying process (or when they use the product), about the incentives and constraints placed on them by their organization or society, and/or their basic expectations with respect to life and work (see "A Broader Scope for Consumer Insight").

A Broader Scope for Consumer Insight

Teams have not only to considerably broaden the categories of data they collect about customers but change the way they gather, record, and present that data. The vast majority of the methods firms use to do their customer research—from B2B's voice of the customer to B2C's bewildering array of survey techniques—rely on narrow focus to gain depth of understanding. The surveys and questions focus on precisely defined piece parts of what people experience. They ask customers to recall and rate how valuable they find each individual feature of Brand X and Brand Y, or they ask them for their satisfaction with breadth of selection at a particular store. They restrict both what's being asked about (to a feature or a functionality or an attribute of a channel) and what customers can say about it (only that it is/isn't valuable, rather than that it reminds them of something their mother would do). And in doing so, they miss the full scope and connected nature of what customers really remember about things. Fortunately, there are more holistic and synthetic research methods, for example, metaphor elicitation techniques, which can be used to more accurately map customers' memories. [47] These techniques are often a bit costlier and cumbersome to use than the traditional panel-based, email quantitative survey. The yield from such techniques is, however, far, far higher. Our point isn't that the traditional methods should be abandoned but that they should be used much more sparingly, and that the results of more synthetic forms of research need to be the centerpiece of the beliefs and attitudes portion of the CBF.

FIGURE 7-5

Guiding Questions: Preexisting Beliefs and Attitudes

Product and Channel

- What are their memories and expectations, both positive and negative, about the accessibility, functionality, features, performance, and short term and life cycle costs (financial, psychological and opportunity) of:
  - *The company's product/brand*
  - *Competitor's products/brands*
  - *The category within which the company's product/brand sits*
  - *Substitute or other related categories*
- Where/when do they think it most appropriate to purchase or use this category? The company's brand?
- What situations, occasions, and/or experiences (either while purchasing or using the product) do they associate most strongly with the product?
- What do they believe buying or using the product says about the people who buy it or use it? About themselves, if they buy it or use it?
- What are their memories and expectations, both positive and negative, about the accessibility, ease of use/navigation, functionality, features, performance, and cost of various channels that are or could be used during the buying process – in an absolute sense and relative to each other?
- Where/when do they think it most appropriate to utilize each channel?

Buying Process

- What are their memories and expectations, both positive and negative, about the accessibility, functionality (i.e., the output), usefulness, and credibility/reputation of doing:
  - *Each of the basic stages (i.e., the research stage or the evaluation stage, etc.)*
  - *Each of the individual activities it is possible to do during each stage (e.g., searching online, talking to friends, talking to parents, reading magazines, etc.)*
- In what way, if any, do their memories and expectations about accessibility, functionality, etc. change when they do the stage or activity with one or more other people?
- What do they believe doing the buying process activity says about the people who do it (e.g., what does doing exhaustive testing say about the person doing the testing)?
- What do they believe their role is in the buying process?
- When, and in what situations or occasions, do they think it most appropriate to do a stage or a particular activity within a stage? Most valuable?
- What are their general attitudes, memories and expectations, both positive and negative, about the other people involved in the buying process?

General

- Do they place the funding for the product/category, or the product/category itself, in a distinct mental account? If so, why?
- What are their general attitudes and beliefs about the role of work, the value of shopping/purchasing, etc. in their life?
- In what ways does their educational and/or work background shape their approach to purchasing or using/consuming a product? For example, have they absorbed 'standards' about what activities should be performed, or how they should be performed from a particular discipline they've mastered (e.g., value of written documentation to people with legal training, etc.)

Step 1d: Describe social and physical context (situation)

The social and physical context section of the CBF is arguably its most distinctive and important component. It's distinctive in that most conventional approaches to understanding customer decision making that we observe in practice either do not consider these factors or do so in an ad hoc fashion. It's important because there's overwhelming evidence that human decision-making is fundamentally context dependent. Experiment after experiment shows that even subtle changes in people's physical environment (for example, the pace of background music, the color or cleanliness of a room, how tight space is) or in their social setting (for example, their reporting relationships within an organization, whether they're with a friend or a relative when shopping) often causes major changes, even reversals, in their choices.[48] Even if we believe a customer's relative valuation of products or activities is fixed, unchanging over time, if the customer's context changes enough, so will their choice of activity or brand.

There are two pathways by which a segment's social and physical situation shapes what they think and do. The first pathway runs through desired experience. As we noted earlier, what customers want from an activity or a product depends on the specific character of their social or physical environment. The second pathway runs through preexisting beliefs and attitudes. Certain aspects of the social or physical environment trigger, or light up, certain aspects of their memory of the product more than others. What's fresh and top of mind about a product to a customer depends on the cue provided by the context. What this means is that when a customer considers buying something, the particular situation in which their buying process takes place (for example, whether they're alone or not) will strongly affect both what they really want (desired experience) and what they recall is positive and negative about it. Context shapes how people choose among products by influencing what they want from that kind of product and what they believe about how those products might perform.

In practice, this section of the CBF is a record of the typical customer's social, organizational, and physical environment during and just after their buying process. It is a description of their situation that especially highlights those things in the situation that may shape how they think and hence what they do. As the guiding questions in Figure 7-6 illustrate, good descriptions of a segment's social and physical context contain, at a minimum, all of the demographic and firmographic data that form the backbone of traditional customer profiles, for example, size of family/firm, location, income/revenue, and so on. But what we mean by knowing a customer's physical context goes much wider and deeper. For one thing, it includes knowing specifically where the customer is when buying or using the product as well as the physical characteristics of that space, and how hard it was to get to it. In a B2C market this means knowing whether the channel or website is: Large or small? Well or poorly laid out? Brightly or mutely colored? If a channel, is it well or poorly stocked? It means knowing how hard it is to reach the channel or website. In a B2B market: Does the customer work at a cubicle in a vast office, or in a comfortable private office—or do they have to do their work on the go? Do the customers' technicians have access to the best testing equipment? Do they have the time and capacity for a detailed evaluation of products or not? While an exact and complete description of physical environment may not be achievable, teams should strive to capture the characteristics of the physical environment that might change a customer's thinking.

Similarly, the things that matter for social and organizational context go deeper and wider than what's captured in most traditional profiles. It's always important to document the buyer's place or role in the various social entities to which they belong (for example, families or firms). In B2C markets: What is their status in society? Are they married or single? How many friends do they have? Are they the primary caregiver or not? In B2B markets: Where are they located in the firm's or organization's hierarchy? Are they the owner or an agent? What department or sub organization do the buyers belong to? What is their title and role? What are the rights and responsibilities that go along with that title and role? Beyond the buyer's place in their social environment, it's important to document the policies, incentives (and punishments), expectations, and traditions that govern customers' interactions within their social unit. How does the department the buyer works within measure performance? What does it use to reward good performance, and to punish poor performance? Are there strong functional mindsets and expectations at work, for example, does the department largely use functional or professional standards in judging work?

FIGURE 7-6

Guiding Questions: Social, Organizational, and Physical Context

Organizational Context

- What is the full range of roles involved in the purchase decision? At the stage in the buying process where the high-yield behavior occurs?
- What is the nature of typical relationships among the roles involved (e.g., hierarchical vs. peer-to-peer, formal vs. informal)?
- What is the organizational setting in which these roles interact (e.g., formal vs. informal, planned meeting vs. change encounter)?
- What is the nature of the relationship among the roles during the stage in the buying process where the high-yield behavior occurs? During the actual high-yield behavior?
- What formal and informal metrics are used to assess overall performance of the key roles (e.g., functional, financial)? What metrics are used to assess performance of the key buying roles during the buying process itself?
- What are the metrics – both formal and informal –used to assess overall performance of the key roles, e.g., functional, financial, etc.? What are the metrics used to assess performance of the key buying roles during the buying process itself?
- Is the buying process part of a larger process (e.g., new product development, capital appropriation)? If so, what metrics are applied to the larger process? Is the buying process routine or an unusual event?
- What are the potential rewards/punishments from doing the key buying behavior/buying activity well or poorly, and what is their size and nature?

Legal/Regulatory Context

- What laws or regulations strongly affect what buying process activities occur (e.g., formal vs. informal tendering of bids)? How are those activities performed (e.g., requirement for disclosure of certain information)?

Social Context

- What is the typical background of the individuals in the key roles within the customer's organization (e.g., age, education, prior experience)?
- What are the characteristics of the personal relationships among the individiuals in key roles within the customer's organization (e.g., transactional, long-standing)?
- How important are these personal relationships to these individuals? That is, how much does the approval of another matter to the key individual?
- What cultural norms affect the buying process/high-yield activity (e.g., role/gender/age expectations)?
- Who are the key buyer's peers/reference groups outside the customer's organization? Where and when do they interact, and what are the norms/expectations for gaining status among peers?

Physical/Economic Context

- What are the physical characteristics of the setting in which the high-yield behavior occurs (e.g., spacious vs. crowded, well-stocked vs. poorly stocked, time of day)?
- How easily can customers access the buying activity (e.g., physical distance of store, navigability of website)?
- How easily can customers access alternatives and/or functional substitutes?
- What is the actual, controllable budget of the key roles (e.g., money on hand, money in the bank)?

The purpose of this part of the CBF, therefore, is to succinctly record those aspects of the physical and social environment customers in a segment typically encounter during their buying process that may influence their expectations or their recall. The description of the context immediately surrounding the high-yield behavior(s) in the buying process is especially important. Ideally, teams would document the specific physical cues that trigger selective recall and the relationships or people that are most influential. In practice, it may be hard to identify these things at the outset of the analysis. That's why we advocate thorough and comprehensive efforts to gather as much data as possible on the various elements of context.

The model in motion: Seeing the CBF as a whole

The purpose of the CBF is, of course, to explain each segment's characteristic pattern of buying process behaviors and purchases, and especially the segment's propensity to do high-yield behaviors. The general form of that explanation is given by the diagram in Figure 7-2, namely that the segment's social and physical context sets the stage, both triggering the selective or preferential recall of specific preexisting thoughts and attitudes about buying process activities and brands and largely determining what kind of experience the customer would like to have in that situation. Taken together, these factors lead to customer behaviors and outcomes. Put somewhat differently, customers' choices emerge as they balance their (preexisting) beliefs about what kind of experience a product or activity can deliver for them against the experience they'd like to have. And both their desired experience and what they remember about previous experiences are strongly shaped by the specific situation they're in (see "Situation-Based Consumption").

Situation-Based Consumption

Consider, for example, a young adult who has clear preferences among different beverage categories, strongly preferring soft drinks over either sparkling water or alcohol. When alone, she will nearly always choose to consume a soft drink. But when out on a first date, she does something different. She is much more likely to order a cocktail or a sparkling water. This isn't just a B2C market phenomenon but something that happens in B2B markets as well. A procurement manager with the authority to negotiate and conclude a deal independently will often choose a vendor that they believe will never let them down, even at a somewhat higher price, rather than simply selecting the vendor with the lowest price. They may act quite differently if they're making the choice as the chair of a procurement committee.

Why did the people in these examples override their seemingly fixed preferences? In a nutshell, it's because their new environment led them to alter their product associations and desired experience. The person choosing a cocktail over a soda had a different desired experience because of the context in which this buying process unfolded. She wanted, above all, to look sophisticated and worldly in the presence of her date. The context also influenced her beliefs and attitudes by triggering recall of certain negative perceptions of soft drinks (for example, that sweet stuff is for kids). The point is that the social and physical context of a segment's buying process simultaneously shapes what they actually remember (or remember most vividly) about a product or buying process activity and how they frame or evaluate the situation they're in. This is as true in B2B as in B2C markets. What a procurement manager wants out of a one-on-one meeting with a vendor—for example, the chance to demonstrate mastery and be in charge—may not be what she wants when accompanying her vice president to a meeting with the same vendor, where she may wish to show that she's a team player.

What emerges from this multifactor, explanatory model of customer behavior is thus much more than a list of facts and observations. The different factors influence and comment upon one another in subtle and interesting ways to build up a complete picture of individuals and their behaviors in a selected segment. The power of the CBF is that it considers all these pieces in motion as it were—rather than as fixed and static lumps of data. Another distinctive feature of the CBF is its orientation toward the high-yield behaviors that matter most for growth. The data collected in the framework helps illuminate specific factors that encourage or impede these key behaviors.

As we've seen, however, the sheer quantity and complexity of the data synthesized in the CBF can sometimes be overwhelming. It's for this reason that we developed the second step of the process, the customer narrative. It synthesizes the important facts and insights of the CBF analysis as a story about a customer.

Step 2: Write the customer narrative

In the early years of the *Playbook*, we conducted driver and barrier workshops to review and draw conclusions about each part of a segment's CBF. We soon found, however, that every discussion of the CBF turned into a *storytelling* session. Stories are superb vehicles for articulating the tensions and intertwined subplots that characterize real human decision making.[49] To make sense of the mass of data in a segment's CBF, team members instinctively began weaving key insights about various parts of the analysis back into a whole, laying out the complete emotional and rational logic behind customers' propensity to the high-yield behavior in the form of a story. Vigorous debate always ensued, and alternative versions of the story were proposed by team members. We therefore formalized the development of customer narratives as a distinct step in our approach in order to harness this creative and beneficial storytelling process. What we're aiming for is a clear, coherent picture of a segment that accommodates *all* the facts and data of the CBF in a compelling and manageable way.

Including this intermediate step turned out to be valuable for at least two reasons. First, constructing a version of the CBF in story form for each segment provides additional insight, insight that may not surface (or is hard to see) when analyzing one fact at a time. For instance, while the EnServ team was able to glean a good deal of valuable information about a key customer segment from the CBF analysis, the real a-ha moment came only when they put these pieces together in a cohesive narrative. They knew, for example, that facilities managers recognized that energy service projects often received low priority in the capital budgeting process. They also knew that facilities managers typically had modest discretionary budgets of their own to manage. The CBF made clear as well that facilities managers greatly valued being recognized as cutting edge operators and innovators by their professional peers and as key contributors to business outcomes in their own organizations. Despite knowing all these things, the insights that led the team to uncover a key driver for this segment—that modularizing energy projects to fit within facilities managers' discretionary budgets would boost the likelihood of purchase—didn't really pop until they started to describe the trials and tribulations of a recognizable individual. Once the story line emerged, however, the team was able to draw on additional data from the CBF to test and refine their conclusions. As this example makes clear, the customer narrative applies just as much in a B2B context as it does in B2C.

Secondly, the story form is especially useful for ensuring that the various functions (sales, marketing, R&D, and so on) are truly aligned in their understanding of a segment. We've often seen marketing teams share the customer narratives they've constructed with their sales colleagues and received a reaction of, "Sure—I know that guy!" Sometimes, the salespeople even give the protagonist of the narrative the name of one of their actual customers. This is usually a good indication that the team is on the right track and that the analysis makes sense to others in the organization who will need to adopt and act upon these insights. The customer narrative can therefore operate as a compelling and mentally sticky North Star for aligning functions within the business.

Once the guiding questions of a segment's CBF have been answered, writing the customer narrative usually turns out to be a relatively straightforward task. One reason is that humans are naturally inclined to construct stories. Another is that the structure of the CBF positively lends itself to the development of causal stories. There is, in fact, a near one to one correspondence between the components of the customer decision-making model that underpins the CBF (that is, context, desired experience, and beliefs and attitudes) and the basic structure of stories.

Most stories begin by identifying a protagonist and describing the setting of the story. As the familiar format goes: "Once upon a time in a faraway land, there was a handsome prince..." The protagonist of a customer narrative is, of course, the target customer and the kingdom in this fairy tale is documented in the CBF's social and physical context section. Good stories also look backward and inward, providing the reader with a rich view of the protagonist's past and mindset, of what has happened to them, factually and emotionally, and what conclusions they've drawn from those experiences—their beliefs and attitudes. Finally, stories need a plot—some challenge or aspiration that the protagonist faces, something that their current circumstances lead them to want to achieve: they want to save their family, slay the dragon, or fight the evil empire. There's a desired experience that drives the protagonist to take action.

Once people shed their inhibitions and get into the spirit of the exercise, we usually find that they have little trouble developing rich and insightful stories about customers—provided, of course, that they've done the work of completing a thorough CBF. It may take a few iterations to capture the essence of the segment story and bring it to life, but the key elements: the protagonist, their world, their character, and the challenges that set the story in motion flow naturally from the CBF.

Before moving on to the final step in our approach, we should mention an optional exercise that some teams find useful in transitioning from the customer narrative to the articulation of drivers and barriers. This is the identification of key themes in the segment story. Themes are coherent motifs running through the narrative that articulate the fundamental conditions and motivations shaping customer behavior. Naming them can help teams zero in on key drivers and barriers, which are usually directly related to these important themes. For example, a central theme in the Sparkle team's narrative about teen cosmetics buyers was the importance for these young women of fitting in and being appropriate as they transitioned from childhood to adulthood. Calling out these themes helped focus the team on the social dimension that shopping for cosmetics played in the lives of these customers and how this context shaped their decision making. It helped the team better appreciate the role of teens' close social circles and aspirational peers as both drivers and barriers to the target behaviors. As noted, identifying themes is optional but can be a useful device in continuing to narrow the analysis begun in the CBF to pinpoint drivers and barriers.

Step 3: Extract the drivers and barriers

The third step in the process, developing the list of drivers and barriers, involves extracting and articulating insights out of the pieces developed earlier. While the customer narrative offers a holistic explanation of segment behavior drawn from the CBF data, the purpose of this exercise is to anatomize it into the discrete, concrete, actionable requirements for changing the segment's behavior. Each barrier or driver distills a key insight about customer decision making in a form useful for taking action.

Defining drivers and barriers takes judgment and iteration, along with a sense of what good looks like. That sense can be gained faster by studying the examples provided by the client stories, and by using the taxonomy of drivers and barriers discussed earlier in this chapter to systematically sift through the themes and insights generated in doing the customer narrative. We've found that taxonomy to be particularly helpful in jump-starting work on drivers and barriers, and so share a richer explanation and illustration of each in the next few paragraphs.

Physical drivers and barriers are the easiest to understand and to spot. If a product is out of stock, or is delivered or packaged in quantities a customer can't easily move, store, or use, customers exit the buying process pretty rapidly. Similarly, they exit if the product is only available in channels that are difficult or expensive for customers to visit, or if they don't possess the space, expertise, or equipment to try out a new product. But the notion of physical drivers and barriers goes beyond these kinds of stop/go situations to include the way that the size, shape, color, quality, or complexity of the physical environment subtly shapes customers' thinking. As we pointed out in the CBF discussion, people's willingness to engage in an activity or to buy something is noticeably affected by their physical surroundings. Loud, fast-paced music or hard and not too comfortable seating subliminally tell consumers in quick service restaurants to eat quickly and turn over the table. Physical drivers and barriers are just that—physical aspects of the environment or the product that make it easier or harder for customers to get through their buying process.

Economic drivers and barriers are also intuitive, perhaps even more so than physical drivers or barriers. Not having enough money for something is an economic barrier that has happened to nearly everyone while the stimulating effect of having nearly unlimited funds has been virtually experienced by all through books, movies, and imagination. However, these kinds of absolute economic drivers and barriers are less interesting and less prevalent than those that are relative. Customers often find, for example, that while they might have more than enough money in general to pay for a brand or product, they simply don't have room in the budget, that is, they don't have enough relative to all their competing demands to purchase that particular one. EnServ found, for example, that facilities managers had a discretionary budget of about $75,000. This created a sharp, clear break point barrier for selling energy services. If the new service was priced below $75,000, the facilities manager had total control—if they liked the idea they could buy it; economics didn't deter purchase at all. But if the new service cost more than that, they had to put together a business case, present it to their company's capital expenditure committee, and so on. At these higher price points, economics definitely were a barrier—in two ways: one, they greatly raised the psychological cost—the hassle—of even proposing that energy project, and two, they forced the project to compete against many other projects, including those that were revenue producing.

As we've noted earlier, the high-yield behaviors teams identify are often upstream in the buying process, in the origination, information gathering, and information evaluation phases. This makes the group of drivers and barriers that arise from the *nature, availability, and credibility of information sources* customers encounter or seek out especially important. The ease or difficulty of learning about a category or brand directly by trying a sample (before buying it) is probably the most powerful information-related driver or barrier. Credibility of the source is also hugely important; it's common knowledge that a recommendation or even a mention of a brand or product from a trusted friend, a parent, or a well-known maven, can have a powerful effect on customers' thinking.[50] The point is that the same data or evaluation, when delivered by a parent, a trusted friend, or a highly regarded enthusiast is believed—and influences people's thinking—far more than the same data when delivered through a company website or a sales person. The number of information sources a customer taps, and the order in which they do so, for instance, also form significant drivers and barriers. There are some categories, for example, where having too many sources of information can actually be a barrier—performing too much research can cause customers to drop out at a higher rate as each additional source increases the odds that they will encounter something off-putting about the product or the category.[51]

The influence of barriers and drivers related to *social context* is thoroughly documented, and often has a greater effect on what happens than their physical environment.[52] Indeed, the behavioral economics literature describes a wide range of specific biases and behaviors that derive from the influence of social context on people's decision making. It's well known that consumers often buy things to badge themselves as part of a group they aspire to belong to; this is the taproot of fashion movements, for instance. But social context affects both how and what things are bought. Who a customer is with (or not with), and their relationship to their companion or colleague, has a strong effect on whether a certain buying behavior gets done, or how thoroughly, or how frequently. A teenager looking for clothes will, for example, look into different shops, spend different amounts of time in them, try on more and different clothes when they're on their own than when they do so in company with a close friend, and their buying process behavior will change even more when they're out with their mother instead.

The phenomenon is as strong in B2B markets as it is in B2C (although people often don't think of it that way). The norms and attitudes of the professional community someone in a company belongs to, or wants to belong to, matter a great deal in determining how they approach evaluating old and new products. As we saw in the EnServ case study, one of the strongest motivations facilities managers had for doing energy projects, and thus for consulting with a vendor early and often, was the prospect of gaining a reputation among their peers as cutting edge or up to date.

The *institutional* arrangements under which customers live and operate also can form or shape drivers and barriers for them as they move through the buying process. Institutional is our term for the defining characteristics and arrangements of organizations and societies, things such as structure and hierarchy, process, laws and policies, formal/explicit measures and metrics, rewards and punishments, and so on. Institutional drivers abound in every market. Some are external to firms or households, like regulations, laws, and societal customs. Building codes or toxicity laws, for example, may require buyers or sellers to add steps to their buying process (for example, completing certain tests), or restrict what product may be used where and by whom. These external barriers and drivers may even have indirect effects in which customers go above and beyond the basic requirements. As EnServ found, facilities managers in states with strict energy requirements in their building codes often were interested in projects that took them beyond what was required by statute.

Conclusion

While the CBF is the analytical centerpiece of the third principle, its focus— the payoff for all the work that goes into the CBF and customer narrative— is the drivers and barriers. This is because the list of drivers and barriers is what drives all the subsequent how-to-win choices. It is, in IT jargon, the requirements document for segment-specific growth campaigns. Indeed, each component of the tremendously successful go-to-market plans recounted in our client case studies can be traced back to one or more of the drivers or barriers identified in this phase of the *Playbook*.

For instance, think back to Sam Wilcox's plan for revitalizing Terrafix. It had three major elements: making the objective tests for the disease easy and low/no cost to take, convincing college educated women in their fifties (the target segment) that a key additional part of their normal health and beauty regime should be taking the test to spot the disease early, and motivating doctors to make ordering the objective test a routine part of physicals. Every part of the plan can be traced back to the drivers and barriers Sam's team unearthed when studying why patients or doctors might ask for a test. For instance, the initiatives to expand the number of testing centers and to get insurance companies to reimburse the cost of the test were designed to reduce the barriers of inconvenience or inability to reach a tester and out of pocket cost of the test. And the main thrust of the patient advertising campaign— that watching for this disease should be a natural part of taking care of one's best self—tied back to the drivers concerning the segment's attitudes toward health and beauty in general.

Thus the third principle, and the process described in this chapter, is a kind of keystone in the *Playbook* methodology. It marks the connection point between the where-to-play choices and principles and the how-to-win choices and principles described in subsequent chapters. Our focus moving forward will be on activating the specific behaviors identified as drivers and barriers for particular segments. Looking ahead, Chapters 8 and 9 frame the novel idea of a behavior change value proposition, which essentially lays out the roadmap for how teams organize segment-specific behavior change campaigns. Chapter 10 then delves into the most effective ways for deploying resources and tactics to implement successful growth campaigns.

Chapter 8

Caesar Financial: "We Need the Whole Client Portfolio!"

Eugene Shin recalled the excitement he had felt on joining Caesar Financial as the new EVP of wealth and investment management. With over a century of experience as a full-service bank and mortgage lender, Caesar was a widely recognized institution with deep roots in communities across the United States. Its foray into wealth management, however, stemmed from the more recent acquisition of a troubled investment house. Looking to diversify its traditional business lines, Caesar's CEO had championed the growth of the investment group. The CEO had declared a goal of catapulting Caesar from the second tier of wealth managers into the top ten in terms of assets under management. It was for this task that the company had recruited Eugene from his position as a managing director at another global financial company. Six months into the role, he faced mounting anxiety over how to achieve the ambitious growth targets set by senior management.

The previous year, the company had launched a nationwide advertising campaign touting its wealth management offerings. Caesar's marketing messages had historically emphasized the strength and reliability of the institution, its association with main street America, and a fundamental optimism about the future. The new campaign sought to reposition the company as a more modern and nimble wealth manager. Print and television advertisements contained hardly any references to the well-known symbols and imagery associated with the Caesar brand. Rather, the campaign focused primarily on performance and financial returns for its wealth management clients.

This was in line with how other large firms positioned themselves and reflected accepted norms of the industry—from traditional players like JPMorgan to lower cost advisors such as Charles Schwab to high-end investment firms such as Goldman Sachs. Since most individual advisors earned their fees based on a percentage of total assets managed (and not in a fee-for-service way), their primary goal was to increase the total assets managed per customer. This could be accomplished either by cross-selling to them (that is, selling multiple products) or by increasing the percentage of a customer's money held by the institution. Indeed, most advisors strongly believed that customers should allow them to manage *all* of their investable funds. The rationale was that doing so enabled the investment advisors to create and execute an optimal, financial plan, one that would generate the highest returns for the customer while minimizing risk through appropriate diversification. As a result, firms competed fiercely to increase the share of wallet of existing customers and to draw clients and their portfolios away from competitors.

Eugene knew the conventional wisdom by heart. The trouble was, he didn't believe it anymore. Having participated in a long and largely unsuccessful effort to woo new customers through aggressive advertising at his previous company, he was dismayed to find a similar campaign underway at Caesar Financial. "If I covered up the logos on the two companies' advertisements, they were basically indistinguishable," he recalled. "All the advisors were basically offering the same value proposition: let us manage all your money and we'll get you the best return. Trust us." Perhaps not surprisingly, the new Caesar campaign did little to stimulate growth. While the effort had begun before Eugene's arrival, senior management now looked to him for new answers.

The buying process and high-yield behavior change

Eugene's doubts about this conventional approach had been building for a number of years. His decision to use a new approach, one focusing on customer behavior, was driven by two observations. The first was the low yield of the recent advertising campaign and the second was his personal observation of the high drop out rate among potential wealth management clients. Many—if not most—customers who initiated conversations with financial advisors never followed through on the initial meetings. Eugene, like every other wealth manager, had accepted this yield loss as simply one of those things about the industry. Now he wondered whether the path to faster growth required a deeper understanding of why customers behaved so capriciously so often.

The first discovery in mapping the buying process waterfall was that there were certain triggering events that often led customers to explore investing with a new institution or advisor. A significant life event or the inflow of new money was often the mechanism that caused people to assess the appropriateness of their current investment choices and consider new options. This was the point at which they often sought out information or contacted a new financial advisor. While Caesar Financial advisors knew this at some level and often asked about these motivations in their initial meetings with clients, they had not fully appreciated the impact that these different triggers had on subsequent behaviors. There was a tendency to engage all new customers in similar ways, regardless of what brought them in the door. As Eugene pointed out, this was because the real, interesting target was the client's whole portfolio and the comprehensive plan for managing total wealth. The fleeting issues that customers might have on their minds on a given day were of much less concern to most advisors.

The analysis also found that the window for taking action following a triggering event could be fairly short. In general, if an individual didn't take action within sixty days of the motivating trigger, they were much less likely to follow through on the original intention to engage in a new advisory relationship. This prompted a deeper look at these early stages of the buying process.

Following the initial triggers, customers researched and evaluated options—which often included a meeting with a financial advisor. These face-to-face meetings typically took place in the advisor's office and were a way for financial advisors to get a sense of potential clients' needs and their attractiveness as customers (that is, how much they had to invest with Caesar). To this end, advisors typically asked prospective clients to complete a detailed form describing their assets and investment goals. These forms could run to more than twenty pages and were often tedious and time-consuming to complete. Many of the questions were framed in language common to the financial industry, for example, "How much of your portfolio do you want to invest in fixed income versus equity?"

"When you look at the things we'd ask about on these forms, I would compare it to a root canal in terms of how invasive it was," mused Eugene. "But for the last twenty years I'd been asking people to do them, because we needed the information to craft a comprehensive financial plan for the client." Many clients didn't complete the forms and simply vanished after these initial

FIGURE 8-1

Triggering Events and Objectives in Wealth Management Buying Process

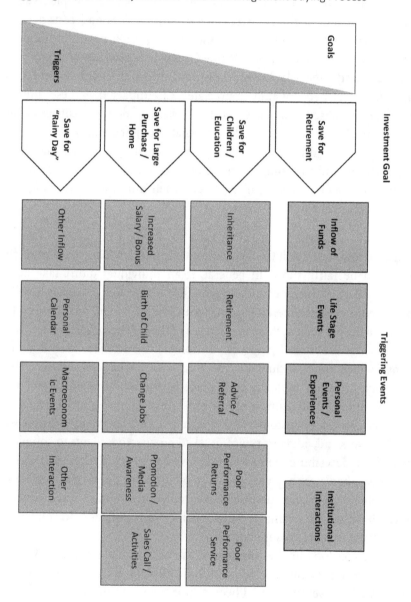

consultations. "In a way, we almost saw it as a good thing," said Eugene. "If they weren't serious enough to fill out the forms and commit to a plan, then maybe they weren't the kind of clients we wanted to work with. That was the thinking." It was simple math for a financial professional like Eugene to recognize that if Caesar could find a way to prevent even a fraction of these clients from leaking away after the initial meeting, it could have a tremendous impact on growth.

A key finding was that behaviors further downstream in the buying process were strongly linked to the confluence of initial triggers and investment goals that brought customers into the buying process. For example, one of the few situations that led customers to consider switching their entire portfolios to new advisors or institutions was if they had had a bad recent service experience with one of their existing institutions. The numbers showed, however, that this type of switching behavior was actually quite uncommon. Moving assets away from one advisor to another required a high-activation energy to overcome inertia. Clients typically had to complete onerous administrative tasks and pay transaction costs (for example, fees to brokers for buying and selling securities to form a new portfolio) to switch institutions. By contrast, customers were more likely to initiate a new advisory relationship—without transferring assets away from a current advisor—when they had "new money" to invest, for example, after receiving an unexpectedly large bonus or an inheritance. Customers often maintained relationships with multiple institutions despite advisors' promptings to consolidate the management of their assets.

One of the most striking findings from the research, which included numerous qualitative interviews with wealth management clients, was that people didn't think about managing their money in the way that the professionals did. Professional advisors typically took a holistic, money-is-money view of an investment portfolio. The right thing to do was thus to invest the whole to get the greatest total return. Customers could then decide how to allocate these returns among different things like retirement or vacation or education.

Customers, however, took a different view. They tended to engage in mental accounting. They designated different pots of money for different goals and treated each pot separately and differently. The purpose—the job they wanted done—came first and required setting aside enough money and managing it separately for that purpose. That way, they would *know* they had done what needed to be done. So, for example, if the goal was to fund a child's education, they would create a dedicated account that was invested a certain way and wasn't to be touched for other reasons. Along with treating money with different purposes separately, they also thought money received from different sources should be handled and invested differently. Money received from an inheritance was usually invested differently from the same sum received through a work-related bonus or salary increase.

"As financial professionals, we tend to believe that the *rational* thing for people to care about is total investment return balanced with appropriate risk over the relevant investment period," Eugene noted. "The thing is, people aren't really all that rational when it comes to money. It's actually highly emotional. It was time for us to stop being right all the time and listen to what customers were telling us they wanted."

As the buying process picture started to come together, it became increasingly clear that the actions that Caesar Financial—and its competitors—were trying to encourage, namely, getting customers to move all their funds to a single advisor and to commit to a comprehensive investment plan for all their assets, flew in the teeth of how customers actually thought and behaved. A much more common behavior was to initiate new advisory relationships when investing discrete amounts of new money for specific objectives. "We were pushing the heaviest rock up the steepest hill," reflected Eugene. "First, we were asking people to switch their relationships to Caesar Financial. Then we wanted them to transfer all their assets to us. That's actually two difficult things we were trying to do at the same time. The buying process analysis showed us how rare those behaviors actually were. But that was basically the strategy we had, along with just about everyone else in the industry."

So Eugene made a bold and seemingly risky change in his group's strategy. Rather than continue to pitch a comprehensive plan for the client's entire portfolio, advisors would instead identify and focus their discussion and pitch to customers around the particular jobs to be done that the investor already had in mind when seeking investment advice. The specific customer behaviors Eugene's team wanted to encourage were:

- Calling Caesar Financial to learn about the best way to accomplish particular financial jobs (for example, retirement, health care, education, and so on).
- Letting the advisor help the customer invest the new funds in a purpose-specific way, that is, by putting the money into investments and accounts that were best suited for, and transparently linked to, the particular job the customer was interested in at the moment.

- Investing additional funds with Caesar over time for future jobs to be done.

This marked a radical departure from the previous objective of getting customers to establish an exclusive relationship with Caesar Financial for the management of their entire portfolio. The next step was to segment the market based on different customer groups' propensity to engage in the desired behaviors.

Rethinking segmentation

The way Caesar Financial traditionally segmented the market was straightforward and based on two factors: investable assets and demographic characteristics. Customers were first categorized by wealth (based on their responses to the forms they were asked to complete) as: mass, mass affluent, affluent, and family fortune (that is, the very rich), and then by some version of age, gender, and marital status/size of household. This segmentation was attractive to the institution because it precisely identified the size of the prize and provided guidance about acceptable levels of cost to serve. Another appealing aspect of this segmentation was that it permitted an easy internal division of labor, with certain advisors specializing, for example, in serving affluent or very rich customers. Since fees were based on total assets under management, institutions generally prioritized these high net worth investors and sought to manage as much of their wealth as possible.

Despite its simplicity and ability to address certain internal needs (for example, organizational focus) it was actually a poor segmentation. It didn't provide useful insight into *either* customer behaviors or needs—two mass affluent customers, even of the same age and gender, could be starkly different. Furthermore, it was a *dangerous* segmentation because nearly every wealth management business used some version of these customer characteristics to segment the market. Because they all looked at the market the same way, firms tended to prioritize customers the same way—and devoted most of their resources to the same few segments. The result? Head-to-head battles over the same customers with largely identical products, leading to disappointing growth won at exceptionally high cost. The lackluster and forgettable marketing campaign previously launched by Caesar Financial reflected this undifferentiated approach.

FIGURE 8-2

Propensity-Based Segmentation of New Wealth Management Clients

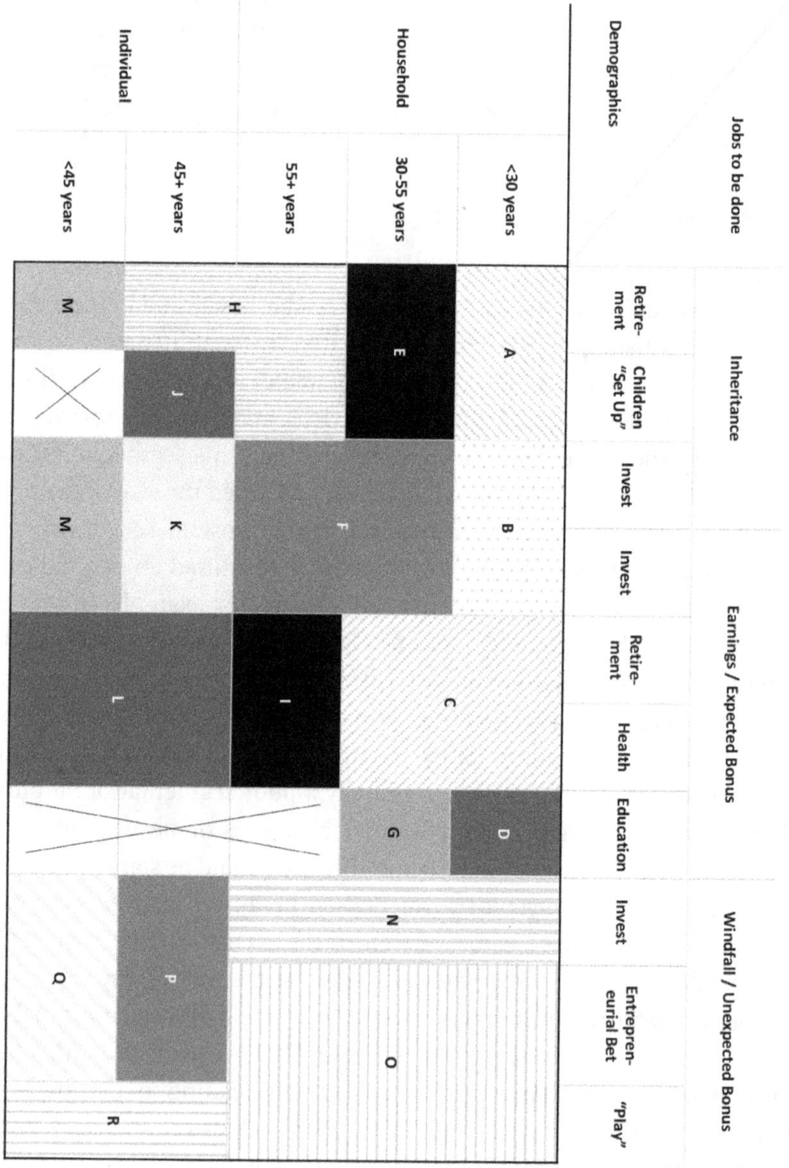

Eugene's team went in a different direction, abandoning the standard market map used throughout the industry. Rather than join the mob chasing after the portfolios of the wealthiest investors, they designed a way of finding and targeting customers investing money from a new source who might consider working with a Caesar financial advisor. As shown in Figure 8-2, while this propensity-based segmentation shared some attributes of the industry's standard segmentation, it really was dramatically different.

The segmentation frame they developed had one axis representing key aspects of the customer's situation (driving their desired experience) and another representing intrinsic characteristics of customers, for example, demographics. It was the horizontal or situational axis that was really novel. It focused on two things: the source of new investable money (for example, inheritance versus promotion versus unexpected bonus) and, most importantly, the purpose the customer had in mind for the new money. These were actionable segmentation variables because they could be easily discerned in initial conversations with prospective clients, and they had been shown in the buying process work to be hugely meaningful in terms of customers' propensity to engage in the behavioral objectives. The vertical axis, by contrast, hewed closer to the industry standard, identifying customers based on marital/household status and age.

The new segmentation was more complex than most, comprising a number of distinct segments. This was an indication that the market was, in fact, quite fragmented—customers had many different jobs they wanted to invest in to achieve. Indeed, the segmentation frame above essentially consists of three separate frames (divided by columns indicating the sources of new investable funds) with a few areas of crossover between columns.

The team identified Segment E as an initial target segment based on these customers' propensity to engage with a new institution to invest new money.[53] These investors treated funds received from a one-time event, such as an inheritance, differently from money coming from a step function change in income (for example, promotion), and tended to allocate the funds to specific goals. These households headed by thirty- to fifty-five-year-olds, often with children, typically applied inherited money to family concerns, such as providing for education or helping children with major purchases. While the sums invested by this segment weren't always large, this segment did represent an important opportunity for Caesar Financial to acquire new advisory relationships that could develop and grow over time.

"The idea that we would target people based on the highly specific goals they had for a newly obtained portion of their assets, rather than the size of their total portfolio, was pretty mind-blowing for a lot of people," said Eugene. "It was hard for us to think this way, but the new segmentation showed us that there was a lot of overlooked growth opportunity from converting even a portion of these customers." The firm needed to reach these key segments with communications and targeted offers that directly addressed their specific needs. To do so, however, the team needed to delve more deeply into the reasons and motivations for their behaviors to identify drivers and barriers to action.

Drivers and barriers to behavior change

The buying process interviews and analysis uncovered a number of surprising findings about how customers engaged in financial advisory relationships. It showed that most believed they had a financial plan; that they typically spread their investments across two or three institutions; that they were prone to drop out of any process investigating new institutions; that when they did engage with a new institution it tended to increase the total number they worked with (that is, they rarely abandoned existing advisory relationships totally); and that they almost never put their whole portfolio in the hands of one advisor. It also offered several insights into how differently customers thought about investing than professional advisors did. Investors tended to engage in tacit mental accounting with regard to different chunks of money rather than treating them as part of a single portfolio to be optimized. Furthermore, decision making about money matters was heavily freighted with strong (often negative) emotions for many customers.

The challenge for Eugene and his team was to explain Segment E's particular pattern of behaviors and outcomes. They worked toward that understanding using the CBF and the customer narrative. From that work they were able to identify the key factors—drivers and barriers—that shaped these customers' behaviors.

Jumping ahead in the analysis to the list of drivers and barriers (Figure 8-3) reveals the many different types of factors (economic, physical, social/psychological, and so on) that played a role in Segment E's thinking and behaviors. While a few of these barriers and drivers involved physical or economic constraints (for example, the complexity and amount of work required to engage a new advisor), the majority were about social and emotional factors. The analysis made abundantly clear that these emotional considerations—for example, the way advisors' questions made potential customers feel they were being graded on their past financial decisions, or the desire customers felt to honor the source of their new funds in the way they invested them—largely dictated what customers did.

This set of drivers and barriers emerged from the CBF analysis (Figure 8-4). The team conducted additional data collection and information-gathering interviews about Segment E to fill out the picture of their context, attitudes, and desired behaviors that led these customers to behave as they did.

The segment's story began with its social and physical context: they were multiperson households with many demands on their time that had money invested with two or three institutions. The decision to engage with a new advisor could be logistically challenging for these busy customers. Referrals from trusted sources were often a key factor in the decision to reach out to an advisor when investing newly inherited funds. However, having to wade through reams of paperwork or meet repeatedly with different members of an investment advisory team could easily turn customers off. These circumstances factored significantly into customers' desired experience: they wanted to deal with real experts and be treated seriously by investment advisors who would not waste their precious time.

Among the beliefs and attitudes of Segment E, the key findings related to the strong—even overwhelming—emotions that customers often experienced with regard to investment decision making and interactions with advisors. They expressed fear, confusion, vulnerability, and distrust about their investment experiences. Many people weren't deeply versed in money management and were afraid of making a mistake in handling their inheritance. As a result, there was a strong tendency to avoid making decisions. On the other hand, these customers usually felt that they had an adequate financial plan for the majority of their assets, even if it wasn't a formal one. They had worked hard to figure out where to place their money and believed those investments were appropriate. They found it off-putting when advisors suggested that they needed a "real" plan for all their assets when what they really wanted was help with a particular job to be done. Finally, they believed that the unique—almost sacred—nature of an inheritance warranted treating these funds in a special way.

FIGURE 8-3

Drivers and Barriers to Engaging in New Advisor Relationship for Segment E

Drivers	Barriers
• New money to invest from an inheritance – intrinsic desire to put funds to "good use" for recipient or recipient's family	• Actions/words by advisor that suggest current management of existing portfolio is inadequate – feeling of being "graded" by advisor
• Clarity about degree to which financial instrument or plan is specific to particular goals	• Actions/words by advisor that signal interest in putting inheritance into "general investments," i.e., investments not specific to one of the jobs identified by customer
• Clear, easy to execute plan to "do the job" : no more than 3 steps, minimal paperwork, data required easy to lay hands on	• Time spent discussing "extraneous" matters not directly related to inheritance and associated job
• Validation of soundness of intent and plan by prospective institution	• Size of "set up" costs, i.e., cost to establish relationship with new institution (especially if felt to be not related to job specific investment)
• Recommendation/testimonial from someone "like them" (or friend) in similar situation	• Need to work with more than one person / no single person to handle transaction end to end
• Interactions with advisor/expert that signal greater knowledge of specific job than current institutions/advisors and don't waste time on other "extraneous" issues, opportunities, or products	• Having to provide hard to gather data, especially if not directly related to the job they want to accomplish
	• Signals – words, actions – that advisor is not a world class expert on the job to be done

Again, these factors shaped elements of the desired experience for these customers. While financial professionals tended to emphasize the importance of investment performance and returns, customers wanted something different. They were deeply afraid of making the wrong choice and worried that they didn't understand the jargon and math surrounding products and services. Moreover, they disliked facing a battery of questions and suggestions from advisors that could make them feel that their prior decisions were poor, even misguided. What they wanted was clear information on product benefits, features, and pricing, and an appropriate level of advice to accomplish the *specific jobs* they wanted done delivered in a respectful way. Financial professionals often exacerbated negative ideas and emotions in the way they interacted with customers. For a financial advisor, asking questions about customers' current investments and gathering information about assets

FIGURE 8-4

Customer Behavior Framework for 30- to 55-Year-Old Heads of
Households Investing Funds from an Inheritance

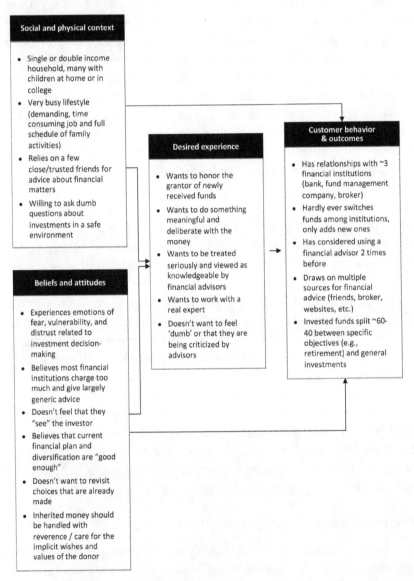

Social and physical context

- Single or double income household, many with children at home or in college
- Very busy lifestyle (demanding, time consuming job and full schedule of family activities)
- Relies on a few close/trusted friends for advice about financial matters
- Willing to ask dumb questions about investments in a safe environment

Beliefs and attitudes

- Experiences emotions of fear, vulnerability, and distrust related to investment decision-making
- Believes most financial institutions charge too much and give largely generic advice
- Doesn't feel that they "see" the investor
- Believes that current financial plan and diversification are "good enough"
- Doesn't want to revisit choices that are already made
- Inherited money should be handled with reverence / care for the implicit wishes and values of the donor

Desired experience

- Wants to honor the grantor of newly received funds
- Wants to do something meaningful and deliberate with the money
- Wants to be treated seriously and viewed as knowledgeable by financial advisors
- Wants to work with a real expert
- Doesn't want to feel 'dumb' or that they are being criticized by advisors

Customer behavior & outcomes

- Has relationships with ~3 financial institutions (bank, fund management company, broker)
- Hardly ever switches funds among institutions, only adds new ones
- Has considered using a financial advisor 2 times before
- Draws on multiple sources for financial advice (friends, broker, websites, etc.)
- Invested funds split ~60-40 between specific objectives (e.g., retirement) and general investments

in order to develop a comprehensive financial plan was a normal part of being a responsible and professional advisor. Many customers, however, experienced these conversations quite differently.

Insight into these motivating factors helped explain the behaviors and outcomes that Eugene's team observed about these customers. Breaking down investment goals into smaller, discrete jobs to be done and avoiding major decisions—such as moving all their assets to a new advisor—were ways of dealing with the negative and fearful emotions they often experienced with regard to investing. They preferred to build relationships with advisors incrementally, one job at a time. They broke down investment objectives into manageable jobs, investing specific increments of money for a particular job. The analysis showed that these investors often didn't trust themselves to save and invest sufficiently for specific goals without earmarking funds in separate funds for different purposes. They also distrusted assurances from advisors that a comprehensive investment plan for their assets would enable them to achieve all their goals.

"With the best intentions, we were shooting ourselves in the foot," said Eugene. "The point is, people don't make these decisions in a detached, calculating way. It takes a lot for them to take the step of setting up an appointment with a new advisor, and then we use that precious time to increase the fear and loathing they have for the process! Instead of helping them accomplish the goals they have, we tell them that their previous investment decisions weren't so good. That they don't have a *real* plan. We ask them to fill out tons of paperwork. No wonder we were seeing such high dropout rates after the first conversation. We gave them every reason and opportunity to bail out. This process helped us step into the shoes of the customer and understand where they want our help and where they don't."

The next step for Eugene and his team was to take a fresh look at how Caesar Financial crafted messages and touchpoints with customers to overcome the emotional and practical barriers that prevented them from taking action. They also considered what changes to make in the products they offered and the way they served clients to capitalize on key drivers.

Behavior change value proposition

Eugene's team spent a lot of time discussing the list of drivers and barriers for Segment E. Through debate and discussion, they sorted out how the various drivers and barriers reinforced or negated each other, and which were most important. They then synthesized the discussion in a behavior change value proposition (BCVP), a statement of what they believed it would take to convince a Segment E customer to actually work through a job-specific financial plan with an advisor (hopefully from Caesar).

Though the format of the BCVP (Figure 8-5) was similar to value proposition statements they had developed for prior campaigns, its intent and content were dramatically different. The value propositions they'd created in the past were fundamentally product and/or brand centric. They were intended to articulate the benefits to the customer of Caesar's products or of the Caesar brand. The BCVP, by contrast, wasn't about a product or a brand. It was about the benefits to a customer of *taking a different action* somewhere in the buying process. In this case, the BCVP centered on the value of working with a professional financial advisor to craft *a job-specific financial plan for* inherited money. In the language of the *Playbook*, the BCVP for Segment E articulated which behavioral benefits (that is, drivers) Caesar would accentuate, and which behavioral impediments (that is, barriers) it would mitigate to increase the likelihood of Segment E customers engaging in the desired behaviors.

The key to convincing someone to put their money to work through Caesar was, first, to avoid doing anything to trigger customers' just-below-the-surface feelings of fear and distrust. The new approach aimed to eliminate the subtle (or not-so-subtle) signals that customers often received that advisors judged them to be poor investors or that they were squandering money. The marketing team wanted Caesar advisors to enhance customer drivers by affirming that investors had done a good job with their financial planning and were acting responsibly. Secondly, the team wanted to demonstrate that Caesar was superbly equipped to enable chunk by chunk job-focused investing by making clear that Caesar's products were job-specific and that each advisor was a genuine expert in accomplishing these customer-defined jobs. This involved refocusing the initial meeting with potential investors entirely on what the customer was interested in (that is, how to use their new money), and not on what the advisor wanted to know (that is, how big a customer they might be). The BCVP thus expressed an approach to engaging customers in a virtuous psychological cycle—validating that the direction they thought they wanted to go was a good one and making it easy for them to take action.

FIGURE 8-5

Segment E Behavior Change Value Proposition

For:	30-55 year-old head of household investing funds received from an inheritance (Segment E)
Doing Behavior:	Seeking help from expert advisor to invest appropriate portions of a recent inheritance to meet specific goals related to family's education or housing needs
Instead of Behavior:	Adding inherited funds to their general investment account or leaving funds uninvested (i.e., dropping out)
Will produce value for customers by:	Ensuring that they are respecting the wishes of the grantor of the inheritance by putting the money to good uses and "doing the right thing" for their families

Our behavior change campaign will therefore seek to enhance the value of the targeted Behavior to the customer and their propensity to do the Behavior through:

Tapping key Drivers to the Desired Behavior by:	Offering solutions / products specifically tailored to the goals and "jobs to be done" with inherited funds
	Designing initial customer meeting around developing a plan to achieve the specific goals the customer has for discrete "chunk" of investable funds from an inheritance
	Demonstrating Caesar Financial's experience and expertise in helping "customers like you" meet their specific goals
And eliminating Barriers to the Desired Behavior by:	Minimizing time, cost, hand-offs, and paperwork not focused on specific goals and jobs to be done, e.g., short forms (1-2pp), no data on rest of portfolio, questions fully answered within 1 hour, etc.
	Not asking about or implicitly criticizing current plan for customer's larger investment portfolio

The BCVP was, in effect, a blueprint for Eugene and his team to follow, one that would lead to more positive and effective interactions with Segment E customers. It highlighted the need to redesign both the substance of Caesar's approach (for example, its products, its focus on all dollars) and the emotional impact of its processes and communications (the tone and tempo of communications, the use of the dreaded questionnaire, and so on).

The first task was to rework or create products that truly would be effective vehicles for job-focused investing. They began by tweaking existing products for customer jobs they already knew about, for example, saving for college education, to make them even more focused. The team then constructed new investment bundles that mirrored the additional jobs the analysis had revealed were in customers' minds, such as travel, or buying a second home. Changing the product lineup this way had the benefit of communicating to the customer how seriously Caesar took their mental accounting as well as improving performance for them.

The team's second task was to develop a new media campaign with the dual objectives of validating customers' subconscious notion that new dollars ought to be used for specific purposes, and positioning Caesar as uniquely suited to help them take action. The campaign was built to show how new money from bonuses or inheritances motivated people to act on the jobs that they knew they should do—but had not yet—with assistance from Caesar's experts who knew just how to match investment vehicles to the job the customer had in mind. The emotional tone running through all these communications was affirmation. They tried to make it clear that the way customers thought about investing money was sensible and good and that Caesar knew how to help them succeed in carrying out their intentions. In doing so the team was able to tap into Caesar's hundred-year heritage as a workingman's bank, artfully incorporating iconic elements of past campaigns (for example, logos, color, tunes) to remind people of its ability to support them in accomplishing their goals.

Third, the team set out to dramatically reduce the snags and chores that made working with a financial institution so aggravating to customers. Redesigning the initial meeting was critically important, because it was there that many of those obstacles first surfaced and where most of the drop off occurred. The goal was to make this a positive, nonjudgmental experience for customers and streamline the path to taking action. Rather than quiz potential clients about their entire portfolio, advisors were instructed to zero in quickly on more tangible goals and focus the discussion on how straightforward it would be to use the new funds to accomplish them. They eliminated the lengthy asset disclosure questionnaire, substituting just a few questions about the potential customer's recent inflow of money, their risk tolerance, and so on. The advisor was asked to then sketch out the available options—products or plans—for achieving one or more of their goals, going through both pros and cons, but emphasizing that any choice was a good one as they all would do the job, albeit in different ways.

The advisor would then offer to complete the first steps of the investment process right then and there, while showing the potential customer how to work through the rest of the streamlined purchase process. This more personal and limited conversation helped reduce the feelings of fear and mistrust that many people brought to these encounters and created a sense that they were making rapid and substantive progress on specific goals. Demonstrating understanding and commitment to achieving these jobs helped build investors' confidence and comfort, encouraging them to continue to the next stage of the buying process.

Another aspect of streamlining the buying process was to minimize the number of hand-offs among investment professionals. In the past, team members would pass off customers—sometimes two or three times—to different specialists who handled specific types of investments. But every hand off and time gap was an opportunity for customers to feel that progress had halted, to renew their doubts, and to drop out of the process. The redesign called for each team member to wear two hats: acting as the single point of contact and advice for a potential customer while reaching out to and dealing with other team members with specific expertise as needed. This expedited process eliminated interruptions and reduced the total amount of time customers spent in understanding and evaluating options by an order of magnitude. Again, the objective was to move customers quickly and seamlessly through the early phases of the buying process to reduce dropout and encourage customers to proceed to the purchase stage. Once a customer had retained a Caesar Financial advisor, the advisor looked to deepen that relationship and gradually grow the share of funds invested one job at a time.

"Some of the things we did were pretty simple, really," said Eugene. "But there was a lot of thought that went into this. We realized that getting people to engage in the buying process in the first place usually required a combination of triggers. Instead of trying to draw more people into the process with advertisements, we focused instead on making sure that Caesar was part of their consideration set when they went looking for an advisor to help them with specific jobs. So we were widening the funnel at the top and then doing everything we could to keep people engaged with a different kind of conversation about their needs. The hard part was accepting that people didn't really like talking to us! Everyone wants to be liked—but we had to earn that trust and relationship."

FIGURE 8-6

Redesigned Customer Experience

From		To
Lecturing customers about financial planning and options for investing entire portfolio	→	Brief credentialing followed by questions to gather information about customer "job to be done"
Extensive documentation on assets and investment objectives to be filled out by client, requiring follow-up meeting with advisor	→	Streamlined documentation focused on discrete assets to be invested for specific purpose – ideally completed by advisor during initial client conversation
Additional meeting with advisor to go over portfolio plan and gain agreement	→	Advisor presents information on options and bundled offerings tailored to customer objectives
Multiple meetings and hand-offs to different product specialists to discuss elements of plan	→	Lead advisor orchestrates contacts with specialist experts, acting as single point of contact
Hand-off to administrators to obtain necessary paperwork and permissions to execute plan	→	Expedited decision and execution of initial investment with follow-up opportunities for cross-selling

Disproportionate investment

The final stage of the process, while conceptually simple, turned out to be one of the most challenging aspects of the new strategy. "It wasn't just about shifting marketing spend around and launching new TV spots. That part was relatively easy. It was about changing the way we do business and earn a living, down to the level of each individual advisor," said Eugene.

The first element of this was to prioritize and sequence the campaign around target segments that were most likely to engage. Rather than go after all the jobs to be done at once, the new approach and advertising resources were disproportionately focused on specific investment triggers (that is, receiving an inheritance) and investment goals. The next wave of the campaign extended the reach to investors receiving an unexpected windfall or influx of new money from other sources. While the one-time nature of this new money was similar to that of an inheritance, investors tended to have different jobs in mind for these types of funds. They were much more likely, for example, to invest these dollars for personal projects or in entrepreneurial ventures and thus required different product bundles. Accordingly, Caesar shifted its marketing spend for the first few years away from a scattershot approach to a more focused attempt to attract these target segments.

As discussed earlier, a large part of the redesigned campaign depended upon the ability and willingness of individual advisors to adopt a new approach in dealing with potential clients. Because advisors were traditionally compensated on a percentage of client assets under management, the incentives rewarded those who could attract a few large investors and convince them to place most or all of their assets with Caesar. The new jobs to be done strategy, however, required advisors to engage with more clients around smaller initial investments.

The task of selling the new growth strategy to senior management and to Caesar's pool of investment advisors was thus a daunting one for Eugene. He was aided in this, however, by the unflagging support of the company's CEO. "When we showed him the analysis, he got it at once," said Eugene. "It made a big difference to know the CEO had my back in conversations with the Board and other stakeholders. But it was pretty clear to me that it was *my* job and *my* career on the line. Having done the work, I couldn't accept a return to the status quo knowing that it wasn't going to get us to our growth targets. I was ready to walk away if I had to—I was all in."

With the backing of the CEO, and working with key line executives and HR, Eugene's team created training programs for advisors on the new offerings and drafted revised protocols for customer conversations focused around jobs to be done. Financial incentives were also restructured to reward advisors based on the number of client initiations and new client engagements they converted in addition to the value of assets managed. Inevitably, some advisors resisted these changes. There were therefore some difficult choices to make about separating from long-tenured advisors (who often took a substantial portion of their advisory clients with them when they left).

Epilogue

The full transformation of wealth management services at Caesar Financial didn't take place overnight. But the results of the new strategy to focus on discrete jobs to be done for investors started to be felt fairly quickly. Following the introduction of the new, goal-specific investment bundles, there was a substantial increase in the number of potential clients approaching Caesar to speak with a specialist and a dramatic increase in the rate at which these initial meetings were converted to sales. By the third year of the campaign, the number of initial conversations with advisors was up by more than 25 percent. And the conversion rate from first meeting to initiation of a new advisory relationship more than doubled, from around 18 percent to 48 percent. While some of these initial investments could be fairly modest, they often led to additional investments over time for the other jobs customers needed done.

Assets under management also grew faster than the industry average every year following the rollout of the new products and advertising campaign. In the first year, assets under management grew by 7 percent (versus 3 percent for the industry as a whole). The growth rate increased to 10 percent in the second year, and 12 percent in the third year. While other firms continued to slug it out, trying to lure large investors to transfer their entire portfolios, Caesar built a leading position and vastly expanded its client base by addressing customers' need for targeted help with specific investment goals that others in the industry had largely overlooked.

Chapter 9

Fourth Principle: Develop a Behavior Change Value Proposition

Early in his tenure at Caesar Financial, Eugene Shin confronted the uncomfortable reality that all wealth management firms were offering largely the same product value proposition. In a nutshell, their message to investors was this: let us manage all your money and we'll provide the best financial returns. The reasons to believe this claim—Caesar's highly educated financial advisors, suite of proprietary analytical tools, wide range of financial products, and so on—were largely indistinguishable from those being touted by their competitors. As a result, the marketplace was intensely competitive with similar firms offering similar services and value propositions. Eugene's situation was not unique. Indeed, it's highly representative of the situations of many companies who market good enough but largely undifferentiated products.

A common response to this predicament is for marketers to redouble efforts to distinguish their products through louder, more frequent, more expensive communications and promotional campaigns. Seeing the poor results of Caesar's attempts to do just this, Eugene opted for a different solution. Rather than try to change customers' perceptions of the firm's brand or its offerings, he focused Caesar's new strategy on certain frequently observed behaviors in the buying process. Recognizing that many investors sought out investment advice to help them with a specific job to be done with new funds (for example, from an inheritance), the new approach sought to facilitate this behavior and remove obstacles that investors frequently faced.

While most advisors actively discouraged customers from fragmenting their investment portfolios or threw up impediments, such as asking them to complete lengthy financial disclosure forms about *all* their wealth, Eugene decided instead to boost customers' propensity to engage in this type of behavior.

Rather than pitch a comprehensive plan for clients' entire portfolio, the new approach aimed to validate and reinforce the behavior of investing discrete amounts for particular purposes. Note that this was *not* about promoting a product or brand. Rather, this approach signaled to customers the value of the new behavior of consulting with a financial advisor when they had new money to invest. Promoting this behavior change value proposition (BCVP) became the centerpiece of Caesar's redesigned campaign, which also included tailoring offerings and services to support this behavior and eliminate barriers. By changing how they went to market in a crowded field of players with fairly undifferentiated offerings, Caesar was able to rapidly grow its number of advisory relationships and assets under management relative to competitors.

There are, of course, companies with highly differentiated—even revolutionary—products. Terrafix is an example. Yet, despite offering a first-of-its-kind, highly effective therapeutic benefit for a serious disease, it too found its growth rate faltering. We don't mean to suggest that having a product with a compelling and differentiated value proposition is irrelevant—far from it. Distinctive, credible product value propositions form the foundations of growth. But a strong product value proposition isn't enough to guarantee growth.[54] Nor will strengthening an already solid product value proposition always deliver faster growth. In fact, creating memorable positive associations in customers' minds—even incredibly powerful ones (for example, BMW as the "ultimate driving machine")—may or may not drive growth. The reason, as we've pointed out in previous chapters, is that faster growth reliably occurs only when customers are induced to change certain high-yield behaviors in the buying process in favorable ways.

The concept of a BCVP may be new to you. But you're probably familiar with the idea of a product value proposition (PVP) or positioning statement. In this chapter, we explain how a BCVP is analogous to—but distinctly different from—a PVP. While conventional wisdom has long stressed the importance of developing coherent, compelling, and differentiated PVPs, we argue that you'll typically achieve much higher growth by focusing instead on building marketing campaigns around a cogent BCVP.

Conventional wisdom

The precise form and content of a typical PVP varies among individual companies and marketers, but nearly all contain the same basic elements. At heart, a PVP is a statement of how the company seeks to position a product or offering to convince target customers of its differentiated value relative to competitors' offerings.[55] Accordingly, a PVP first specifies the customer segment or segments targeted by the value proposition. Second, a PVP identifies the specific functional benefits that the product or brand offers to the target customer. A good PVP usually focuses on just a few core benefits that are easy to convey. Even though an offering may have many benefits that customers value, a simple benefit message is more likely to be memorable (for example, Disney World is the "happiest place on earth").

Third, a PVP recognizes that all products or offerings will be assessed by customers relative to the next best alternative. So it usually defines, in detail, how or how much the product's functional benefits are better or different from those of competitors. Finally, a PVP usually includes a set of reasons to believe that the product attributes, firm resources, assets, or capabilities, or customer-facing services provide the superior benefit claimed. Hence, firms may say they are superior on a core benefit (for example, the most reliable airline service), but only those that can demonstrate proof of their assertions (for example, higher performance on industry metrics of on-time departures and arrivals) can lay claim to real reasons for customers to believe in the promised benefit. A compelling and differentiated PVP is the linchpin of the marketing plan in the standard approach. It provides the platform for a growth campaign whose aim is to fix the chosen benefits in the minds of target customers by reinforcing the reasons to believe in the superiority of the firm's offering relative to competitors.

So, what's the problem? From our perspective, there are four fundamental limitations to the conventional approach. First, while marketing orthodoxy emphasizes the critical importance of having a differentiated value proposition and establishing a unique position in the mind of the customer, the fact is that there are plenty of products and services that just aren't particularly exceptional. Despite the best efforts of engineers to design in and marketers to tease out distinctive points of their offering, significant and meaningful product differentiation can be hard to come by in many heavily competed markets.[56] This was certainly the case for the Sparkle, Caesar, and EnServ teams. They all had very good products and services, and each could point to key selling points of their products relative to rivals. But no matter how much or how cleverly they pointed out these selling points, customers didn't really see much difference between them and their rivals. These companies' product-focused campaigns fell flat because their central product claims weren't credible enough to motivate people.

Second, and very importantly, the traditional PVP-driven model is all about the upside of the product. PVPs are nearly always geared toward the benefits of product purchase—there's no attention paid to the negatives of the product or to the barriers that get in the way of purchase. But for many consumer situations, the key isn't improving the benefits but removing the downsides associated with the product, service, or offering. For example, as noted earlier, while airlines have long emphasized the pleasures and comfort of air travel, the issue for most business travelers is actually one of pain reduction. Many recent innovations in the industry—for example, flight delay notifications delivered to mobile phones and at-home check-in with boarding passes—are about removing the pain of travel. Effective marketing campaigns thus need to address both the potential upsides and downsides of the end-to-end buying experience. The traditional PVP rarely takes this balanced view of customer benefits.

The third and fourth limitations of the traditional PVP-based approach arise from its implicit focus on just one stage of the buying process. This causes teams to ignore many potential growth opportunities and to underestimate the various things that can happen in customers' thinking when they are out shopping. The PVP approach focuses on behaviors that occur far downstream in the buying process, at the stage of brand choice. In effect, a PVP campaign is aimed directly at getting customers who have made up their minds to buy something in a category to choose Brand A instead of Brand B. In this approach, growth comes solely from gaining share or retaining share. The trouble is that by ignoring all the other stages of the buying process it ignores the opportunities for growth (and getting their fair share of that growth) either by drawing new customers into the category or by increasing the amount or intensity of product use among existing customers. As we've seen, critical high-yield behaviors can occur at any stage—upstream or downstream—in the buying process and may affect more than simply brand or product choice (see Finding Leverage in Different Stages of the Buying Process).

Finding Leverage in Different Stages of the Buying Process

The pharmaceutical industry provides numerous examples of companies finding leverage points at different stages in the buying process. For example, Viagra focused heavily on the origination stage of the buying process to create awareness of the condition it was meant to treat. As the first to market in this category and the market share leader, increasing the number of customers at the top of the funnel benefited Viagra relative to the competition. Meanwhile, other pharmaceutical makers have focused efforts at the opposite end of the buying process to ensure that patients take their medications as prescribed. Through the use of RFID-enabled blister packs or even ingestible sensors, they have sought to drive growth by increasing post-purchase compliance with therapies. Neither of these growth strategies is focused on product or brand choice, but on other stages in the overall buying process.

Finally, and most importantly, the standard approach assumes that a customer with a clear preference for Product X will look for and buy the product they prefer. While this may seem logical, it doesn't reflect the reality of how customers shop. As we've seen, regardless of people's initial preferences, the things that happen to them in the course of the buying process can significantly affect their thinking and behavior. Brand preference often doesn't determine actual purchase behaviors because something happened while they were shopping. The same dynamic can play out in B2B and B2C settings. For instance, a product manager might prefer one vendor but choose a different one because of the constraints of a corporate procurement process (see Moving from Attitude to Action).

Moving from Attitude to Action

Take the example of the Uber ride-sharing service. Over the last few years, the company has built an enviable position in the minds of young, urban, smartphone users as offering a low-cost and convenient alternative to taxis. Despite having a compelling and differentiated value proposition, however, Uber needs customers to not only believe in its benefits, but also to *do* something. Specifically, they need target customers to download the Uber app on their smartphones as a prerequisite for using the service. Having a strong PVP may help persuade people to engage in this behavior, but there's not necessarily a direct path from believing in the benefits to taking action. In this case, a campaign focused on getting target customers to take action around downloading the app—by showing them the value of this behavior and removing barriers to doing it—may be more effective in driving growth than ads and promotions extolling the benefits of the service. The point is simply that stuff happens in the course of the buying process that can have a profound effect on outcomes. Getting customers to prefer your brand doesn't pay off unless they actually follow through on that preference.

In sum, the traditional reliance on PVPs has some significant limitations. Even a highly differentiated PVP doesn't necessarily lead to revenue growth. Moreover, customers often purchase undifferentiated or good enough products because of other factors influencing the buying process. While we're certainly not suggesting that product differentiation is unimportant, we're saying that it's often insufficient for growth. Our approach advocates a more balanced view of the importance of a strong PVP *and* a compelling BCVP.

The *Playbook* approach: Behavior change value proposition

Our view is that while a good PVP is a necessary element of a product's growth strategy, it's insufficient to deliver faster growth. To be clear, bad products just don't make it—no matter how they're marketed or sold. What enables good products to thrive is ensuring that customers see, learn about, or engage with them at the most favorable times, places, and conditions during the buying process, that is, that customers engage in high-yield behaviors. The BCVP is the formula for persuading customers to do those behaviors, to engage in activities at those favorable points in the buying process. The BCVP helps you articulate two specific things. First, it expresses the *value to the potential customer* of doing a high-yield behavior relative to other possible buying process behaviors. And secondly, it describes how you can boost that behavior's value to customers, thus increasing their propensity to do it. A compelling BCVP is thus an essential complement of the PVP that provides a complete and reliable blueprint for driving faster growth.

Remember that the key insight for the EnServ team was that facility managers who consulted with a vendor early in the buying process for energy services projects were more likely to complete a project and were five times more likely to choose the vendor they initially consulted over other vendors. The implications were clear. Engaging these customers more frequently at an earlier stage of the process was much more likely to steer them onto a pathway of subsequent activities that led them to purchase a project from EnServ. The company's growth campaign therefore included multiple activities aimed at changing this specific upstream behavior.

Notice, however, what it did *not* include. It did not include spending money to advertise the benefits of doing an energy saving project with EnServ instead of with one of its competitors. It did not include reasons to believe that EnServ's equipment or services were superior to others. And it did not include positioning key product benefits in the mind of the customer. Rather, the driver of faster organic growth was to increase the value of the high-yield behavior (that is, consulting with a qualified vendor when developing energy saving ideas to put in next year's plan) in the mind of the target customer. The company trained its salespeople and equipped them to provide more accurate, practical insights on all aspects of energy management, thus tapping into drivers of the behavior, and made it very easy to reach them and get the advice, so reducing barriers to it. Boosting the value of this otherwise unremarkable buying process behavior led customers to do it more frequently because they got more out of consulting with EnServ than they did from alternative buying behaviors. In turn and in time, this led them to purchase energy projects from EnServ more frequently than they had before.

We should note how deeply uncomfortable many product managers and marketers will be with this notion. In a number of our consulting engagements, we've had clients stare at us with a mix of horror and incredulity and say something to this effect: "You mean, you want me to spend 70 percent of my marketing budget *not* talking about the product?" In some cases, that's exactly what we mean. Recall that the key to turning around Terrafix's fortunes was an *unbranded* information campaign focused on encouraging middle-aged women to ask their doctors for a diagnostic test. It did so by showing them how valuable the behavior of asking for a test was in terms of their deeply felt need to take care of their own health and well-being—not by promoting the therapeutic benefits of the drug. The Terrafix team struggled with this seeming diversion of time and money away from promoting the drug until they saw a remarkable jump in sales over the first few months.

The intent of the BCVP is to make engaging in the desired behavior more valuable to the customer, both intrinsically (as an activity) and as a gateway to making the best possible purchase decision. As such, the BCVP is analogous to a PVP, but different in important ways. As the names suggest, the goal of both the PVP and the BCVP is to propose and establish the value of something in the mind of the target customer. The focus of the PVP is on the benefits of Product X that will induce the customer to choose Product X over other products (or other options). Essentially, it conveys the value of *one* specific behavior. That is, buying or using the particular brand or product. The BCVP extends this to the entire buying process, or—more precisely—to particular high-yield behaviors that may occur *at any stage* in the buying process.

An effective BCVP clearly articulates how customers will be better off by engaging in the desired behavior as compared to the status quo. It also lays out the general game plan for how to induce the behavior change. The BCVP therefore has two parts: 1) articulating the value of a behavior to a segment, and 2) defining what's required to boost the value of the behavior to that segment. Specifically, a BCVP:

- Identifies a specific customer segment.
- Articulates the targeted behavior change (that is, what behavior you want customers to do instead of current behaviors).
- Describes the benefit for the customer of engaging in the desired behavior.
- Specifies drivers to increase the propensity of target customers to do the desired behavior.
- Specifies barriers that hinder the propensity of target customers to do the desired behavior.

The first three components of the BCVP are about the value of the targeted high-yield behavior. The fourth and fifth components are about how to build up the value of that behavior.

In many cases, it makes sense to develop both a PVP and a BCVP. Indeed, our approach rests on the assumption that the product or brand offers at least a good enough value proposition that customers are willing to purchase it. And, as we've said, having a clear and differentiated PVP that's valued by the target segment goes a long way to supporting other behaviors targeted by the

BCVP. Going back to the Uber example, if the ride-sharing service is viewed as safe, convenient, and cost effective relative to traditional taxis, this belief in the product benefits can bolster a campaign to induce customers to undertake a related behavior change (that is, downloading the app).

As shown in Figure 9-1, a firm that has both a differentiated PVP and a differentiated BCVP will be in the strongest position. In the case of Terrafix, Sam Wilcox had the good fortune to begin with a highly differentiated product with clear and distinctive therapeutic benefits that were well understood by physicians (putting him in the upper-left cell of the matrix). The catalyst for faster sustained growth, however, was the addition of a clearly articulated BCVP that enabled his team to craft and execute an effective campaign to change behaviors related to asking for and prescribing an objective test for the disease.

FIGURE 9-1

Mapping Differentiation of PVP and BCVP: Terrafix

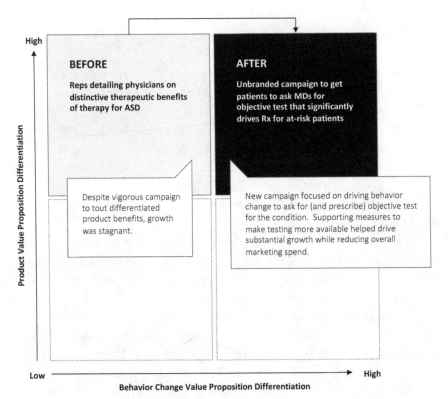

As the Caesar Financial case study illustrates, however, it's not necessary to begin by establishing a strong product differentiation. At the outset, Eugene Shin found himself firmly wedged in the lower-left cell of the matrix with a "me too" product value proposition and no BCVP. Building off the insights of the buying process analysis, his team constructed a compelling behavior change value proposition for target customers based on the notion of financial jobs to be done. Once they established the value of the desired behavior of engaging an advisor to help invest discrete chunks of money for specific purposes, they were able to enhance the PVP of their financial products. At some level, the actual content of these products (for example, the underlying analytics and investment algorithms) didn't change all that much. The firm was, however, able to create investment bundles specifically tailored for certain jobs to be done (for example, funding an education, saving for retirement, or planning for a vacation). This enabled them to differentiate these rebranded products relative to other firms' offerings (see "One Campaign or Two?").

One Campaign or Two?

Since having both a good PVP and a strong BCVP is important, should you actually have two campaigns, that is, one to establish or maintain your PVP and another to establish and drive your BCVP? From a practical perspective, you often have to keep talking about a product's value proposition to maintain its relevance in the market. Rarely would we advocate pulling the plug on all product-centered marketing. But you'll generally need to do more—often much more—to establish a compelling BCVP. This is particularly true when the desired behavior change occurs at a point in the buying process that's distant from the product choice stage.

In general, three factors affect the degree of emphasis you should put on the BCVP relative to the PVP: the strength of the existing PVP, the location of the desired behavior within the buying process, and the degree to which the desired behavior differs from current behavior. In situations where the PVP is well-established and where the desired behavior is unusual for the market and occurs either far upstream or downstream of product choice, we recommend focusing almost exclusively on the BCVP. This was the situation in the EnServ case study, where the firm's products were well-regarded but the desired behavior (consulting with a vendor to come up with ideas for energy services projects) was quite novel in the industry. By contrast, in cases where the PVP is weak, you may need to devote more resources to shoring up the reputation and appeal of your offerings in order for the BCVP to be effective. In these instances, you may require separate organizational efforts to address the PVP and the BCVP.

In sum, a good BCVP should be simple and easy to understand. It should make clear to everyone involved in designing and executing a marketing campaign what the behavior change is and how it's to be achieved. In the next section, we explain in detail how to construct an effective behavior change value proposition. Also, in a sidebar discussion, we briefly consider a model of behavioral change you can use to assess whether a proposed BCVP meets the conditions required for behavior change to occur (see The MOA Model).

The fourth principle explained

To assist teams in constructing effective BCVPs, we've developed a simple template that draws together critical elements of the previous analysis. It's intended to guide you step by step in creating the design document for each of the segment-specific behavior change campaigns you'll implement. Since these campaigns require you to make unambiguous choices about where, how, and when to invest marketing resources (as discussed further in Chapter 10), it's important that the BCVP be clear and accessible. It also must contain a credible and compelling statement of how the targeted behavior change is to be accomplished.

The BCVP template

Figure 9-2 provides a template for constructing a segment-level BCVP statement. The format of the BCVP is, at first glance, similar to that of a PVP, but its focus and components are actually quite different. The most important difference is that the BCVP focuses on the benefits that doing the target high-yield behavior provides to those in the target segment, rather than the benefits associated with purchase and use of the product. The BCVP therefore also provides guidance on how to get customers to want to do the high-yield behavior more frequently, rather than listing reasons to believe in the product. Taken together, the pieces of the BCVP yield a clear and concise statement of the behavior change to be achieved, the value to the segment of engaging in that behavior, and the key elements of the approach the company will take to activate the change. It serves as the marching orders for the teams engaged in the creative, operational, and promotional aspects of segment-specific campaigns.

It's important to build, and understand, the template in two parts. The first part defines the target segment (*who*), the target behavior change (*what*), and the value proposition for doing the high-yield behavior more frequently (*why*). The who and the what naturally go together, since, as explained in Chapter 5, segments are defined by the propensity of people in a particular role to do the target behavior. The crux of the first part of the BCVP, though, is the behavior value proposition statement itself, which explains why doing the target behavior instead of some other possible behavior at that stage of the buying process is valuable for customers in the target segment. Unlike a PVP that describes the benefits a customer will receive as a result of the purchase, possession, and/or use of the product, the BCVP expresses the beneficial value of the behavior itself.

The second part of the BCVP template transitions toward action. It identifies the few critical drivers and barriers around which you'll build the campaign for the segment and how you'll address them. In effect, these statements document how you can increase the net value that the high-yield behavior has for customers by enhancing incentives or clearing away obstacles. As noted in Chapter 7, you can increase the value of doing an activity by either providing more of something people find attractive about it or making it easier or less aggravating to do. Oftentimes the most cost-effective way to boost the value of an activity is to address both drivers and barriers simultaneously.

Figure 9-3 uses the example of one of the Caesar team's key segments to illustrate what a filled-in BCVP template looks like and how all its pieces work together. In this case, the target segment was heads of households aged thirty to fifty-five who were investing funds from an inheritance. The key behavior to trigger was that customers would seek help from an expert advisor when investing these funds for specific purposes related to education or housing, rather than simply adding inherited funds to a general investment account. As the buying process and customer behavior framework revealed,

FIGURE 9-2

Behavior Change Value Proposition (BCVP) Template

For [Target Segment]:	
Doing Behavior [Desired Behavior]:	
Instead of Behavior [Current / Common Behaviors]:	
Will produce value for customers by [Benefits of Behavior Change]:	

Our behavior change campaign will therefore seek to enhance the value of the targeted Behavior to the customer and their propensity to do the Behavior through:

Tapping key Drivers to the Desired Behavior by [Mechanisms for activating chosen Drivers]:	
And eliminating Barriers to the Desired Behavior by [Mechanisms for overcoming chosen Barriers]:	

these customers were already favorably inclined to this behavior. Investing specific funds for specific goals made sense to them as a way of respecting the wishes of the grantor of the inheritance by putting the money to good use for their family.

While customers in this segment thus recognized the potential value of the target behavior, there were barriers that needed to be removed and drivers that could be accentuated for the value proposition to be realized. For example, the firm needed to craft investment solutions that were more sharply and intuitively "about" the jobs to be done and to design first meetings that focused on the inflow of these funds. On the barriers side, the firm needed to shift its focus from winning customers' entire investment portfolio to simplifying the paperwork and processes to help them follow through on investing for the specific jobs to be done.

Defining who, what, and why

Who and what: Defining the targets

Our experience is that when teams have already made clear choices throughout the *Playbook* process, they should be able to specify target segments and specify target behavior changes fairly quickly. If the team struggles at this stage, it's likely that there are gaps in the foregoing analysis or that the team simply hasn't agreed on the core choices. Rather than try to force or—even worse—fake agreement on these critical issues for the sake of completing the BCVP, the better course is to a return to the earlier steps of the analysis.

The thing we want to emphasize here is that the BCVP requires you to identify both the specific behavior you want to see more of (the target high-yield behavior) *and* the specific behavior you want to see less of. You may implicitly define behavioral objectives solely in terms of the new, desired behaviors you want to drive. But the BCVP is actually, as the name implies, about a specific *change* in behavior—that is, moving from Behavior X to Behavior Y. The goal is to markedly increase the value of the target behavior (say, calling a vendor) relative to the value of doing another behavior at the same stage of the buying process (for example, doing research on the internet) or dropping out of the process altogether. To get the BCVP right, then, you have to define and deeply understand exactly what it is that the target behavior—the one you want people to do—is competing with in the minds of customers.

FIGURE 9-3

Behavior Change Value Proposition for Caesar Financial

For:	30-55 year-old head of household investing funds received from an inheritance
Doing Behavior:	Seeking help from expert advisor to invest appropriate portions of a recent inheritance to meet specific goals related to family's education or housing needs
Instead of Behavior:	Adding inherited funds to their general investment account or leaving funds uninvested (i.e., dropping out)
Will produce value for customers by:	Ensuring that they are respecting the wishes of the grantor of the inheritance by putting the money to good uses and "doing the right thing" for their families

Our behavior change campaign will therefore seek to enhance the value of the targeted Behavior to the customer and their propensity to do the Behavior through:

Tapping key Drivers to the Desired Behavior by:	Offering solutions / products specifically tailored to the goals and "jobs to be done" with inherited funds
	Designing initial customer meeting around developing a plan to achieve the specific goals the customer has for discrete "chunk" of investable funds from an inheritance
	Demonstrating Caesar Financial's experience and expertise in helping "customers like you" meet their specific goals
And eliminating Barriers to the Desired Behavior by:	Minimizing time, cost, hand-offs, and paperwork not focused on specific goals and jobs to be done, e.g., short forms (1-2pp), no data on rest of portfolio, questions fully answered within 1 hour, etc.
	Not asking about or implicitly criticizing current plan for customer's larger investment portfolio

Figure 9-4 illustrates this point, using the behavioral objectives identified in the company case studies in earlier chapters. It shows both the target high-yield behavior each team identified through its buying process work and the most important alternative behavior that they wanted customers to stop doing (or do less frequently). In some cases, the change is straightforward (for example, trying color cosmetics in the store instead of not trying them). In others, the team had to scrutinize the current buying process to articulate as precisely as possible the alternative behaviors they wanted to replace. The more precise you can be in specifying the current behavior, the clearer you can be about the change you want to produce.

FIGURE 9-4

Examples of To-From Behavior Changes

Company / Brand	Segment	Does	Instead of
Terrafix	Highly Educated, Female, 55-65, Previously Unassessed For ASD	Asking her doctor for an objective test for ASD	Waiting for the physician to recommend action
EnServ	Facilities Manager responsible for a portfolio of medium/ large buildings who regularly monitors energy use and has completed 2+ energy projects in the past	Consulting with vendors early in the planning process when considering energy services projects	Waiting to the RFP stage to contact vendors, or doing nothing (i.e., failing to consider and follow through on projects)
Sparkle	Pre-teen / teen girls who are starting to shop for cosmetics	Testing whether Sparkle's colors look good on them by trying them at the point of purchase	Not trying colors in the store

The key is to be as clear and crisp as possible in describing the targeted behavior change in terms that are observable and measurable. Indeed, the whole *Playbook* approach is predicated on the idea that changing this specific behavior in a particular segment will drive disproportionate growth with these customers. The next step is to make clear *why* customers would want to change their behavior.

Why: The value proposition for buying process behavior (change)

The next piece in the BCVP is the value proposition itself. It articulates why the target customer would want to do the behavior—what's in it for them—instead of doing something else. Unless there's a clear benefit of engaging in the new behavior for its own sake, you're likely to find yourself fighting an uphill battle trying to activate the desired behavior change.

This is often the most difficult part of the BCVP to articulate because it's the most unfamiliar element of the process. It is, after all, *not* about the product or why customers do or do not like it. It's purely about the value that customers place on one of the many activities they do during the buying process. Often, the target behavior occurs far away in the buying process from the actual product selection, which can make it harder to see its relevance. But it is, in fact, the heart and soul of the *Playbook* process and the key to ensuring faster growth.

As discussed earlier, Caesar Financial recognized that the benefit to customers of investing inherited money for specific jobs to be done was the sense that they were respecting the wishes of the grantor by putting the money to good use and doing the right thing for their families. As Eugene and his team learned, customers naturally gravitated toward and saw the value of this behavior. They commonly engaged in mental accounting that allocated special funds for special purposes. Very often, however, they encountered resistance from investment advisors urging them to take a holistic view of their investment portfolio—essentially belittling the value of the behavior. By recognizing and validating the value that customers placed on this behavior, Caesar was able to find a novel growth opportunity.

One of the best places to identify the benefits of behavior change for the customer is in the customer narrative, which uses the CBF analysis to tell a multidimensional story about customers and what they want. In the case of EnServ, the customer narrative played a pivotal role in fleshing out the profile of the long-overlooked facilities managers. The narrative helped establish the importance that facilities managers in the target segment placed on building a reputation among their professional peers and the part that undertaking innovative, forward-thinking energy projects played in this. The benefit to them of consulting more actively and more frequently with vendors at an early stage was that it helped them conceive and develop cutting-edge ideas to include in energy and cost saving plans for the buildings they managed. This was a subtle but important finding. Again, while the buying process made clear the *benefit to EnServ* of getting facilities managers to consult vendors early on, the team had to understand the potential *benefit to the customer* of engaging in this behavior in order to activate it.

The Terrafix team did a particularly good job of zeroing in on the benefits of the desired behavior change for the target segment of highly educated, older women. One thing that came through loud and clear from the customer narrative was the importance that these women placed on taking charge of choices affecting their health and lifestyle. In addition to wanting to look and feel healthy, they put a premium on exercising control over their well-being. The unbranded magazine ads that the Terrafix team ran as part of its campaign successfully tapped into these motivations by positioning "asking for an ASD test" as an affirmative part of taking care of oneself at every age. Similarly, the Sparkle team reinforced the benefits of trying on cosmetics to teen customers by tapping into the fun, social aspect of shopping for and experimenting with makeup with mothers and friends (see Changing Customer Behavior).

Changing Customer Behavior

Our discussion is solely about identifying the value that customers place on certain behaviors, not about how susceptible the behavior is to change.[57] As anyone who's ever struggled to take off—and keep off—unwanted weight can attest, some behavior changes are hard to achieve. In the pharmaceutical industry, noncompliance with lifesaving medications to prevent recurrence of heart attacks is mind-bogglingly high. Despite understanding and acknowledging the benefits of losing weight or taking their prescriptions, people sometimes fall short in following through on a behavior change. While you need to be realistic about the type and degree of change that's possible, the first step is to make clear why the change is worth doing from the customer's perspective.

Defining how to activate the value of the target behavior

The second part of the BCVP focuses on how to accomplish the desired behavior change. While the first part of the BCVP statement is all about the customer and the value of behavior change to a given segment, this second part delves into how to activate the change. In effect, having identified the value of the activity, you now shift to identifying how to incentivize customers to engage in the target activity. The starting point for this is the list of drivers and barriers generated from the CBF and customer narrative. The BCVP highlights a subset of these as the center of gravity for a behavior change campaign and explores options for taking action.

In many situations, you may begin with a long list of drivers and barriers. Eugene's team at Caesar Financial, for example, generated six drivers and seven barriers to behavior change (see Figure 8-3). Although all of these were valid, focusing on thirteen change levers simultaneously would have been both impractical and costly. In practice, you should aim to reduce the list to a more manageable set of two to three critical drivers and two to three critical barriers. While there's no strict methodology for doing this, it's often helpful to think about themes related to the value of the desired behavior. These themes can help you hone in on certain elements among a laundry list of drivers and barriers. The Caesar team thus focused on drivers and barriers that were most clearly linked to the theme of investing around specific jobs to be done (rather than more general ones about the expertise of Caesar's investment advisors). By tailoring their approach and offerings around the most common jobs to be done and eliminating time-consuming paperwork and hand-offs among financial advisors, the firm facilitated the behavior of investing discrete funds for specific purposes and signaled to customers that this kind of behavior was valuable and appropriate.

For the EnServ team, "confidence" emerged as a key theme in prompting facilities managers to shift from doing online research to holding face-to-face meetings with vendors. Increasing these customers' confidence that they could identify, propose, and get approval for energy projects and implement them smoothly was for them a key element of the value of engaging in the new behavior. The team therefore focused on this theme that showed up in various ways across the set of drivers and barriers initially identified. The MOA Model (see below) can also be a helpful guide in selecting a short list of elements. You should work to ensure that the combination of chosen activities results in customers having the *motivation*, *opportunity*, and *ability* to engage in the desired behavior change.

The MOA Model

There's a vast amount of literature devoted to how human behavior change works. The topic is at the heart of fields as diverse as economics, employee management, weight loss and nutrition, and, of course, sales and marketing. There are, however, some core commonalities among the various explanations of the phenomenon of change that are captured in the MOA Model.[58] Quite simply, the model states that for behavior change to occur, people need three things: *motivation, opportunity,* and *ability* to change. Motivation can be a function of external incentives (for example, rewards and punishments) or intrinsic factors (for example, beliefs and attitudes about the value of the behavior change). Opportunity refers to the impact of a person's situation (physical, social, and so on) on their capacity for change. Ability to change includes things such as skills, knowledge, and capabilities that make change possible. If these three conditions aren't met, behavior change is unlikely to occur.

The guiding questions of the customer behavior framework (CBF) discussed in Chapter 7 are designed to elicit information related to all three MOA factors. By focusing attention on the context, beliefs, and desired experience of customers, the framework can help you understand and articulate the forces that support or impede the desired behaviors. These insights are synthesized in the customer narrative and ultimately expressed in the list of drivers and barriers for each segment.

The MOA model is a useful tool to assess and test the BCVP statements you develop. An effective behavior change campaign should ensure that target customers have sufficient motivation, opportunity, and ability to engage in the desired behavior—either as a result of existing conditions or of actions undertaken by the team. In the case of Caesar Financial, the company's marketing campaign aimed to boost motivation by validating customers' natural inclination to engage in mental accounting and invest separately for specific goals. The main thrust of the campaign was to ensure that customers had the opportunity and ability to follow through on these intentions by clearing away the obstacles that financial advisors typically placed in the way and offering new financial products that made it easy to invest in this way.

We've mentioned several times the decisive impact that removing barriers can have on unleashing desired behaviors. This was certainly the case for the Sparkle brand. Their redesigned point-of-sale displays with single-use product samples and large mirrors removed the impediments to trying the product that teens shopping in mass merchandise channels typically encountered, boosting the opportunity for in-store trial. These innovations also increased the sense of fun and social bonding that were important elements of the shopping experience for these young customers. Expanding the range of colors that appealed to teens while keeping the price point of individual products low also ensured that these customers could find and purchase products that were right for them. Importantly, the Sparkle team recognized that changing just a few of these factors was not enough. While redesigning in-store displays might be highly motivating in encouraging product trial and offering an opportunity to do so, if the price points were not right—that is, teens were unable to purchase the products—there would be no behavior change. Again, it's important to consider all factors of the MOA Model.

Conclusion

The concept of a behavior change value proposition (BCVP) introduced in this chapter may be new if you're steeped in the practice of writing product value propositions. A traditional PVP can be a useful expression of the differentiated positioning for a brand or product that you seek to establish in customers' minds. In our experience, however, it's not enough. While you may be in the happy position of having truly distinctive products to market, most are not so lucky. And, as we've seen, having a differentiated value proposition may not produce reliable growth unless customers actually change their behavior. A surer path is therefore to target the desired behavior change itself by articulating and reinforcing the value to the customer of doing the new behavior.

The BCVP thus serves as a roadmap for the development of segment-specific behavior change campaigns. The following chapter explores how you can best focus and concentrate your marketing resources to execute effective growth campaigns.

Chapter 10

Fifth Principle: Invest Disproportionately

Returning to the story of Caesar Financial, Eugene Shin did a few extraordinary things. First, he recognized that the industry as a whole was in the grip of a powerful—but misguided—notion that the only way to grow was to attract the whole portfolio of wealthy investors. In many cases, this meant getting them to abandon their current financial advisors and switch allegiance to a new institution. Eugene broke with this conventional wisdom by focusing on the discrete jobs to be done and increments of new money that investors wanted help to invest. Secondly, he abandoned the standard, unimaginative market segmentation based on investable assets that prevailed in the industry. Instead, Caesar sought to identify customers and situations that yielded a high propensity to consult with a new advisor when investing for specific tasks.

But he also did a third thing differently: he put a stop to the peanut butter marketing and sales efforts of the past. Instead of spreading marketing resources across multiple segments, messages, customer engagement points, and media channels, he redirected efforts into a series of highly tailored, segment-specific campaigns aimed at changing behaviors with one segment at a time. Specifically, he concentrated the impact of these moves by directing disproportionate resources—roughly 60 to 70 percent of the marketing spend over two and a half years—to changing behaviors in just a couple of segments in the initial implementation wave. Although these segments didn't represent the largest or wealthiest groups of customers, Eugene reasoned—correctly— that if Caesar could produce a spike in growth among these segments while keeping pace with the industry in others, it would drive overall growth faster than its competitors. Meanwhile, Eugene's team prepared to launch a second wave effort aimed at two additional segments with messages and channels tailored to them. As they tapered down the wave one campaign, they again directed approximately 70 percent of resources to wave two over a sustained period before launching a wave three effort at yet another group of segments.

The core principle discussed in this chapter is about changing customer behaviors in a *segment-by-segment* way by marshaling and concentrating resources effectively. Though the idea of making disproportionate, sequential investments may be conceptually simple, it can be hard to achieve in practice. There are many reasons for this, which we explore further in this chapter and in Chapter 12, where we discuss common organizational roadblocks to organic growth. Not least among these obstacles is the persistence of entrenched attitudes within an organization.

Consider, for example, the case of EnServ's residential air HVAC business. Following the successful implementation of the *Playbook* approach in Susan Gomez's commercial energy services business unit, the methodology was extended to other parts of the organization. A dedicated marketing team in the residential air conditioning business used the approach to identify a key leverage point in the customer buying process: the first hot day of the year when homeowners turned on their air conditioning for the first time in several months and often found that it was not working properly. The team devised an innovative marketing campaign around this upstream leverage point with the goal of getting customers in key segments to anticipate this event and contact a professional HVAC dealer early in the season to address potential problems before they occurred. The research showed that EnServ's extensive and highly trained dealer network tended to benefit disproportionately from this customer behavior relative to other dealers and small-scale outfits. The team conceived an unbranded public awareness campaign using fairly low-cost media, such as radio spots and door-drop pamphlets in targeted neighborhoods and successfully piloted the approach in a few markets. When the time came for the broader rollout of the campaign, however, the effort hit a brick wall.

In this case, the obstacle was the division's own chief marketing officer. While the CMO had been involved and regularly briefed on the project from the start and agreed in principle with the logic of the new approach, he resisted pulling the trigger on the new campaign. The apparent reason was that he was too deeply enamored of the glamorous television commercials he had recently commissioned touting the superior power and style of the company's A/C products. And, in truth, they were great ads that won multiple advertising industry awards! The problem was that running these expensive ads barely moved the needle on the critical behavioral objective of getting customers to visit a dealer preventively. They also ate up the majority of the marketing budget. As a result, the newly planned, unbranded campaign was shelved and the hoped for growth didn't materialize.

As this example demonstrates, the problem is often not a failure of analysis but of institutional will. You can make all the preparations, check and double-check that your parachute is in working order, and take an airplane up to 12,000 feet—but you're not actually skydiving until you step out the open door. Committing to a disproportionate allocation of marketing resources that may be radically different from past patterns of marketing spend can feel like a step into the unknown. It takes a strong stomach. More importantly, it takes discipline and conviction to follow through on the analysis. The disciplined and rigorous approach provided by the *Playbook* can help managers take this decisive step.

Conventional wisdom

Before delving into the conventional attitudes and approaches to funding and focusing marketing campaigns, let's consider again the challenges that the *Playbook* was designed to solve. As stated at the outset, the main focus of our approach is on generating strong, reliable organic growth in highly competed markets where there are many similar, good enough products available. In these situations, companies often focus on the distinctive features of their products to try to differentiate themselves from the competition. In the absence of any real innovations or breakthroughs in product functionality, however, firms tend to direct similar messages about similar products to the same customers and, as a result, make little headway. The fact is, it's hard to gain share against your identical twin by doing the same things in the same ways.

Rather than offer another way for companies to continue beating each other's brains out over the same slim pickings, the *Playbook* seeks to unlock new avenues of growth by identifying and leveraging key customer behaviors. In the end, however, all the insight in the world will produce precious little in the way of organic growth unless companies choose to act differently on the basis of these insights. Aligning marketing spend with growth insights is where the rubber meets the road in this process. The three main dimensions of conventional wisdom regarding how to deploy marketing spend relate to the:

- Stages of the buying process to which marketing resources are allocated.
- Customer segments to prioritize.

- Marketing tactics to employ.

As you'll see, the *Playbook* approach departs substantially from the conventional wisdom on all three fronts.

Allocate spend across buying process stages

Surprisingly, the academic literature is fairly silent on the subject of rolling out commercial campaigns. There is, however, a prevailing point of view in the marketing field about how to allocate spend across the buying process. This conventional wisdom is best summarized in the following quote from a leading marketing textbook: Marketers must develop activities and programs that reach consumers at all decision stages.[59] The theory is that customers need to be ushered through each step of the process, and the implication is that firms should therefore allocate marketing spend at each stage (and usually roughly equally).

The underlying logic of distributing resources across the buying process is that consumers need to be nudged along at each stage to keep them engaged and reduce the likelihood of dropping out along the way. On the surface, this makes some sense. It would seem appropriate, for example, for a car company to invest at successive stages of the buying process funnel to make customers aware of their product, to provide information that enables them compare their brand to other models, to incentivize them to visit a dealership, to provide sales support materials, and continue to provide post-purchase outreach and service.

The problem is that it ignores the disproportionate impact of certain decisions and behaviors at high-yield leverage points within the process. In the car example, for instance, a finding that customers who test drive the company's brand are much more likely to buy that brand would dictate shifting efforts and resources toward promoting the test driving behavior. The conventional approach misses the fact that some stages of the buying process are simply more important than others for driving growth. Too often, firms overfund inconsequential initiatives while diluting the resources available to influence behaviors at key leverage points.

Allocate spend across segments

Some younger firms introducing distinctive new products have found success without paying a lot of attention to market segmentation. Typically, this success is driven by understanding and fulfilling a truly unmet customer need. As competitors begin to catch up in vying for this business with more complete offerings of their own, however, the importance of identifying and prioritizing segments grows. Mature firms in contested markets tend to have more highly developed market segmentation maps. However, as we've discussed in earlier chapters, they tend to have the *same* (or similar) maps as everyone else and thus don't gain advantage through their segmentation.

The greater problem, however, is that they tend to go after the same segments as competitors, jostling for the same shelf space, mind share, and purchase dollars with similar products and messages. Part of the issue here has to do with lousy segmentation based on conventional wisdom about the market. The other aspect of conventional wisdom, however, has to do with the prioritization and sequencing of segments. This may be even more insidious, since there's a certain logic to the conventional approach that can seem persuasive.

First, many firms effectively don't prioritize segments at all. Even if they've done the work of creating a segmentation map, they don't want to miss out on opportunities by ignoring some customers. They therefore go after all segments simultaneously, thus spreading efforts across all targets. Again, while it can seem sensible to pursue all opportunities, it's not necessary to do so to drive growth. Furthermore, the resulting dilution of focus and resources usually means that growth suffers instead.

The second issue has to do with how firms typically choose which segments to go after. Lay a market segmentation map in front of a group of marketers and ask them which segments they want to target and chances are they will instinctively say, "We want the biggest ones." The problem, of course, is that everyone else is looking at the same segments and saying the same thing. While it can seem risky *not* to target the largest or most affluent segments, a better approach is to prioritize segments based on their propensity to engage in certain behaviors that uniquely benefit us *and* where we have the ability to influence those behaviors efficiently (at reasonable cost) and effectively.

The third point we typically observe is that firms *say* they're prioritizing certain customer groups but aren't actually doing so. The issue here is often that the salesforce or other important stakeholders aren't on board with the stated segmentation strategy. This can happen because the incentives are misaligned to drive the desired actions or because the logic of segment choice has not been effectively or convincingly explained. As a result, the salesforce often ignores the corporate segmentation plan and simply goes out and sells the product. The actual segmentation in use may not be truly revealed until and unless someone analyzes which customers the salesforce has actually been selling to.

To summarize, the conventional approach we have observed in business after business is to go after too many segments at a time, to choose segments based on size rather than ability to influence and serve, and to exercise limited control over selling discipline. As a result, marketing resources tend to be spread too thinly across too many targets or squandered outright.

Allocate spend across media channels and tactics

In terms of determining the overall size of marketing budgets, the approach of making incremental adjustments to prior years spend is nearly universal. Rarely do we see zero-based budgeting that determines total marketing spend and allocation from the ground up each year. The reason is largely due to the nature of large organizations. The advertising group, sales support group, social media group, and other units establish their budget, headcount, and set of activities. These become hardwired into the life of the organization, its resource allocation, and the career paths of the individuals in those groups. While this may be part of the reality of organizations, we need to acknowledge that it often leads to actions that are the *exact opposite* of using customer behavior insights to drive the allocation of marketing spend! One of the extraordinary aspects of the Terrafix story is that Sam Wilcox actually requested a *smaller* budget to implement the new marketing strategy and was able to achieve much more with less by focusing on key segments and leverage points.

We also observe that organizations will often benchmark their spending allocation to match what competitors are doing. They will also add new marketing and sales capabilities to address changing dynamics in the market (for example, digital marketing) but rarely make corresponding cuts elsewhere. Marketing budgets therefore tend to grow over time while continuing to be spread thin across more and more activities.

In summary, the conventional wisdom about how and where to deploy marketing spend seems to be driven by a desire—perhaps even a paranoia—to cover all possible bases at once. We therefore see many organizations allocating spend across multiple buying process stages, many different customer segments, and a multitude of marketing tactics. As the reader probably expects by now, our approach is rather different.

The *Playbook* approach: Sequence segments and spend disproportionately

The *Playbook* approach to investing marketing resources can be summed up in a short phrase: sequence segment-specific efforts and spend disproportionately. This idea of disciplined, disproportionate investment operates at three levels: within the buying process, among segments, and across tactics. The idea is to create sequential bursts of growth in targeted parts of the market that drive overall growth for a business that is higher than the rest of the industry.

If you've followed us to this stage of the argument, then the idea of directing spend against a small number of specific stages and behaviors in the buying process should come as little surprise. A key principle of military doctrine is to mass force at the point of attack by synchronizing all the elements of combat power at the decisive place and time to produce an overwhelming effect as quickly as possible. We're essentially making this same point: a growth strategy should be focused on the one or (at most) two high-yield behavioral objectives that are likely to produce growth, in the segments where those behaviors will be easiest to change. Consequently, the bulk of marketing resources should be massed around these objectives. The *Playbook* approach of mapping segments based on propensities to engage in key behaviors, identifying drivers and barriers to these behaviors among key segments, and developing behavior change value propositions provides a roadmap for focusing effort.

The basic approach, described in more detailed in the following section, consists of three linked choices. The first choice is about grouping and prioritizing segments for a sequenced rollout of marketing campaigns. These prioritized groups will typically include one or two segments—rarely more— to address for a period of time with disproportionate effort. We use the term *wave* to denote each group of segments identified for parallel implementation.

The next choice is to disproportionately fund each wave. This involves making choices about the amount and type of investment required and the period of time needed to effect a substantial change in behavior in the chosen segment(s). There are, of course, two sides to the coin of disproportionate investment. While some segments and tactics will receive the lion's share of investment, others will necessarily get less. Again, it's about making choices and having the discipline to see them through. The final choice is about designing tailored, segment-specific campaigns around the behavior change value propositions and high-yield behaviors for each targeted segment.

The overall effect of this patient, methodical approach is to produce a succession of growth spurts. Rather than try to grow all parts of the market at the same rate at the same time, our approach is to win decisively in one area after another. As illustrated in Figure 10-1 below, a business running a disproportionately funded effort in one or two segments for a couple of years will grow faster than it would otherwise. Once that initial burst starts to taper off, another disproportionately funded effort focused on additional segments will enable the business to continue to grow faster than it would otherwise. Hence, we find it helpful to conceive of these efforts as *waves of investments*.

FIGURE 10-1

Sequenced Growth from Segment-Targeted Campaigns

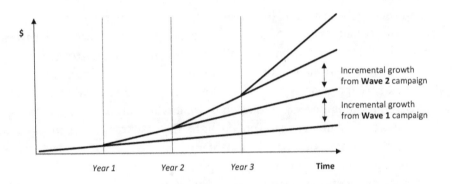

As we said at the start of the chapter, the idea of sequencing and allocating marketing resources disproportionately at key segments and activities is conceptually fairly simple. But it takes some thoughtful planning, discipline, and nerve to do it—especially in the context of large organizations that tend toward stasis. Below, we outline a series of steps to help managers take action.

The fifth principle explained

The first four principles of the *Playbook* focused on identifying specific high-yield behaviors and the factors that motivate behaviors for different customer groups. Our fifth principle addresses the timeless managerial question of where and how to implement a marketing plan. At the heart of the issue lies a set of choices about focusing and funding new organic growth efforts relative to current activities.

In most organizations, we find some managers who strongly advocate launching a campaign aimed at the whole market. They typically argue for a single, marketwide campaign, in effect replacing their current one-size-fits-all program with a new and improved one-size-fits-all program. A more nuanced version of this broad approach is to heed the lessons of segmentation by launching a slew of segment-specific campaigns more or less simultaneously. Against these voices, we nearly always encounter a set of managers arguing for a much narrower and cautious approach. They advocate beginning by developing and running a limited campaign for a single segment to see how well it works before committing to a broader effort.

Underlying this debate are the real constraints faced by organizations: most firms don't have the money, capabilities, or management bandwidth to do everything all at once and do it well. A common compromise, therefore, is to try to act on the insights of the *Playbook* analysis by designing a market-wide campaign that addresses a subset of the most important drivers and barriers. They believe that a broad-based implementation of a more narrowly focused campaign will yield the maximum return on investment. In our experience, however, this approach typically leaves a great deal of growth on the table. Moreover, it's an unnecessary solution to what is actually a false dilemma.

The simple truth is that you *do* have the resources, capabilities, and bandwidth to address each target segment in an optimal way—if you factor time into the equation. The most effective approach to implementing the *Playbook* is through a sequence of disproportionately funded waves. Each wave consists of a campaign designed specifically for a small number of key segments that is fully funded for a substantial period of time (perhaps several years). Because each wave's constituent campaigns are carefully tailored to these segments' particular drivers and barriers and are funded heavily enough to cut through the competitive clutter, each successive wave yields a burst of growth that is big enough to lift the business' overall growth rate. And, critically, each wave is a manageable task. Designing and running, say, two distinct campaigns over an eighteen to thirty month period is well within the reach of most teams.

Below, we elaborate on how teams can implement this approach in two phases. The first phase involves establishing the parameters of a sustained *Playbook* growth plan over a period of four to six years. This overall plan includes the sequencing and timing of segment-based implementation waves and, critically, the proportion of marketing spend to be allocated to the segments in each wave. The second phase focuses on the design of the segment-level plans with particular emphasis on the disproportionate investment of effort and resources in particular tactics and high-yield behaviors. In effect, the principle of disproportionate spending plays itself out at two levels—first at the macro level in the allocation of total spend across segments, and secondly at the micro level in the distribution of segment-level spend across stages and specific activities in the buying process.

Define the overall plan

The overall *Playbook* implementation plan, as illustrated in Figure 10-2, is really quite simple. It's a table listing the segments to be targeted in each implementation wave along with estimates of the percentage of resources to be allocated to just those segments and the length of time each wave is expected to last. So, in wave 1, we see that its duration was 18 months and that it consumed 55 percent of the total budget focused entirely on Segment A. In wave 2, 70 percent of total spending was allocated to the target segments (F and G), while the remainder was used to continue funding a reduced level of wave 1 activities and other market segments. More generally, the process consists of three basic steps: characterizing the attractiveness and the feasibility of activating each segment, prioritizing and grouping the segments into time-bound waves, and estimating the time and funding that should be devoted to each wave.

Identifying which segments should comprise a wave, as well as the order in which the waves should be addressed, involves a judgment call—the choice isn't always straightforward. Rather, it requires managers to assess a number of factors from the perspective of a sustained, multiyear growth agenda. It may be tempting to simply target the most attractive segments in the initial wave (in order to get the most results as quickly as possible) and shift the focus to less attractive segments in successive waves. The problem is that some segments that may seem attractive due to their large size or strong intrinsic growth rate may be hard to activate because those customers have a lower propensity toward the high-yield behavior or because the business lacks the capabilities to reach them. We therefore need to consider multiple factors in establishing the attractiveness of individual segments and combinations of segments to sequence and prioritize. There's no neat formula for evaluating and weighing these factors. There are, however, rules of thumb that can guide teams toward better choices.

FIGURE 10-2

Sequence and Funding of Implementation Waves

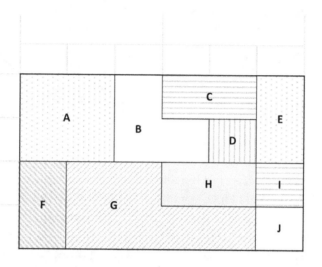

Wave	Segment(s)	Duration of Focus	% Total Funding While Wave is Focus	% of Total Funding After Focus
1	A	18 months	55%	–
2	F G	24 months	30% (F) 40% (G)	20% (Wave 1) 10% (Rest of market)
3	E J	30 months	30% (E) 25% (J)	15% (Wave 1) 20% (Wave 2) 10% (Rest of market)

Characterize the segments

Characterizing segments so that the team can group and sequence them effectively involves assessing five types of data about them: magnitude, influence, propensity, feasibility, and competitive sensitivity.

Magnitude—the absolute size of a segment measured by volume, revenue, total profit, or intrinsic growth rate—typically receives the most attention. The logic is clear: targeting the biggest and fastest growing segments will yield the highest returns most quickly—bigger pond, bigger fish. While the size of the prize undoubtedly matters, it should not be the only consideration in prioritizing a segment.

The second factor, what we call *influence*, also plays an important role. Some customer segments have an impact on the market that is out of proportion to their absolute size or profitability. Winning in these segments can influence the behavior of customers in other segments so that these high-influence segments actually deliver more overall growth per marketing dollar spent than may appear at first. This may be because customers in these segments are regarded as bellwethers whose actions are seen as aspirational (or anathema) to customers in other segments. Another dimension of influence is the impact that targeting this segment may have on the firm's own capabilities and experience. Assets and know-how needed to activate one segment may be foundational for activating other segments that might otherwise be deemed too big a stretch for the current organization. Building capabilities for successfully targeting these segments may thus ease entry and boost the effectiveness of campaigns in other segments in later waves.

More important than either of these, however, is propensity to do the target high-yield behavior. Recall that the *Playbook*'s segments are literally defined in terms of their propensity to engage in particular high-yield behaviors. As illustrated in our propensity heat maps in Chapter 5, segments vary considerably in terms of frequency and likelihood of acting on behavioral objectives (for example, visiting a particular channel, calling a dealer, or asking for a test). Segments that already tend to do and find value in the desired behaviors are more likely to respond favorably to even basic campaigns to encourage these behaviors. For example, we've found that simply reminding people in these high-propensity segments about the high-yield behavior (that is, an ad that simply says "ask for a test" or "talk to your mom about cosmetics") is sufficient to increase the frequency with which they do the behavior by three to five percentage points. Changing behaviors in these segments is like pushing on a half-open door, and their propensity toward the desired behaviors makes them attractive regardless of size or growth rate. By contrast, some segments will be naturally less inclined toward the desired behaviors and therefore require a higher activation energy—usually at higher cost—to stimulate behavior change.

These three factors—magnitude, influence, and especially propensity to high-yield behavior— characterize a segment's absolute attractiveness, that is, the value that you might realize from a successful behavior change campaign. There may, however, be thorny obstacles to plucking these low-hanging fruit. So you need to assess the impact of such impediments on segment attractiveness.

There's usually a gap between what a business needs to do to boost the frequency of high-yield behavior in a segment and what it's currently capable of doing. That is, given current assets (brand equity, channel reach, and so on) and skills, a business will find that it's more feasible to change behavior in some segments than in others. To evaluate the feasibility gap, teams need to review drivers and barriers for each segment, sketch out what kind of tactics and assets would be needed to reduce barriers or boost drivers for that segment, and then take a clear-eyed look at what they're capable of doing. We have found over the years that firms that have configured themselves to address the market in conventional ways often face significant feasibility gaps when they adopt new, *Playbook*-based segmentation schemes. The good news is that they have a differentiated view of the market that allows them to identify attractive customers and behaviors that others have overlooked. The bad news is that they often lack the capabilities needed to address these new segments effectively. Undertaking an honest assessment of the cost and effort required is thus an important step.

Finally, teams need to recognize that some segments may be especially important to particular competitors. Going head on with one or more competitors in a segment that is vital to them is likely to draw a quick and concerted response, thereby reducing the potential effectiveness of spending on a behavior-focused campaign in that segment. Sheer weight of arms does matter, at least at the margin. Of course, teams using a propensity-based segmentation scheme are almost always looking at the market differently than their competitors (that is, they literally have a different map), meaning that their segments don't correspond exactly to those used by the rest of the industry. Instead, a propensity-based segment will typically overlay pieces of several traditionally defined segments. While this reduces the risk of inadvertently sparking a competitive barroom brawl over a specific segment, the possibility of competitive reaction remains and needs to be identified and sized in judging a segment's attractiveness.

There's no right way or prescribed formula for rating the importance of these various factors. Often, the five factors will pull in different directions. The marketing team can use these criteria to score segments in a consistent and disciplined manner and assess the relative pros and cons of each. In the end, however, there's a judgment call to make on which segments should be targeted for growth. Furthermore, the selection and ranking of segments needs to take place within the context of an overall plan and phased implementation program, as described in more detail below.

Prioritize and group segments into implementation waves

The second step in developing an overall plan is to prioritize and group segments into sequential implementation waves (Figure 10-3). The goal is to identify two to four distinct groups of one or two segments and order them in a way that delivers consistent rapid growth for the business overall through successive bursts of growth from the sequenced waves.

Again, this exercise requires the team to make a judgment call. There are, however, a few heuristics to help make the choice of how to group segments into meaningful waves. One clear lesson from our experience is that less is more in the earliest waves. That is, teams should target fewer segments—one or, at most, two—in Wave 1, and probably no more than two segments in Wave 2. Because these marketing campaigns tend to be quite different than past programs, it pays to focus attention and effort disproportionately on a small number of segments in the early going.

The second consideration is that the early waves should typically involve the highest propensity and most feasible segments—that is, those that are easiest to activate. Recall that in the case of Terrafix, the company chose to focus initial efforts on just one critical patient segment (older, educated women who were comfortable asking for the objective test) who were most likely to adopt the behavioral objective. The usual default is to prioritize segments based on their propensity to engage in the high leverage behavior. This is because the team is trying to demonstrate that rapid bursts of growth are achievable by changing the targeted buying behaviors. Focusing on segments that require the least work to convince customers of the behavior change value proposition generally makes the most sense.

An important caveat to this is that the chosen segment(s) be large

FIGURE 10-3

Sequencing Waves for Successive Marketing Campaigns

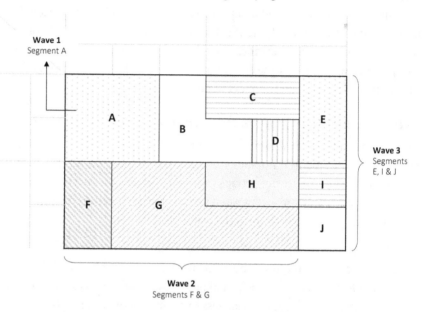

enough that a successful behavior change campaign with these customers will be sufficient to produce noticeable improvement in the business' overall rate of growth. This is a question of simple arithmetic: how big must a wave be so that growing those segments at, say, 5 to 8 percent yields a noticeable change in overall growth? There are thus some tradeoffs to make between ease of activation and size of the prize in the choice of initial segments.

A third consideration in sequencing waves is the idea that certain segments can act as stepping stones to others—either by targeting customers with broader influence in the market or by building the internal capabilities required to launch successive waves. Returning to the Terrafix example, part of the Wave 1 effort focused on working with third party providers to make objective diagnostic tests more easily available to patients who could be readily persuaded to ask for them. Once this testing infrastructure was in place, it facilitated the Wave 2 and 3 campaigns to encourage the asking for the test behavior with other segments. All else being equal, firms may also choose to avoid going after segments that are likely to provoke a strong competitive response in Waves 1 and 2.

Estimate funding and timing

The final piece of the overall plan is the budgeting of resources and time to each wave. Sounds simple—but this is where we've seen some teams struggle to make strong choices. When we say disproportionate spend, we really mean it! Mapping out funding and timing needs in the overall plan helps combat the tendency toward peanut butter marketing: the common practice of spreading a thin, ineffective coat of marketing resources across too many targets.

We would argue that, as a rule of thumb, each segment that is part of an active implementation wave should get no less than 25 percent of the business' total growth spend. Particularly large or influential segments might each get 30 to 40 percent of total growth spend. For a wave with two segments then, 55 to 65 percent of total spend might be dedicated to just those segments, with the remainder allocated to other segments and activities.

While these numbers may seem large, we have found that it usually takes this kind of overwhelming force at targeted points for teams to develop new campaigns that can cut through the competitive clutter in the market. As noted, these campaigns often also involve novel efforts to activate new channels or introduce new activities that require dedicated time and resources to create and deliver. In many cases, delivering a knockout punch in targeted segments also requires a good deal of internal retooling and retraining to ensure that skills and incentives are aligned with strategic goals.

An instinctive response among marketers to this unbalanced allocation of resources is that starving nontargeted segments of sales and marketing spending for a considerable period of time will result in revenue declines that will offset any gains in the prioritized segments. This would, indeed, vitiate the effectiveness of the strategy. Fortunately, the risk of this happening is actually quite low. A number of studies have shown that there's a great deal of momentum in spending patterns and that customers continue to buy accustomed brands even during periods when the business isn't actively promoting them. Indeed, the notion of staging pulsed campaigns is part of the entrenched wisdom of Madison Avenue. Very few firms advertise and actively promote their products at the same rate throughout the year. An interesting area of marketing research is actually dedicated to quantifying the amount of wasted or unnecessary advertising dollars spent on continuous promotions that don't produce incremental growth.[60]

A second response to this concern is simply that we're not advocating going dark in all non-wave segments. There will still be some funding of marketing, sales, and innovation activities in these other areas, just less of it over a given period of time. Most of our clients find that the disproportionate reallocation of budget actually forces them to think carefully about their sales and marketing practices in the non-wave segments and be more rigorous about determining which are most effective. And, of course, we're not proposing an indefinite halt to activities in these other areas of the market—merely a temporary reduction.

This disciplined, sequenced approach not only produces higher growth overall, but enables concerted, behavior-focused efforts in place of the semi-random promotional campaigns that exist in many companies. As Wave 1 growth stabilizes, teams have a plan in place to taper spending in those segments and transition to Wave 2. What we usually see at these transition points is that sales remain robust in Wave 1 segments even after funds are reallocated to new priorities because of the more effective efforts focused on specific drivers and barriers that teams have put in place. Sales continue to rise in those segments, though not at the same hot house pace, as attention shifts to the next wave.

Develop disproportionately focused segment-specific campaigns

The key message of principle four discussed in Chapter 9 is that behavior change efforts should specifically target the drivers and barriers of chosen segments. Principle five builds on this notion, arguing that segment-specific content must be brought to bear at the right place and time in the segment's buying process. The impact of tailored products, service experiences, and messages is greatly magnified if these activities reach customers when they're in the neighborhood of the critical, high-yield behaviors as they move through the buying process. Once the team has laid out the overall, multi-year plan for prioritizing and sequencing implementation waves at the macro level, the attention then shifts to the mix of tactics and media that create disproportionate impact at these key points in the segment's buying process (as illustrated in Figure 10-4).

Recall that for EnServ the most important high-yield behavior occurred early in the customer's buying processes, as they were generating new ideas for their next year's plan and doing preliminary research on those ideas. What

FIGURE 10-4

Segment-Specific Marketing Tactics to Activate High-Yield Behaviors

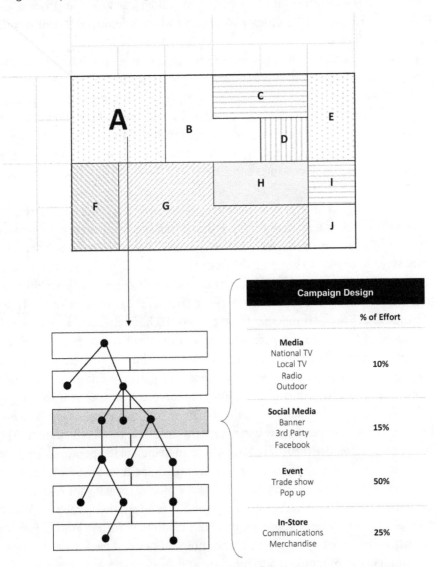

this meant was that information about EnServ's capabilities and offers had far, far more impact on customers' thinking and behavior when it reached them during this planning process. The same information delivered at a more downstream stage of the buying process—for example, as part of a formal RFP and bid evaluation phase—had considerably less impact. This insight about the importance of being consulted early in the process led EnServ to dramatically reallocate where and when it deployed its selling and marketing efforts.

It also changed the nature and mix of communications vehicles that the company used to reach customers. Salespeople started to make more frequent, brief informational calls on a larger number of customers and increased their presence at local conferences, seminars, and trade shows that facilities managers attended. EnServ also began writing and distributing white papers and technical tracts concerning energy cost management. It funded this redirected effort by allocating funds previously used for more general brand marketing and for chasing after RFPs.

As the diagram in Figure 10-4 conveys, the particular stages and activities involved in high-yield behaviors are specific to a segment—as are the drivers and barriers to those behaviors. The BCVP articulates the approach that the team seeks to deploy to increase the frequency of the high-yield behavior. The choice facing the team is how to deliver the BCVP through some combination of available marketing mechanisms (for example, types of salesforces, types of physical delivery, arrangements with physical channels, media, and so on).

Some of these delivery mechanisms will naturally be more relevant and powerful in reaching customers at key stages of the buying process and should therefore be over-represented in implementation plans. In EnServ's case, trade shows, local conferences, and short informational conversations with experts were critical parts of facilities managers' ideation and exploration process. EnServ therefore built its new campaign around these types of activities. The Sparkle team likewise reallocated the where and when of its spending. The vast majority of its time and effort had previously been spent on brand-focused TV and print advertising. In addition, most of the money set aside for cooperative marketing with their retail customers went to funding the retailer's TV and print ads. The new campaign aimed at teen customers focused much further downstream in the buying process at the point of sale and use. The majority of their budgets were redirected to building and stocking try-on kiosks in retail stores and other activities to encourage trial at the wall.

There are many different ways that firms interact with customers, and some will be inherently better suited for reaching and affecting customers at particular stages of the buying process. For example, webinars can be a great way of reaching technical buyers in the origination or research phases of a buying process. They're less effective for influencing customers' decision-making deep in the evaluation or negotiation stages. Again, the choice of specific tactics and messages needs to be left to the judgment of individual marketing teams. The key principle that should guide these choices, however, is that effort and spending should be disproportionately focused on just the few tactics and vehicles that are best suited to changing one or two high-yield behaviors for a given segment.

Conclusion

The central message of this chapter and the principle that it describes can be briefly summarized as "see the job through!" That is, having done the hard work and painstaking analysis of mapping the customer buying process, identifying segments, and pinpointing drivers and barriers, the next step is to ensure that your marketing plans reflect these insights and choices. We fully recognize, however, that the approach we've described of disproportionately funding certain activities while deemphasizing others can be both psychologically daunting and fraught with organizational obstacles. We address a number of the institutional barriers to change that exist in most large firms in Chapter 12.

Any change process has to contend with the forces of convention and inertia. There will also be winners and losers within an organization resulting from a reallocation of resources. Those who stand to lose funding or power may be inclined to resist the change. The reason the *Playbook* has been successful in many different kinds of organizations, we believe, is because it provides a step-by-step, evidence-based case for how a behavior-focused approach can fuel organic growth. Time after time, we've seen managers make a successful case for change based on the *Playbook* analysis and the confidence it gives them to make the tough choices.

Implementing the *Playbook*

In the next section, we discuss how to implement the *Playbook* in different situations and types of organizations. In Chapter 11 we share some key lessons about how to get the most out of using the *Playbook* in different types of markets. In particular, we provide guidance for teams who intend to use the *Playbook* in emerging markets (especially fast-growing ones) and B2B markets (especially concentrated or high-tech B2B markets). Each of these sections follows a similar pattern. We begin by briefly describing what managers typically believe are the unique characteristics of these markets, the ones that make them concerned about the applicability of the *Playbook*. We then examine how the core principles can be adjusted to best execute under these market situations.

In Chapter 12, we complete our journey by focusing on organizational roadblocks that we have observed across almost all of our client engagements. These roadblocks range from issues related to organizational structure (for example, organizational silos within firms), to human resource policies, and other issues (for example, the systematic underfunding of market intelligence). For each of the roadblocks, we provide concrete recommendations that have been shown to be effective in practice.

In sum, Chapters 11 and 12 focus on how to best fit the *Playbook* to your circumstances. Chapter 11 focuses at the level of market conditions and Chapter 12 focuses on dynamics within organizations. Our aim is to help you begin the journey of implementing the *Playbook* within your unique situation.

Chapter 11

Applying the *Playbook* in Different Markets

We're often asked by clients whether the *Playbook* will work in their market. The answer is, quite simply, yes. As noted in Chapter 1, the methodology has been applied successfully in hundreds of firms across all types of markets: both business-to-consumer (B2C) and business-to-business (B2B) within every kind and level of geopolitical entity, including both highly developed and developing countries. The five principles and the methods and tools associated with them yield the powerful insights organizations need to develop compelling new offers and campaigns to change high-yield behaviors and accelerate growth.

We want, however, to acknowledge the concerns that often lie behind this question. Managers raise it because they're keenly aware of how their category or market is different from what they perceive to be the average market. They worry that methodologies like the *Playbook* were created for other types of companies or industries but may not fit their own situation. They know, for example, that their infrastructure or channels are substandard, or that the culture of their country or category is distinctive, or that they have either fewer or more competitors than normal, or that product cycles and innovation run much faster (or slower) than the textbook market. They believe that the distinctive structure or competition in their market means that any kind of playbook developed for ordinary circumstances will either be invalid or will need to be significantly modified to meet their needs. Given that there's no one-size-fits-all growth *strategy*, it may seem natural to question whether any one growth *methodology* can apply across different contexts and circumstances.

We recognize that each market is distinctive in important ways. Our work with companies and leaders in a wide spectrum of countries and industries has convinced us of two things. The first is that the organic growth principles laid out in the preceding chapters really do work everywhere and have proven their value time and time again. The second is that some customization of how the

Playbook is applied in different markets can be valuable. The adaptations may be straightforward—for example, changing research methods to compensate for issues such as having only a small number of customers or difficulties reaching customers in markets with poor infrastructure. In other cases, the modifications can involve a more subtle shift of emphasis in the degree of detail or breadth required in applying different elements of the methodology in a given context. The purpose of this chapter is to provide advice, tips, and recommendations for how to apply the *Playbook* in situations where the question of whether it will work is most often raised. In particular, we address the unique aspects of specific country markets (especially less developed markets) and various types of B2B markets.

This is one chapter where you may find it useful to skip around to the sections that apply most specifically to your firm. There are three sections. The first addresses issues specific to creating growth strategies in less developed economies. The second addresses whether and how to adjust the *Playbook* for use in more traditional B2B markets. The third section considers the case of special B2B markets, including heavily regulated industries and innovation-driven, high-tech markets. Each section follows a similar pattern. We begin by briefly describing the distinctive features of these markets that can pose unique challenges in applying the *Playbook*. We then examine how these circumstances may impact the ways in which the choices or principles can be applied and suggest some approaches for adapting the methodology to unlock organic growth in these situations.[61]

Less developed economy markets

Most managers are comfortable with the notion that their offers and campaigns should be tailored to the varying circumstances encountered in different geopolitical spheres, be it a megacity, a country, or a region. Hard experience has taught them that what works well in one place does not always work in another. The idea of geographical adaptation is often reinforced by the way companies are structured. Geography—region and country, typically—is a standard dimension of organizational design; some companies make it the primary dimension (that is, their profit and loss statements are defined and run based on geography), while others make it a secondary consideration (that is, only some decisions and activities are taken based on geography). Built into the job description of the regional or country manager is the expectation that some or all aspects of the business—product, price, sales and marketing approach, and so on—should be tailored to reflect the particular needs and realities of their part of the world.

Given the vast and easily observable differences among country markets as diverse as China, Germany, Morocco, Ecuador, and Indonesia, it's perhaps not surprising that some managers might extend the idea of taking a tailored approach even further. They may, in fact, question whether the same organic growth methodology can possibly be applicable across these different markets. In doing so, they seem to be extrapolating backward from the clear need for different outcomes from the growth planning process (that is, campaigns with different messages, prices, product variants, and so on) to a hypothesis that the process itself should be different. The underlying assumption seems to be that different circumstances require different methods: for example, because the market in Ecuador is smaller and more dominated by mom and pop shops than the German market, the approach to determining product positioning should be simpler—or at least distinct. While one can see the reasoning behind this belief, in our experience, it's simply incorrect. Great growth campaigns are born of a robust and rigorous understanding of customers and competition, which is the result of applying the right approach and methods.

The fact is that the *Playbook* approach has worked everywhere, producing country-specific growth plans that deliver faster growth. Indeed, most of the early *Playbook* work was done in less developed markets or rapidly developing ones, including Peru, Venezuela, Indonesia, Pakistan, India, Turkey, South Africa, and Brazil. The country teams all used the same principles and the same tools and did the same types of analysis. Of course, the growth plan each team produced differed as greatly in its specifics as did the countries in their channel structures, cultures, and so on. Yet all were centered on changing a few high-yield behaviors, and they all resulted in a dramatic acceleration of growth rates for the company involved (see Unique Challenges of Less Developed Country Markets).

Unique Challenges of Less Developed Country Markets

While developing countries vary widely in their character and stages of development, there are a number of dimensions in which they differ from more developed economies, including:

- Logistics/transportation infrastructure: While developed countries typically have extensive and well-functioning transportation infrastructure (including intercity and intracity rail and road, ports, and air travel), developing countries often lack these facilities. For example, roads can be poor or non-existent, or may be too small for motorized transport.
- Type/mix of channels: A far greater percentage of goods are sold through big box and chain stores in developed countries relative to developing countries, where small-scale mom and pop channels may account for a much higher share of commerce.
- Availability of media: In developed countries there are a huge number of media outlets (radio, TV, print, direct mail, and so on) with wide coverage of the population. Developing countries tend to have fewer types of media or more limited coverage provided by those media. In some cases, there may be a greater reliance on certain technologies and communications channels that are widespread in developing economies, such as mobile phones, relative to developed markets.
- Structure of the economy: While developed countries have a host of institutions and facilities supporting a fully functioning market economy (for example, established markets and financial intermediaries), some developing countries have much larger proportions of the economy that operate at subsistence or near subsistence levels.
- Demographic profile: While many developed countries have rapidly aging populations, a number of developing countries have a much higher proportion of younger workers and consumers.

Working in developing countries, however, led us to understand that even faster growth was possible by adjusting where and how we used the methodology. In particular, we learned that these countries usually harbored multiple economies at different stages of development that are so distinct that taking each of these separate economies within a single country as the unit of analysis for the *Playbook* process often produced higher growth than if the *Playbook* approach were applied to the country as a whole. Indeed, the internal social and economic variations *within* these countries are often more pronounced than the differences among more developed nations. In practice, this means that teams striving for growth in less developed countries may need to do the whole *Playbook* approach (buying process maps, segmentation, and so on) separately for each distinct economy. We also learned that the research and analytics behind many of the principles and choices needed to be done at an even *greater* level of granularity than might be required in developed country markets.

Finally, we learned that it was best to dedicate a separate team, with sufficient time and resources, to develop and implement the behavior-driven campaign for each separate economy. The campaigns were always different in nature, and asking one country team to manage them all while keeping their distinctive focus and tactics was simply too much; teams tasked to design and execute two or three really different major campaigns inevitably combined, shared, and generally mushed them together into one campaign that didn't work very well. This can seem like a big ask for senior regional managers who may question whether this additional level of investment can be justified (particularly in lower-income markets) and whether they can muster the extra resources. The return on investment of well-designed, targeted campaigns, however, can be quite high—more than worth the extra investment and extra management burden.

Separate economies within less developed markets

The economies of many, if not all, developing countries consist of two or more distinct economies: a developed or global economy, an aspiring middle-class economy, and often a subsistence economy. Each is a more or less self-contained and distinct cluster of customers, channels, and competitors. In the early years of working out the *Playbook*, we found all three of these separate economies existing side by side in countries all over the world, such as South Africa, Peru, India, Brazil, and Pakistan, to name a few. Sometimes, these multiple economies are physically located in different places; the subsistence economy, for instance, is largely found in rural areas, while the developed or global economy is largely found in cities. But particularly in the cities, and especially megacities, all three of these economies often exist within city blocks of one another.

In virtually every country we've worked in there's a top end, a relatively narrow slice of the economy that looks and acts much like that of any wealthy European country. This is the small group of consumers whose per capita income, adjusted for cost of living, would put them in the middle and upper classes in a highly developed economy. Their lifestyle looks very much like that of their peers living in highly developed economies: the product choices available in upscale shopping districts in Shanghai, Cairo, or Johannesburg bear a much closer resemblance to those in similar swaths of London or New York than to other areas within those countries. The buying behaviors of these customers (how and when they shop, and so on), the retail channels in which they shop, and the firms that supply brands and products to them, are likewise similar to those of the elite in the world's most developed economies.

These countries almost always also have an aspirant middle class that buys, with a distinctly different pattern and type of purchasing activities, from a different set of suppliers through a broader and more local range of channels. These emerging middle classes are often the largest part of the economy in terms of total spending power and number of customers, although they also usually have several layers and sub-segments within them, including both urban/rural and ethnic divisions. Their channel options are quite varied. At one end of the range, they may shop in the super- and hypermarkets that operate in developing and developed countries; at the other, they have myriad small, specialized mom-and-pop shops and regional chains all to themselves. The choice of and access to buying channels in this subeconomy is often distinctive to a particular society. (In Malaysia, for example, tea shops catering specifically to ethnically Malay, Chinese, or Indian customers are configured differently and offer different products.) The firms that supply these channels are often local or regional and focus on making good enough (or simply cheap enough) products for their customers.

This emerging middle class economy has its own characteristic way of buying things as well. These consumers usually don't have the time or the means to do extensive searches for items; they find themselves searching nearby—often only hundreds of meters from their home. They rely heavily on word of mouth—from relatives and friends—and only consider the few options available nearby or those that are close at hand along the route of their daily commute on foot, bike, or bus. Purchasing (and consumption) is strongly affected by the cultural and social mores of the aspiring middle class, often in subtle ways (see Different Buying Processes in Different Types of Economies).

Different Buying Processes in Different Types of Economies

In many developed or global economies, soft drinks are a minor item. The buying process for these ordinary goods is largely indistinguishable from the process for many other similar items. We found, however, that the way that middle class laborers in low-income countries approach this category can be vastly different. For these consumers, the price of a Coke or a Pepsi can exceed the wages of a half day's labor. It is thus treated as a near luxury product, one usually reserved as a gift. In one country where we worked, Sunday lunch was a major weekly event that brought together friends as well as family. It was a custom to dispatch one of the children after the meal to the local store for a liter of a soft drink, with strict instructions to bring back the coldest soft drink they could find (meaning that the actual buying activity in the store consisted of touching every bottle to see which was coldest). On return, the adult guests were served shot glass sized portions as an after meal treat—a gift to the guests. The point is that understanding the particular nuances of the buying process and customer narratives within distinct economies is key to designing effective campaigns.

Of course, this somewhat archetypal picture of an aspiring middle class buying process must be tempered by the rapid changes being wrought by the access that many consumers at this level in developing economies have to the internet through their mobile phones. In certain categories and certain parts of a country, the aspiring middle class may indeed buy in a way that is similar to the buying behaviors of consumers in more mature markets. In some cases, these consumers may use technology to leapfrog the buying patterns of more developed markets. Even in areas where roads are poor, wired communications are patchy, and formal commercial institutions are nonexistent, consumers may have access to information or payment services delivered through mobile technology. So it's important to understand at a granular level how the particular conditions and constraints in a market shape the specific buying behaviors. From a *Playbook* perspective, the key is to comprehensively map the channels, buying methods and technologies in use and how they impact behaviors. The trick here is to avoid being constrained by developed country models—rather one needs to painstakingly map the processes within a particular local economy.

Virtually all countries also harbor a substantial subsistence or near-subsistence economy. This economy is large and visible in many developing countries, such as India, Vietnam, or Nigeria, but it also exists in France and the United States. The ratios of these three subeconomies in the overall economy vary by country, but they're present nearly everywhere. The subsistence economy again looks different from other segments of the same society. Companies seeking to serve this population need to understand at a fine-grained level what and how these consumers purchase and what substitutes exist to the use of their products in this part of the market.

As the foregoing discussion suggests, a detailed and nuanced understanding of drivers and barriers often turns out to be most critical in portions of a country market consisting of customers with limited income. For example, one has to pay particular attention to disposable income at the point of sale and to logistical obstacles. Infrastructural barriers tend to loom large—in many places it's still difficult to reach stores due to poor public transport, bad roads, and narrow congested streets. Sales channels may therefore look quite different in these parts of the market. Consumer products may be sold primarily in small stores or kiosks whose ability to stock multiple brands, packages, and sizes is limited.

The implication of the foregoing discussion for marketers working in less mature country markets is that the *Playbook* process can and should be applied at the level of the separate economies that exist within a single geography to uncover and tap into the high-yield behaviors that can drive growth. One of the key challenges for global companies wading into these less familiar markets, however, is the relative dearth of market research that exists and the obstacles to collecting quantitative customer information. Teams therefore need to pay special attention to the details of how and where information is gathered to overcome these constraints.

While we have argued that robust quantification of buying behaviors and purchasing pathways based on comprehensive customer surveys is the gold standard, and required where the burden of proof for decision making is especially high (for example, pharma markets), in other cases such precision may be neither feasible nor necessary. Much of the research we have performed in less developed markets—particularly in lower income economies—has been more qualitative and observational in nature. This demands a distinctive set of resources and skills for deploying an on-the-ground presence to generate nuanced and actionable insights. Knowing the unique characteristics of a particular set of customers (for example, how much money a worker carries around in his pocket on his way home, or how much storage space a typical household has available) can be key to understanding behaviors and what drives them. Sometimes, there's no substitute for looking around and talking to people to really understand how and why they act as they do.

Building off our earlier example, we spent a good deal of time in poor South African townships observing the behavior of customers in *spaza* shops, informal convenience stores selling everyday household items that are often run out of people's homes. As noted earlier, we observed children coming into the shop running their fingers down the sides of every refrigerated bottle before making a beverage selection. When we asked them what they were doing, we discovered that they were looking for the coldest drink, one that would still be cold when they arrived back home after a long walk under a hot sun. In many cases, we found that the coldness of the bottle trumped the beverage brand in determining which product was selected. This detailed insight led our client to redirect investment to enhancing the integrity of their refrigerated cold chain to ensure that their products arrived and stayed cold.

The key adaptation of the *Playbook* for these markets revolves around the need to find high-value leverage points and behavioral objectives appropriate to the different economies and to segment these opportunities accordingly. The implication is that teams should build separate growth plans for each distinct market—urban rich, urban middle, rural middle, rural subsistence, and so on. A company may choose to address some or all of these markets but needs to do so differently for each and may have different levels of penetration in different parts of the market. The most common mistake we see companies make is to center their country market strategies on a single type of economy (for example, urban middle class) and then apply the same campaign across multiple markets that differ widely.

To summarize, the special circumstances of economically diverse, developing country markets may require certain adjustments in the application of the standard *Playbook* approach:

- Higher reliance on qualitative, observational market research—in the absence of quantitative data on consumer behaviors, research needs to be designed to effectively uncover distinctive patterns of behavior at key leverage points.

- Even more painstaking attention to detail—there's usually no substitute for on-the-ground research to probe the nuances of circumstances and behaviors among distinct economies that exist within a single country market.
- Dedicated teams for different campaigns—understanding and serving different economies usually requires specialized plans and resources dedicated to each distinct opportunity.

Our experience is that global companies (whose headquarters may be located far from the local markets they serve) often push back on the need to do primary market research on buying processes in different country markets. More often, marketing strategies are merely transferred from home country markets to other countries, or to markets within those countries that are thought to most closely resemble established markets. We often see this approach justified by marketing leaders as supporting a single, global brand positioning for their products. While there may be virtue in projecting a consistent set of brand messages across markets, in many cases this overlooks the real organic growth opportunities. As the discussion above points out, it's absolutely essential to do a deep dive into the nuances not only of a country market, but also of the distinct economies within that country to identify and influence buying behaviors in a targeted way.

Traditional B2B markets

B2B teams are often skeptical—at least initially—of the effectiveness of a systematic marketing approach like the *Playbook*. They will point to a number of distinctive characteristics of B2B markets and suggest that these differences invalidate or diminish the usefulness of approaches that were developed for (and hence really only apply to) B2C markets. Our B2B clients often point out, for example, that they have far fewer customers and a higher concentration of purchases in the hands of the biggest customers than is the case in B2C markets. Indeed, they often argue that their biggest customers are segments of one. They will describe the much greater complexity and sophistication of buying processes dominated by professional procurement managers placed at many removes from the end users. Many believe that B2B suppliers' lack of meaningful direct contact with end users makes traditional marketing concepts largely irrelevant. Finally, they will argue that the no-nonsense, by-the-numbers rationality of B2B purchasing tends to override the human factor in buying decisions and makes an approach focused on behaviors pointless.

Ironically, the biggest difference we've observed between our B2B and B2C clients is the degree to which B2B marketers typically believe they know their market and their customers. Indeed, many of these markets have been stable for decades, and industry wisdom can be specific and strongly held. They *know*, for example, that rapid growth isn't really possible (at least not without a breakthrough product). They *know* what customers care about (which usually comes down to some variation on price). Yet, despite this radical certainty about the stability of market dynamics, we have helped countless B2B teams—like the EnServ and Terrafix teams—unlock faster growth by discovering and acting upon unexplored insights about their markets. The biggest impediment to effectively implementing the *Playbook* in B2B markets may thus be the capacity of company leaders to suspend their judgment about how things work and about their ability to shape customer behaviors within their industries. The companies that have been most successful in driving growth in these markets understand the importance of upstream buying process activities, the role of nonproduct factors in consumption, and the different ways to segment markets. We've found that the composition of the team (especially if it includes open-minded folks from R&D and sales) can also make a critical difference in the ability to see things differently and to move the needle on growth.

The truth is that the *Playbook* delivers equally powerful results in both B2C and B2B markets. The core ideas of identifying one or two high-yield behaviors, segmenting the market around propensities to engage in desired behaviors, and building targeted campaigns to convince customers to change key behaviors work in all markets. But B2B managers do have a point. The circumstances of their markets are often different enough from B2C to warrant adapting how the *Playbook* is applied in these markets. For instance, in highly concentrated markets with a small number of players, it's nearly impossible to quantify the buying process in a meaningful way using traditional survey methods. In such cases, it may be better to rely on high quality qualitative research to uncover actionable nuances in behavior patterns.

Below, we outline our learnings from years of successful work with B2B clients on some of the most important particularities of B2B markets and options for adapting the *Playbook* approach in these markets. We begin with several observations about the distinctive nature of the B2B buying process. We then turn to an important, related concept that we call *line of sight*—the need to map activities and influences from the immediate customers who purchase the products all the way through to the end users who ultimately shape demand.

The B2B buying process

As noted already, B2B markets tend to have unique, complex buying processes that must be completely mapped to uncover opportunity. Indeed, a key difference between B2C and B2B markets is that the buying process in B2B markets is often much more elaborate—more players, more steps, more time—than in B2C markets. Typically, the B2B buying process consists of two major stages: an upstream innovation buying process that revolves around customers' development of new products and projects, and a downstream procurement buying process that is typically dictated by customer purchasing departments.

The notion of there being an upstream innovation phase of a B2B buying process can be startling, and even unsettling, for B2B firms. They do know that customers' (or their customers' customers) new product development (NPD) process shapes their portfolio and fundamentally determines the demand for their materials, products or services—and so they should be involved with it. Yet they look past that part of the process. They tell themselves that their salesforce lacks visibility into customers' NPD activities or that they don't have the right contacts, and that getting that visibility and contact would be extremely expensive (our margins won't support that). They've seen their own company's NPD process and know that it contains many steps and many players, with often murky, informal decision-making processes. So they don't acknowledge or address that part of the buying process in a systematic, sustained way.

Yet we would argue that the customer NPD process, which is the backbone of B2B customers' buying processes, is something *always* to be studied—and thoroughly mapped—when trying to grow in B2B markets. Somewhere in the mass of decisions and activities that comprise a new product development process are a few that will make a decisive difference in the "requirements document" the product group will present to procurement, and hence what procurement will go looking for in the market. As is dramatically illustrated by the EnServ case study, influencing customer behavior at that upstream point of leverage can make the downstream interaction with procurement a lot more favorable.

In fact, what we've found over the years is that B2B teams typically discover that the key leverage point for their category often lies in getting some product designer or engineer to talk over technical issues (as in the EnServ situation), or getting them to rethink how they test or evaluate the materials or products they source. B2B firms can thus influence their customers' evaluation approach so that it disproportionately values the functionality or benefits that their product or company possesses. For example by getting the customer to change the test protocol (that is to look for different properties, or set higher standards) or to add a new test, they can effectively tilt the rest of the buying process in their favor.

B2B teams are right on one thing, however—it is, in fact, a more challenging task to map the upstream part of the buying processes they face than it is for a B2C team. But mapping B2B buying processes is quite do-able. What it takes is a detective's (or perhaps a jigsaw puzzler's) approach and patience: the only way to figure out another company's NPD process is to obtain myriad bits of information from multiple sources over time and diligently sift, sort, and fit them together. They need to reach out to ex-executives or participants in the industry and ask detailed questions about how things are done. They need to go to symposia and events that technical people frequent and listen carefully as they talk about the meetings they go to, and the steps they take—what their daily life is like. From all that, it's possible to reconstruct an accurate picture. When EnServ took the time to reconstruct the real end-to-end process that facilities managers used to do their jobs (instead of just restudying the downstream RFP process) it paid huge dividends.

Of course, it's also vital to thoroughly understand the downstream procurement process. Yes, this is where most sales teams spend their time, and they should be— and often are—knowledgeable about what their customers do. But it warrants systematic, third-party study nonetheless. The sales team is necessarily caught up in its selling process and so often doesn't see what the customer's procurement department is actually doing. And, just like in the upstream phase of the process, there are activities that procurement groups do that quite consistently turn out to be high yield if approached properly. An example of this is when a procurement group assigns products into different categories, designating some products as "strategic" and others as "undifferentiated." There is thus enormous value to mapping both the upstream and downstream portions of the buying process. In general, however, we would emphasize the importance of investing in a deeper and more nuanced understanding of customers' upstream decision-making and innovation processes.

Identity of the customer

B2B teams tend to do something odd. They pretend that the customer is a company. They fool themselves into thinking that the customer is a monolithic entity with a single-minded focus on profit maximization in accordance with strictly rational and unyielding practices. Given this view, it may indeed seem unproductive to focus on things like behavioral propensities and customer narratives.

There are actually two issues here. The first, related to the discussion above about understanding the processes within customer organizations, is that B2B companies are actually complex entities, comprising multiple sub-organizations—regions, product business units, brands, plants, and so on—any and all of which may be the real end user or decision-maker for a product. The second issue is that these sub-organizations, in turn, comprise individuals who, while acting on behalf of their company's interests and profit-making goals, are also motivated by individual, personal considerations.

The first issue relates to the choice of the unit of analysis for applying the *Playbook* methodology. One needs to be clear about whether the unit of segmentation, for example, is a whole company, a division of a company or something less than that, such as a brand or a plant. Any of these may be legitimate choices and each implies a different segmentation. Take the example of PPG, a relatively focused maker of paints and specialty coatings that has several divisions: architectural, industrial, marine, and others. Since these divisions serve different markets, it may make sense to consider each division, rather than the parent company, as an individual customer. Moreover, individual manufacturing plants within a division can be treated as unique customers because they have different configurations (for example, the technology of older plants may require different grades or types of products than those with new technology) and hence distinct buyers and buying behaviors. The point is that while you may think your market consists of only ten or thirty or fifty coatings companies—a number too few to be worth segmenting—when properly considered, it actually consists of the key buyers in eighty to one hundred divisions or four hundred to five hundred plants—a universe that demands segmentation.

Sub-organizations within a company nearly always have different circumstances and needs. De-averaging these units within large customers often enables us to see much more opportunity for targeting specific pieces of business. We've seen a number of occasions where teams find that they have uneven penetration or share within a large customer organization. Again, this is evidence that the customer isn't a monolith but a collection of sub-organizations, each of which is a customer. While we may generally be safe in assuming that we know what is meant by the term customer, in most B2B markets it's worth questioning these assumptions and redefining how we draw the boundaries to ensure that we're applying the *Playbook* at the relevant unit of analysis.

The second issue is straightforward. Even a superficial experience with B2B customers should make it clear that they're not hyper-rational, relentless, profit-maximizing machines. In fact, they're a collection of people in roles (housing design engineers, software engineers, product marketers, and so on). Yet we often find a resistance within B2B companies to constructing detailed narratives for specific customer roles, and hence to identifying drivers and barriers that reflect the concerns of an individual in a role. The truth is that B2B purchasing decisions are made not by spreadsheets but by people, individually and collectively, whose decisions and actions are shaped by the social and physical characteristics of their jobs—and who really do comingle their aspirations and concerns with those of their company. Our recommendation to B2B marketers is simply to embrace this reality, identify key roles and the individuals within them, and do a deep dive into the sociology and psychology of consumption.

Scarcity and concentration of customers

Many B2B companies may have less than one hundred total customers, and often as few as ten to twenty, some of whom, inevitably are much larger than the rest. This makes quantitative mapping of the buying process, and quantitative segmentation, problematic—data from ten to twenty customers will not yield statistically significant insights, and it's often quite hard to make sense of data that purports to cover the activities of a large and diverse customer.

The issue is real but not difficult to deal with. First, as explained above, in some markets a small number of companies host a rather large number of real customers (that is, customers defined at the plant or division or regional level). Second, qualitative research and analysis, done properly, can yield the same kind of valid, precise answers about high-yield behaviors and leverage points—and indeed about segments—as does quantitative. There are two key elements to doing this qualitative research properly.

First, it's essential to gather data about how customers' buying processes work from a much broader set of people than the team's own salesforce. Typically, B2B firms turn to their salesforce for customer insights. After all, they tend to be the ones closest to the customer. Companies often literally defer to their sales colleagues, giving them the first and last word on what customers want and what they do. Of course, beginning with the salesforce's knowledge and contacts is generally the right starting point. But it's always only a starting point. All too often a sales team's visibility into how customers make purchasing decisions is strictly limited to the workings of procurement and the RFP process. In fact, part of the role of good procurement departments is to limit the access that salespeople have to the rest of their company to ensure that vendors compete on a level playing field and that transactions occur through a consistent, arm's length process. It can therefore be difficult for the salesforce to get insight into how decisions are made, which level of management really has decision rights, who the critical engineers and influencers are, and so on. Moreover, their perspective on how customers do things is distorted by what they've tried and been successful or unsuccessful with; in saying "well, that person isn't important," or "that step isn't key" they often conflate personal failure with institutional reality (that is, the person really is important but the sales person couldn't change their mind or behavior).

The other key element that's needed, as we pointed out in the section above dealing with the buying process, is for the team to interview a much broader array of people outside as well as inside the buying process. It's valuable to interview other internal sources, like customer service and technical service, who will have invaluable (albeit partial) views of what their customers do and how they do it. It is, of course, essential to interview other industry participants—industry experts, ex-executives of various departments, industry consultants, and trade association staff —about the overall nature of the typical buying process in the industry, and then drill down into details about whatever piece of that process they're most familiar with.

Position in the value system

Another peculiarity of B2B markets is the placement of many firms in the headwaters of an industry value system. Materials makers, for example, typically sell their wares through distributors who, in turn, sell to companies that manufacture parts or components, who sell to brand owners or original equipment manufacturers (OEMs), who then sell—again often through distribution—to the end user. These firms are therefore positioned at several removes from the end users situated far downriver.

In this case, it's possible (and quite valuable) to simply apply the *Playbook* by looking only one step downriver, that is, for a materials manufacturer to try to identify and influence the high-yield behaviors of their direct customers (for example, the component or part manufacturer). But there's nearly always a significant additional opportunity to boost growth by taking the trouble to gain a line of sight to how end users and brand owners behave and think.

We use the term *line of sight* to refer to the process of segmenting players at each step in the value system (for example, direct customers, end users, value added resellers, and so on) in a way that lets you trace which segment in the raw material step sells to which segment in the part manufacturing step, and so on. A line of sight analysis takes the view that one must see how the firm's products and offerings flow through each of these value-added players to the ultimate end user. We can use the analogy of a garden hose to visualize this concept. A kink or obstruction in the hose at any point from spigot to nozzle can choke the flow through the system. Gaining a line of sight through the process allows a company to understand where they can intervene—change someone's behavior—to unkink the hose to allow the flow to be at its maximum. A classic example of this is when a company finds it can't rely on the distributor is sells to and through (their direct customer) to influence the behavior of a design engineer at the part manufacturer the distributor supplies. There's a kink—the design engineer—that the raw material company may not even know exists. This broader view of the market can sometimes suggest novel ways for companies to go to market, either by developing new capabilities themselves or by partnering with others to address the blockage. For example, a line of sight analysis for a component supplier that identified financing or logistics constraints among the ultimate buyers of the products for which they supply parts could suggest a strategy based on an alliance with financial service or technical support providers to increase flow through the system.

Unkinking the garden hose involves two interrelated ideas. First, it's important to figure out which pieces of the value system you are going to segment (for example, distributors, retailers, consumers, or converters, manufacturers, distributors, end users, and so on). Second, it's essential to build a set of market segmentation frames that allow a line of sight from a channel segment to one or more consumer or end user segments. This is a perennial issue—nearly half of our projects wrestle with this idea.

Addressing these issues means that a firm can target and activate segments with much more precision by seeing the whole system. It doesn't help to do a fabulous job of segmenting consumers if the distributors through which you go to market don't reach those key consumer segments or don't have an incentive to target them. The aim is to open the entire hose to enable volume to flow from end to end through the pathways that are most advantageous to the firm.

To summarize the foregoing discussion, there are certain considerations of industrial B2B markets that may require some adaptations or shifts of emphasis in how the *Playbook* approach is applied:

- Extra attention to customers' upstream and innovation activities in the buying process—while the way customers develop new products and specify/evaluate materials can seem like a black box to B2B marketers, understanding the stages, decisions, and gatekeepers in this part of the buying process can pay high dividends.
- Reliance on qualitative research to overcome data limitations—it may not be feasible to obtain statistically valid, survey-based research in B2B markets characterized by small numbers of customers. Instead, companies should try to go deep rather than broad, using qualitative research to understand the steps in the customer buying process that they're not seeing today and the hidden decision points and influencers around which they can craft behavioral objectives and targeted behavior change value propositions.
- Seeking information and insights from multiple sources—B2B companies often rely on their salesforce as the key source of customer insight. Yet, there are some aspects of customers' operations that sales has little visibility into or where there are structural barriers to gaining detailed insights. Companies should draw on insights from other internal sources (for example, technical and engineering support staff or customer service teams) as well as external sources to round out its understanding of buying process waterfalls and customer narratives
- Expanding and refining the definition of the customer—rather than take whole companies as the standard unit of analysis, B2B firms may be better served by applying the *Playbook* concepts at a more fine-grained level to units or sub-organizations within the customer enterprise.

- Tapping the human element—a mechanistic view of customer organizations can lead to a perception that decision making is driven solely by profit-maximizing processes rather than by people. Developing customer narratives that explore the personal motivations and uncover drivers and barriers to behaviors of key role players can be especially powerful in a B2B context.
- Adopting a line of sight through the complete value system—because B2B buying processes tend to be complex, involving multiple stages and players in the value chain, firms should take a holistic view of the buying process all the way to the end customer and develop linked segmentation frames that ensure an unimpeded flow of the firm's goods or services through the most advantageous pathways.

B2B markets: Special cases

Several types of B2B markets have sufficiently unusual structures or competitive dynamics to warrant a separate look at how to apply the *Playbook* most effectively to accelerate growth in these domains. The first group of these special case markets are those that are competitive but heavily regulated, such as life sciences and financial services. The second group are those in which the pace of fundamental technological change is especially swift and complex, as in high-tech industries.

Highly regulated competitive markets

Government and its handmaiden, regulation, play a significant role in all markets. Indeed, one of the fundamental roles of government is to create and enforce the basic rights and rules that underpin market exchange. In some industries, however, the government is either the sole customer (for example, military) or has oversight and veto power over nearly every decision and action of private providers (for example, public utilities). Our focus here isn't, however, on regulated monopolies but on a subset of competitive industries where the government strongly shapes or mandates how firms operate. These markets are often characterized by one or more of the general attributes of B2B markets mentioned above, for example, relatively few and/ or highly concentrated customers, complex buying processes, and so on, so the foregoing discussion is relevant to these cases as well. What's distinctive in these cases is the central role of regulation and other powerful intermediaries that shape the nature of competition in these industries.

In the US pharmaceutical and biotech sector, for example, the government, through the Food and Drug Administration (FDA), exercises extremely detailed supervision of the development and commercialization of all new products. The FDA acts as the final stage gate committee, literally making the go/no go decision about each new product. The FDA also issues explicit instructions on what each company's marketing and sales groups can say and do, right down to reviewing advertising copy. Other government agencies are actual buyers—and major ones. There's a similar pattern in the financial services sector: various government agencies set rules on what kinds of products banks and other financial services firms can offer and exercise a great deal of rulemaking and oversight over what they say and do when marketing and selling their products. And in both the financial services and life sciences sectors there's some ambiguity regarding the role of the end user/consumer as decision maker. Both of these industries involve critical third parties, such as doctors or financial advisors and brokers, who stand in for the end user in making key decisions.

As we have discussed throughout this book and demonstrated through our featured company examples, the *Playbook* works beautifully in these markets. Indeed, we and our colleagues have participated in hundreds of successful growth plans for pharmaceutical, biotech, hospital, and health insurance companies. It's equally true, however, that the particular dynamics and constraints of these markets mean that the methodology works best by emphasizing certain aspects of the process—applying some pieces more thoroughly or extensively or in specific ways—to produce the greatest acceleration in growth. In addition, we have found that it's essential to create a line of sight segmentation of the value system—both vertically and horizontally—to ensure that the critical drivers and barriers are being addressed throughout the market. One characteristic of the segmentation work in these heavily regulated industries is that it's often valuable (or essential) to identify paired behavioral objectives; the Terrafix story, with the paired behavioral objective for doctor and patient is a classic example. Finally, given the size of investments and long time periods over which these investments play out in these industries, we also counsel a relatively heavier investment in precision and proof around key choices.

Full value system

The value system in these special case markets is crowded and interconnected. Pharmaceutical companies, for example, confront a value system which contains not only health care providers and patients, but also drug distributors, group purchasing organizations, private and government insurers, as well as hospitals and integrated delivery networks of various types (nonprofit, for profit, large/small, and so on) that control which products are available to care providers and patients through their formulary committees. As mentioned above, this is an industry in which the primary chooser of the product (that is, the physician) is also distinct from the end user (the patient).

Given this web of interactions and potential obstacles, it's essential for pharma companies to map the interactions of all the downstream players and to segment each distinct group of industry participants in a way that allows their key interactions to be traced. In the case of Terrafix, for example, it was not enough for Sam's team to understand and segment either patients alone or doctors alone. To accelerate growth, they had to identify both the patient segments that would be most likely to ask for the test (push behavior) and the physician segment that would be most likely to order the test (pull behavior). And they had to ascertain whether these groups actually overlapped and interacted so that they could reach the right physicians seeing the right patients. Furthermore, they had to activate multiple levers to ensure that the objective test was widely and conveniently available and covered by health insurers.

In terms of the *Playbook* process, this meant creating a linked propensity-based segmentation scheme around a compatible set of behavioral objectives. In practice, it meant collecting (via survey) accurate data on how decisions and product flowed at each stage in the process. While this approach is similar to that in traditional B2B markets, there tend to be more actors in regulated systems that can play a significant—even decisive—role in facilitating or interrupting the desired behaviors. For example, large hospital systems increasingly shape which branded or generic therapies are available to patients within their networks. The decision about which drugs will be on formulary has an enormous impact on the treatment choices that occur further downstream and creates an important overlay onto how companies segment the market. Simply put, all the hard work to identify physician and patient leverage points could be nullified if these behaviors occurred within a hospital system or insurance regime where the company's therapies weren't available.

Complex, government-shaped buying processes

In highly regulated markets, governments can play multiple roles related to regulation, market access, gatekeeper, advocate, and payer. In the US healthcare market, for example, government shapes funding for research activities, plays an active gatekeeper role related to the design of clinical trials and, ultimately, drug approval, and may also play the role of insurer (for example, through the Centers for Medicare and Medicaid Services).

From a *Playbook* perspective, each of these roles needs to be carefully mapped, understood, and leveraged. The active role of government actors adds complexity relative to the typical B2B buying process, meaning that more care and attention must be paid to the details of the activities, who participates in them, and who really influences various decisions. What we typically find is that the critical growth levers don't involve just a single high-yield behavior tied to one player, but multiple high-yield behaviors by multiple players that have to be identified and targeted.

For example, it's not uncommon to find that there are high-yield behaviors for *patients* both at the top and bottom of the buying process (that is, in how they initiate and investigate different types of treatment *and* in whether they comply with prescribed therapy over time). Likewise, there are high-yield behaviors for doctors both as individuals treating patients and as members of hospital or group practice formulary committees. There are high-yield behaviors for decision makers within insurance companies and within government agencies, and so on. In practice, this means that companies may need to run multiple, highly targeted behavior change campaigns in parallel to activate the linked behaviors among interacting players throughout the value system. Again, we can point to the example of Terrafix, which combined an unbranded campaign aimed at patients with an informational campaign for doctors on the benefits of objective testing, as well as an outreach campaign to government regulators and insurers to ensure that the cost of the test would be reimbursed.

High-innovation (high-tech) markets

While we can't do full justice to the topic here, we want to add a few words about an additional special case of B2B industries characterized by rapid innovation and short product life cycles—notably, the high-tech sector. High-tech markets are more diverse than commonly conceived and include software-driven firms that combine B2B and B2C elements (for example, Facebook, Amazon), software firms that are largely B2B (for example Oracle, Salesforce), hardware-driven firms that have a software and solution wrap around (for example, Texas Instruments and Cisco), and firms that compete largely in the product space but are increasingly looking to monetize digital information flows (for example, ITT).

Despite the substantial differences among these distinct flavors of high-tech firms, a common dynamic across the sector is the speed of product innovation. New generations of high-tech products tend to follow close upon the heels of the last and can represent opportunities for significant market share gains (or losses). Lots of industries move fast, but high-tech markets can be supercharged. The life cycle for a graphics chip is often three months. Compare this to the auto industry where vehicle body styles can remain relatively stable for ten to fifteen years. Undertaking a nine-month buying process analysis (as we might for a new blockbuster drug) for each new chip release would miss three cycles of graphic chip life cycles. The ability to prepare and launch new products swiftly and successfully is thus a key capability for these firms.

One possible response to this situation would be to propose performing a lean or stripped down version of the *Playbook* process to match the pace of these fast-moving markets. For example, we could run the basic frameworks (mapping the buying process waterfall, creating a propensity-based segmentation, and so on) in an abbreviated form—gathering available evidence, relying on qualitative rather than quantitative data, and working from hypotheses and accumulated wisdom within the firm. Following the high-tech industry mantra, we could be prepared to fail fast and adapt plans quickly in response to feedback from the market.

In fact, we *don't* advocate this approach and believe such a technique conflates two distinct things: the rate of change in product innovation and the rate of change in underlying customer buying processes. While product features and benefits may change rapidly with each new product life cycle, in our experience, the way people buy and the high-yield behaviors are actually quite stable over time. Of course, to compete in these industries, a company must possess the research and development (R&D), engineering, and manufacturing capabilities needed to design and produce new things quickly. But the approach to getting B2B customers to try and then buy those new things is less mutable. In our experience, it's worth investing in a robust market analysis to understand the fundamental dynamics of the buying processes in these markets in detail. We may, for example, choose to segment customers on the basis of their propensity to try something new, but we shouldn't let the infatuation with novelty that characterizes many aspects of these industries color our understanding of how customers behave.

Again, this discussion gives relatively short shrift to the vast topic of high-tech markets. Our purpose here is merely to point out how marketers in these areas can adapt or emphasize particular elements of our standard *Playbook* approach to address the special needs of this market.

A few key points thus emerge from the consideration of special B2B markets. While much of this discussion has been focused on particular types of markets (for example, life sciences) there are some general lessons for applying the *Playbook* in complex B2B markets:

- Focus on linked systems and connection points: the additional layer of complexity and scrutiny faced by highly regulated firms above and beyond what's typical for most B2B companies warrants additional efforts to perform a detailed mapping of value systems. This may mean creating segmentation frames at multiple levels to ensure that the firm can activate an aligned set of behaviors with many players, any of which could potentially pose a critical impediment to the growth strategy.
- Identify multiple behavioral objectives: growth in these markets is rarely achieved by pulling on a single behavioral lever. Rather, it's often necessary to influence a few key behaviors with different stakeholders throughout the value system.
- Run multiple behavior change campaigns in parallel: related to the point above, it may be necessary to pursue parallel campaigns (simultaneous or sequenced) with different target groups to change behavior across the system.
- Meet the appropriate burden of proof for decision making: the degree of emphasis and investment in applying the *Playbook* tools may vary depending on the risk and size of investment represented by individual growth opportunities. In high stakes or one shot launch situations, it's often worth doubling down on key analyses. Fostering confidence and certainty around key decision points can help avoid backsliding or loss of focus in allocating resources and effort to behavior change campaigns.
- Emphasize process as a guide through complexity: it's easy for teams to get distracted by the complex dynamics and demands of the markets they serve. Adhering to a disciplined *Playbook* process— and approaching shortcuts with caution—can help marshal scarce resources around the few actions that are likely to drive real growth.

Conclusion

This chapter pointed out a number of challenges related to implementing the *Playbook* in various types of markets. While we can't address the unique aspects of every market, we can draw on decades of experience applying these principles in many different geographies and industries. Our aims here were to argue that the core *Playbook* approach has demonstrated its validity in many different types of markets and to distill a few key lessons for applying this toolset under different circumstances to enhance the impact of the effort. In the next chapter, we'll shift our attention to common institutional roadblocks that firms typically encounter in rolling out and embedding the *Playbook* approach.

Chapter 12

Overcoming Organizational Roadblocks

Curiously, while it's clear that every firm is eager for growth, they often organize and operate in ways that prevent growth. In most companies, the organizational structures (for example, business unit structure, functional silos) inhibit a common, organization-wide view of the marketplace. Moreover, product growth plans often don't follow a common process or playbook—reducing both the prospects for growth and learning about growth over time. While claiming to be customer-oriented, organizations frequently underfund consumer research while boasting publicly about their research and development (R&D) efforts. We often wonder what type of R&D is actually being done in the absence of rigorous, evidence-based views of customer behavior. Furthermore, when these innovations are launched, the marketing and commercial investment tend to be spread across a wide range of marketing and tactics—leaving little room for attacking competitor weak points or high leverage customer behaviors. Finally, marketing and commercial managers are frequently rotated every twenty-four to thirty-six months, and, as a result, hand off a commercial plan in the middle of a campaign. Because of this dynamic, the new manager feels the pressure to do something new—and modifies or abandons the plan mid-course. As a result of these forces, organizations tie their shoelaces together at the starting line. With this starting point, we're absolutely amazed when growth does occur.

As we've engaged with clients over the past couple of decades, we have come to recognize that to implement the *Playbook*, leaders must also address specific firm dynamics to be successful. Thus, in this chapter we shift gears to a look back at the four company stories explored in earlier chapters (as well as other client experiences), to identify organizational roadblocks that we have consistently observed in practice. Importantly, while we designed the *Playbook* to address these roadblocks, we also recognize that the *Playbook* alone may not be sufficient.

While any of these roadblocks alone may derail growth, in combination they most certainly will put the skids on any growth initiative. As such, we conclude this chapter with five specific recommendations that can help overcome the roadblocks. Each of these recommendations has standalone value, but taken together they can have a significant effect on the successful implementation of the *Playbook*.

Conventional industry wisdom

Every industry has an implicit set of rules about where and how to compete. It's as if the industry were a sports league with its own rule book. Over time, seemingly sensible organizational design choices, competitive benchmarking, and intrinsic human biases combine to lead executives in competing firms to share a rather narrow set of assumptions about how growth works in their industry. Most commonly, they come to believe that growth primarily comes from two sources: retaining and expanding their existing customer base (that is, building customer loyalty) and/or taking customers away from weaker competitors (that is, gaining share). This places a hidden but strong brake on their ability to grow rapidly and reliably. Seeing the industry this way, most managers act as if they were in a continuous series of win-lose games. They copy each other as rapidly as they can. Their product line strategies become near mirror images and they invest in the same best internal practices. The result is that all firms' growth rates tend to rise and fall with the industry average. Even those who play the game very well find that they live in a world of two steps forward, one step back, as competitors match (perhaps not perfectly, but reasonably) any effective move on their part.

This was the situation in which Eugene Shin found himself when he joined Caesar Financial as the new EVP of wealth and investment management. Having recently been part of an unsuccessful marketing and advertising campaign at his previous firm, he experienced an unsettling sense of déjà vu at Caesar Financial. The marketing campaigns—as well as the product offerings—were virtually identical from one wealth management institution to the next. The reason for this was that these firms all subscribed to the same conventional wisdom that the right way to advise investors was to devise a comprehensive financial plan that involved the management of their entire portfolio. Everything from the financial disclosure forms that new customers were asked to complete to the way financial advisors were compensated was based on the conventional industry wisdom that they needed the whole client portfolio.

As a veteran of the industry, Eugene himself had long subscribed to this belief. But he also recognized that replicating the same me too offerings and value propositions as the competition was unlikely to deliver the kind of growth he needed to deliver. Pursuing opportunities revealed by the buying process analysis to help customers invest discrete chunks of money set aside for specific purposes required a significant break with industry orthodoxy. With hard data from the analysis and the strong support of the CEO behind him, however, Eugene was able to break the grip of conventional wisdom to launch a successful growth initiative.

Conflicting views and maps: Sales, marketing, and R&D disconnect

In Chapter 5, we noted the often competing views of the market within an organization. This is reflected in the different segmentation schemes that are often in play. This should not be a surprise since different functions have different time horizons and goals.

The salesforce in most organizations is primarily focused on selling *existing* products or devices. Likewise, the R&D function is largely set up to innovate around *new-to-the-world* products (for example, scent of a new cosmetic, a new energy efficient HVAC system, or a new therapy). Finally, marketing is tasked with both knowing what's going on in the minds of customers and, in turn, stimulating demand based on this knowledge. It's no wonder then there's often conflict between functions. In the simplest terms, there's no alignment between these functions unless it is hardwired with new processes.

This issue of different function views is compounded when one shifts the discovery process to look upstream at customer behaviors that precede product selection. Here the key insight is rarely about the product. Rather, it's about altering some aspects of buyer behavior unrelated to product features. We have often seen the R&D organization—which may see itself as the function charged with understanding and anticipating customer needs—left on the sideline in new growth initiatives. If not addressed explicitly, the resulting conflict over the roles and responsibilities of the different functional units can lead to hard feelings, lost momentum, and sub-optimal allocation of resources needed to fuel sustained growth.

The R&D organization at EnServ turned out to be a critical stakeholder for Susan Gomez when she set out to retool the energy services business unit. EnServ's marketing function had historically been fairly weak and decentralized. There were no centralized planning processes and little coordination with other business functions. R&D had stepped into the vacuum, effectively taking on the role of a market intelligence function. R&D leaders came to see themselves as representing the voice of the customer and were therefore somewhat suspicious when Susan launched a business-led (sales and marketing) initiative to resegment the market based on a comprehensive survey of customer buying behaviors.

R&D had championed the development of bundled energy services that had been successfully sold into one industry vertical (which was how EnServ traditionally segmented its market). Leaders in R&D strongly backed the strategy of Susan's predecessor to aggressively expand these offerings to other segments. The findings of the buying process, which showed that such large-scale, bundled offerings actually represented a fairly small opportunity and was out of sync with how decision-makers actually purchased energy services, challenged the wisdom of this approach. Furthermore, Susan and her team developed a wholly new segmentation based on the propensity of facilities managers to consult with vendors early in the planning of energy services projects.

While these changes were initially met with resistance—both by the salesforce and R&D—the evidence from the analysis served as a common basis of understanding of key segments to target. Susan invited multiple stakeholders to participate in the design of the new solutions for these target segments. Here the team relied heavily on product development to help develop a suite of smaller scale, high ROI offerings that facilities managers could purchase and implement without the need for lengthy internal capital budgeting and approval processes. Again, the data-backed insights of the analysis helped meet the burden of proof required to mobilize and foster alignment among the various business functions to implement the new growth strategy.

Underfunding consumer research

Since most firms claim to be customer-driven, the chronic underfunding of rigorous customer research we have observed in many organizations is perplexing. The first issue is simply the overall dollars allocated to marketing research. While iconic B2C companies such as Unilever, Procter & Gamble, and Nestle spend tens of millions on consumer research, they are in the minority. Frequently, B2C firms that are in the $400 to $500 million range will spend perhaps $500,000 on research. Indeed, in many B2B firms, specific divisions and product lines may do no formal market research whatsoever.

The second issue relates to the focus of funding. Most companies devote the overwhelming majority of their research dollars to assess product performance versus competition. Or they spend the money on tracking the impact of current campaigns rather than truly learning about unmet or undermet customer needs. Furthermore, when money is spent on product performance research, it's typically spent on reconfirming customer insights that the firm already knows (for example, customers want lower prices and better service). To test this, we often ask participants in our workshops, "What do you know about customers that your competition does not know?" This is typically a short conversation.

The third issue relates to the market research process itself. While firms tend to significantly underfund primary consumer research, they're simultaneously over reliant on third-party, secondary-research vendors. That is, they outsource critical customer intelligence and market research functions to external vendors (for example, EuroMonitor). While the data is often quite good, the result is that all firms have the same intelligence as their competitors. Thus, there are no proprietary insights specific to the firm. This vendor-centered data naturally leads to the development of similar products and services since they're relying on the same data. A second research process issue relates to the center of gravity of discovery-oriented research. In most cases, firms center their research on the product itself—how it compares to competitors, what new features are desired, and what service could be added to the core product. It does not focus more broadly on the entire buying process. And finally, the discovery-oriented research tends to be allocated to junior marketing research folks who don't have the industry, context, and market knowledge to best exploit their findings. When a chess grand master looks at a chessboard, they know the right move to make. Similarly, when a senior executive participates in discovery-oriented research conversations, they take away a different set of conclusions than someone who's deeply trained in market research techniques.

This lack of attention to discovery research was apparent across all the companies whose stories have been shared in this book. In some cases, such as EnServ, the issue was linked to chronic under-funding and under-development of the marketing function in an industry that relied on a simplistic framing of the market and aggressive sales tactics. In the case of Terrafix, by contrast, the company actually spent quite a lot of money on patient and physician research. The problem there was the focus of the research, which looked narrowly at the therapeutic and prescribing benefits of the product rather than at the broader set of customer behaviors.

The most blatant example, however, may be the case of Caesar Financial (though it was not different from its competitors in this regard). For years, the firm's financial advisors had recognized that many prospective clients discontinued the process after their initial consultation. Rather than investigate the underlying reasons and behaviors leading to the steep drop out at this point, they tended to rationalize it in various ways. Only when they invested the resources to understand the impact of upstream events on the jobs that investors wanted to accomplish with their money were they able to address this large missed opportunity.

Spreading commercial investment across areas

An additional cause of slower organic growth is one that hides in plain sight. It's the *spreading of commercial investment.* Here there are three specific issues. First, firms try to activate too broad a swathe of the market. It's much easier to communicate to senior management that one is targeting several segments—as compared to a narrow focus on one or two segments. It somehow appears less risky—and even more aggressive—if one attempts to address a large portion of the market. The result is that often four to five segments are targeted—or, at times, the entire market is targeted.

Second, with a given target segment money is typically spent across the entire range of communication mix activities—advertising, social media, trade literature, conferences, and other vehicles. The cause for this peanut butter allocation is the belief that all levers need to be activated to get the best marketplace result. Third, and relatedly, it's difficult to defund communication activities once they have budget and a staff behind them. Indeed, this lack of abandonment of activities is compounded by the fact that new media vehicles are arriving almost every day (for example, Twitter and Snapchat). These new media vehicles are simply added to the mix and continue to be funded indefinitely. As a result, the media spend is spread much thinner—across the entire range of media tactics.

In sum, without precise, proprietary information on the location of the one or two opportunities where they can get the most return to incremental investment, managers buy insurance by investing a little money in multiple opportunities. The fragmentation of spending that results is a near guarantee that investment in any truly meaningful opportunity will be too small to cut through the competitive clutter, much less drive customer behavior in a significant enough way to affect results.

Promotion cycles and job rotation

Business leaders' nearly unquenchable desire for initiatives that show results relatively quickly is born of both Wall Street expectations and their own companies' personnel policies and practices. Wall Street's short-term obsession is too well documented to need much explication, but it does play a role in managers' tendency to seek things that work this quarter.

The effect of companies' human resource policies, particularly with respect to promoting people, is less well understood because it operates indirectly and is therefore harder to see. Companies typically arrange for promotions (and/or reshuffling) every eighteen to thirty-six months. This means that, on average, an ambitious, rising manager expects to spend twenty-four to thirty months in a given role before being promoted. If they spend much more time in a role, they start to worry about their career prospects at that company. While the specific policies and criteria vary, companies all sensibly look for managers to demonstrate competence as the rationale for promotion—preferably in the form of tangible results. Aspiring managers respond by trying to demonstrate their competence in a way that bears their stamp, that makes them visible—something that is new and better and notable. And they'd prefer not to incur much risk in doing so. This gives them a strong bias toward initiatives that can be conceived and implemented within six to twelve months and whose results can be seen in what they hope will be the final twelve months of their tenure. This desire for quick, demonstrable wins often leads the manager to engage in short term tactics, superficial refreshes of key campaigns, or new packaging. It rarely lends itself to a more far-reaching reimagination of the strategy to target other avenues of growth.

The pressure to goose growth—and fast—could have spelled disaster for Terrafix. After leading the successful launch of this major new product, Sam Wilcox's prospects for advancement seemed secure. Suddenly, however, he found himself facing a scenario of slowing growth for his product and his career. Had he listened to the urging of many on his team to redouble efforts to promote the therapy's distinctive benefits to physicians he might, perhaps, have eked out enough additional growth—or at least bought some more time—to find a nice new position for himself.

To Sam's credit and the credit of the leadership team that both pressed him for a new approach and allowed him the time and latitude needed for this, he chose to take a different path. Rather than throw marketing resources at short term but unsustainable growth prospects, Sam invested in research on patient and physician behaviors that uncovered the critical importance of asking for and prescribing an under-utilized diagnostic test for the condition. While the ultimate results were unquestionably better for both Sam and the company, it required courage and integrity to adopt this long-term perspective in the face of short-term financial and performance pressures.

The *Playbook* approach

This discussion of the five roadblocks shifts the perspective to the broader context in which the *Playbook* is deployed within organizations. From our experience, these elements of organizational drag or friction can be definitive factors in whether even the most brilliant strategy delivers the desired growth. Nor is addressing these contextual issues an easy fix. (See Figure 12-1 for an overview of the suggested solutions.) As noted earlier, while we designed the *Playbook* to overcome these challenges, there are other levers that an organization can deploy to help lessen the drag.

From conventional wisdom to system-wide replacement

If everyone's playing the same game—by the same set of rules—it's time to change the rules of the game. As we noted in Chapter 1, the entire purpose of the *Playbook* is to change how growth strategies are achieved through market planning. Importantly, we're advocating a system-wide replacement, not just a replacement of a few components of the go-to-market plan. To take an analogy, the West Coast offense in American football is an example of a system wide replacement that requires new plays, new players, new perspective, and a coach/leader who can drive the implementation. One doesn't employ a mix of West Coast and Wishbone offenses on the same team. Similarly, in tennis, one can play a largely back court game or a serve and volley game. This is an either/or choice. In a similar way, we're suggesting that the principles on which the *Playbook* is built act best as an integrated system rather than as standalone components.

FIGURE 12-1

Growth Roadblocks and *Playbook* Solutions

Growth Roadblocks	Potential Solutions
1. Conventional growth wisdom	**1. *Playbook* system solution** System-wide replacement Building transformation campaign Integrating *Playbook* approach into other systems and processes
2. Conflicting maps and views	**2. Create common view of market** Cross-functional steering team with right to recommend one frame Each team member commits own function to use segmentation
3. Underfunding customer research	**3. Fund research in a new way** Exploratory versus confirming research Primary not secondary research Right level for evidence-based management Getting senior management involved
4. Spreading commercial investment	**4. Focus commercial spend** Not spreading across entire buying process Disproportionate spend on one or, at most, two segment-specific campaigns at a time Sequential focus on implementation waves (and maintain but reduce spend for earlier segment-specific campaigns)
5. Promotion Cycles	**5. Alternative promotion paths** Matching metrics to source of growth Longer tenures within job cycles Linking positions across time

The *Playbook* is a different system. It relies on different customer insights, in particular the quantitative drop-off points in the entire end-to-end buying process. The Sparkle team could now answer the simple question, "What do you know that your competition doesn't know?" They knew that 40 percent of women who sampled the Sparkle brand purchased the product as compared to the less than 15 percent who purchased Sparkle without sampling it in the store. This data point drove the entire brand planning process. Using this data point from the buying process as a catalyst, the Sparkle team implemented the entire *Playbook* system and simultaneously abandoned their existing brand planning process.

Since the *Playbook* is a different approach, all of the issues that arise in any change management program need to be incorporated as the firm embeds and deploys the *Playbook* throughout the business. The EnServ approach worked well because the senior executive team was able to identify slow growth as a burning platform issue, set aggressive growth targets and vision for the team, launch pilots to prove the concept, and roll out the program with systematic training and development across the entire commercial team—along with senior folks in the organization.[62]

As you implement the *Playbook*, a second corollary issue arises: how do you integrate the *Playbook* with other systems, processes, structures, and training efforts? That is, how do you align the *Playbook* with yearly budget cycles, yearly job rotations, forecasting, and product launch cycles? This hardwiring of the *Playbook* with other activities doesn't happen overnight. Our observation is that this transition often takes place as a transformation campaign—reinforcing the notion that revamping a company's growth capabilities is truly a process, not a one-time intervention. For EnServ this meant developing new commercial competencies, changing the reward systems, and reworking budgets with the CFO.

From multiple, siloed views to organization-wide views

A significant part of the challenge in creating and managing sustained growth is to make sure that all relevant functions buy into the plan. Indeed, if the plan is built without the input of various functions—there's little chance of buy in. So, the only way that we have seen this work reliably is to put together working teams with the right representation of marketing, R&D, sales, and other key functions of the firm. These working teams must have senior executives and strong cross-functional representation. Furthermore, these working teams must be supported by a powerful, guiding coalition (often termed the steering team) in order for the intervention to be successful.

Firms can establish distinct working teams with meaningful budgets to focus on the most promising sources of growth. And each team should have the scope and authority to design and commission product variants and go-to-market campaigns tailored solely to their strategy, and to do so in parallel with whatever mainstream campaigns the firm is running for acquisition and retention. Pharmaceutical companies routinely establish separate teams to demonstrate to regulators and doctors that the same drug is safe and effective in multiple indications, that is, in treating different diseases or different aspects of a disease. They've learned that it's difficult for one team to do an excellent job addressing different sources of growth. Yet, organizations also need to ensure consistency and alignment across these various efforts by committing to a common understanding of the market and a single segmentation scheme.

Again, EnServ offers a prime example of this. Different functions and individuals within the business had different definitions of what a good customer looked like depending on the particular perspectives and incentives they faced. For a salesperson, for example, a good customer was one that made a major purchase of HVAC equipment (such as a chiller for a large building complex) every few years, which could generate substantial sales commissions. A large part of the task for Susan Gomez and the EnServ working team in revamping the segmentation and go-to-market approach for the energy services business was to gain buy in from multiple groups and to realign incentives to ensure that all parts of the organization worked in tandem.

From underfunding consumer research to market-driven insights

Senior executives need to be accountable and responsible for funding consumer research. To address the three issues raised earlier—they need to allocate more money to consumer research in general, disproportionately focus on discovery-oriented research, insist that teams practice evidence-based construction of marketing plans, and be involved in reviewing, examining, and questioning research findings.

First, the firm must commit to the allocation of funds for market research. Since these funds are typically not budgeted—and R&D does have a budget—it's often easier to take a small chunk of R&D funding. Certainly, R&D will push back initially. But if they believe that this is a good use of funds and that R&D will be more effective, then this shift is possible.

Second, executives need to insist that their teams dig deeper for insights, pushing them to reallocate existing research funds and providing additional funds where needed. Insight about customers and the future is the fuel of growth. If the newly established teams don't see the world differently or see things that others don't, then those teams will not be able to create distinctive growth programs. As noted earlier, most firms spend too little on research, and the vast majority of what they do spend is focused on tracking brand health, share, or advertising effectiveness. Not enough is spent on *discovery*.

Third, executives need to require quantitative mapping of the drop-off points in the buying process. This requirement that all marketing plans show *evidence* of where the firm can intervene successfully—how it can change the behavior, why the customer will want to engage in the new behavior, and how it makes financial sense—is critical to the practice of evidence-based commercial planning. This approach will also lead the team away from purchasing databases of secondary research and handing off research tasks to vendors.

Fourth, senior executives need to demand that working teams show evidence of drop off points in the buying process, segments based on propensity, customer narratives based on drivers and barriers of high leverage behaviors, and other tools from the *Playbook*. For example, the buying process waterfall (Figure 3-5) is an essential discussion vehicle for driving allocation of marketing resources. These outputs must be shown, debated, examined, and discussed in senior steering teams. They must be part of any product or brand plan. If this senior commitment—to learning about markets and to demanding new customer insights and alternative ways to view the market— does not exist then no change will occur.

From a spread of commercial investment to a focused spend

In Chapter 10, we took a deep dive into a process that focuses the commercial spend on specific activities. Maya Stone, head of marketing at Helena Styx Cosmetics, was all too familiar with the peanut butter spreading of resources. Year after year, marketing budgets tended to be divided across the portfolio of brands in proportion to brand sales and allocated in lockstep with common practices within the industry. In effect, this meant that nearly 80 percent of marketing spend was devoted to promoting the brands through print and TV advertisement with most of the rest going to social media advertisement. Indeed, the big fight brewing within the group was about whether this mix of spending should be reallocated more toward online and social media rather than traditional media.

Adopting the *Playbook* process changed all that. Since the analysis showed the critical importance of behaviors and decisions made at the wall in retail channels, Maya's team pivoted to allot significant resources to redesigning the cosmetics shopping experience through changes to the product, the presentation, and the context of purchase. Furthermore, the team decided to invest disproportionately in changing the behaviors of a single segment—point-of-entry teens buying cosmetics for the first time—and to prioritize the flagship Sparkle brand that catered to this segment (wave 1). Once the strategy had begun to work, they then allocated resources to extend this approach to other segments (wave 2) and other brands within the portfolio.

From job rotation to a longer-term perspective

How the leaders of teams dedicated to a new source of growth are measured and promoted also matters a good deal. Typically, a manager's performance is measured against both quantitative goals (for example, revenue growth, market share) and qualitative objectives (for example, completing certain initiatives). Both should be modified if a firm wants to achieve significant growth. This will involve investment in new systems and capabilities to gather new data and changing practices. To begin, each team that is created to pursue a new source of growth will likely have to design and operate a custom-designed tracking system in order to generate metrics that allow a fair evaluation of how successful they've been. Product line revenue numbers are too high level—they're affected by the work of all the teams.

What are needed are metrics appropriate to the growth source. Most firms' tracking research samples only customers in the category and gathers information on overall purchases, consumption, and brand choice, meaning it's only possible to calculate changes in share and retention. So firms have to modify and/or create new tracking research to get the right data for pursuing different growth sources. If you're focused on growth through new-to-the-category customers, you'll have to create a tracking system (or modify the existing one) to sample people both outside and inside the category and carefully track the behavior of transitioning customers. If you're focused on increasing usage, by contrast, you'll need a tracking system that isolates existing customers' behavior in a much more granular way: brand choice and usage by each occasion.

It's equally important to change qualitative measures and promotion policies to get the right level of attention on new sources of growth. The issue is a timing mismatch. Promotion cycles in most companies are generally shorter than the time needed for initiatives and campaigns aimed at the new sources of growth to be designed and implemented properly. If being on track means promotion every twenty to twenty-four months, as is commonly the case, then managers will agree to be measured on only those initiatives that they can design, implement and achieve within twelve to fourteen months. That translates into a bias away from taking the time to develop the deeper insight and the multidimensional, engaging, and educational campaigns needed to draw people into a category or change their usage.

This bias for short cycle, share/retention-oriented initiatives can be countered by changing promotion criteria. Companies can hold aspiring managers accountable for following through on longer term efforts, for example, by making clear that they can't be promoted until they've brought a couple of their predecessor's longer term growth initiatives to a successful conclusion. The key point is to make managers accountable for growth initiatives that last longer than they expect to be in a particular role.

Conclusion

This chapter isolated firm-specific actions and mindsets that get in the way of growth. These issues are often broader, systemic issues (for example, job rotation cycles) that relate to how organizations function. It's perhaps not surprising that organizations desire stability and continuity. Indeed, some of Peter Drucker's most powerful work focused on the need for organizations to abandon activities, processes, and approaches that have worked well in the past. He termed this connection of activities the *theory of the business,* and advocated for revisiting core assumptions of the industry, the mission of the firm, and the strategy every two years. Our message is this: traditional growth approaches don't work—or, at the very least, they don't produce reliable sources of growth. The decision to do a system-wide replacement isn't an easy one. But following conventional wisdom usually doesn't lead to growth. It's time for a new approach.

Acknowledgments

Building and testing the ideas and tools of the *Playbook* in the field, as we did over many years, leaves us in debt to many helping hands and minds among our colleagues, clients, family, and friends—too many to thank individually. We are deeply grateful to each of them.

We owe a special debt to our wonderful colleagues at Monitor Group, whose willingness to apply and critique the *Playbook* as it evolved was essential. First and foremost among these, we'd like to thank Mark Fuller, founder and longtime CEO of Monitor, who has been a driving force in both our careers. Mark is the rare CEO who loves and excels at both the intellectual and practical challenges of finding better ideas and putting them to work within organizations, and his contributions to the *Playbook* span its lifetime. He provided Bob with the initial challenge that led to the *Playbook*, namely, finding a way to accelerate growth that relied on neither individual genius nor team heroics. He provided opportunities to test the ideas in the field and relentlessly pushed to improve both their rigor and ease of use. As the book took shape, he constructively critiqued every draft. We are deeply indebted to Mark—both professionally and personally.

Second, and not far behind, we'd like to thank David Gray, a Monitor colleague and part of the *Playbook* team from early on. David was instrumental in the design and delivery of numerous marketing excellence programs featuring the *Playbook*'s principles. He's been equally instrumental in this project: crafting drafts of the client story chapters, rewriting the principles chapters, and helping with overall editing of the volume. We could not have produced the book without him.

Third, we want to acknowledge the group of Monitor colleagues who played a vital role in developing, testing, and refining the *Playbook*'s core tool set across many different sectors and geographies. Central among these were the leaders, over the years, of Monitor's Market2Customer practice: Toby Thomas, Mark Pocharski, Jonathan Calascione, Tony Siesfeld, Jennifer Barron, Geoffrey Tuff, Jill Bicks, Joe Zale, and Tom Nagle. Each of them pushed the thinking or the process in a key way. But there were many others who should be noted for their willingness to use the alpha and beta versions of the *Playbook*, or for figuring out how to make it work better in different geographies or sectors, among them: Sandi Pocharski, Joe Fuller, Mark Thomas, Jonathan

Goodman, Scott Daniels, Vicky Levy, Stacey Raiche, Sheryl Jacobson, Bansi Nagji, Steve Jennings, Corey Krane, Glenn Goldman, Richard Rawlinson, Carl Engle, Eliette Krakora, Bill Stephens, Karin Stawarky, Michelle Toth, Stacy McManus, John Matthews, Ben Paik, Lisa Thompson, David Maggs, Steve Goldbach, Jennifer Del Carlo, and many others.

Not surprisingly for a practice-based book, our clients have been as much our collaborators as our colleagues. There are literally hundreds we'd like to thank for their willingness to make the *Playbook* a central part of their business and their own management approach. But we'd especially like to thank our visionary early adopters—those who knew they were working with new ideas and were true partners in making them work or improving them: David Anstice, Brian McCloud, Wendy Dixon, Charlie Frenette, Brad Lich, Anne Thistleton.

We also benefited greatly from deep, rich conversations with two of our academic colleagues, Goutam Challagalla and Ajay Kohli, concerning the content and its fit within the marketing literature and traditional marketing practice. Goutam's and Ajay's willingness to challenge our thinking, place the work in context, and "pressure test" the ideas with their executive clients helped us sharpen and fine tune our perspective and approach.

We'd also like to acknowledge our editorial team and AMA colleagues. Andy Friedman, Matt Weingarden, and Russ Klein undertook a major initiative in launching the *Organic Growth Playbook* as the first book in this series. We are forever grateful for their vision to push the envelope on the seven big problems. Melissa Giovagnoli Wilson, our guide and overall editor, was instrumental in pulling together the core team and ushering the book through copyediting, typesetting, and marketing efforts. Kathy Meis and Gretchen Dykstra provided detailed, specific editorial advice and commentary. Euan Monaghan worked with us to typeset and proof the final copy. Bethany Auck was our point person for the book figures.

In addition, we'd like to thank individuals and colleagues who are part of our personal networks.

Bernie

As with all my professional efforts, I wouldn't have completed the book without the full support and love of my wife, Mary. I'm not sure how she put up with all the early morning phone calls with Bob, the constant weekend work, and the inevitable frustrations that come with crafting a book. I've been very fortunate to be on both the Plan A and Plan B journey with her. All my love, as I very much look forward to our continued journey.

My colleagues at the Drucker School also supported the overall effort. In particular, I want to single out my dean, Jenny Darroch, for her continual support, counsel, and leadership, and Vijay Sathe, who was an enthusiastic supporter of the ideas in this volume. I'm fortunate to work with a wonderful set of supportive colleagues.

Special thanks to Ajay Kohli and Jeffrey Rayport. Ajay has been a great friend, special co-author, and wise sage on all things marketing. As noted earlier, he pushed our thinking on the framing of the book and the toolset itself. Special thanks also to Jeffrey Rayport, who has been a co-author, friend, and colleague on numerous projects over many years.

Bob

My deepest thanks first and last to those I owe the most: the Peanut, the Pumpkin, and the B. Their strong, quixotic belief in me, and that this book should, however improbably, "top the charts," bound me to the task of finishing it like nothing else. I'm forever grateful for their conviction that I was doing something useful with all the extra hours I spent working on the principles or the tools, hours that might have been spent with them. I'm forever grateful for their ability to restore my spirits and energy when I (all too frequently) got stuck. And I'm forever grateful for their willingness to read and critique the drafts, and most of all, lovingly but most firmly, make sure I went back to work and "did my job."

But I've been actively working on the *Playbook*, in one form or another, for the better part of two decades now and, as the earlier lists make clear, I was not alone. I've had many helpers, and owe much to many. I do, however, owe special thanks to a special few who made, knowingly or not, major contributions.

So, I want to thank my father, Henry A. Lurie, who by word and deed taught me that the world's most interesting and valuable things happen in the boundaries where disciplines meet and overlap. I cannot thank him in person anymore, but his thought and example are woven in everywhere.

I want to thank Hugh G.J. Aitken, professor of economics at Amherst College, who many years ago introduced to me the idea of path dependency, and show me how to trace outsized effects back to their roots in early on, small choices.

I want to thank Diana Smith, Jamie Higgins, and Anne Thistleton, who at various times and in various ways, sparked and fed my interest in what happens at the boundary where cognitive psychology meets markets and customers.

And finally, a broad but nonetheless heartfelt thank you to all those who took a chance on M2C in the early days, and whose conviction and energy and willingness to try, to fail, to succeed, and, most of all, to learn made all the difference.

Notes

Chapter 1

[1] This and other examples used in the book have been disguised to protect confidentiality. However, all are derived from actual client work in the industries described.

[2] See "Why Revenue Growth Is the CEO's Job, *Axial*, April 28, 2015. www.axial.net/forum/revenue-growth-ceo.

[3] For the past ten years, most CEO surveys—by IBM, Gartner Group, PWC, and others have found that the top CEO priority is revenue growth. See, for example, PWC 18th Annual Global Survey and Gartner Group CEO and Senior Business Executive Survey 2015.

[4] See Rajay Gulati, "How CEOs Manage Growth Agendas," *Harvard Business Review*, July–August 2004.

[5] See Adi Ignatius and Daniel McGinn, "Novo Nordisk CEO Lars Sørensen on What Propelled Him to the Top," *Harvard Business Review*, November 2015. https://hbr.org/2015/11/novo-nordisk-ceo-on-what-propelled-him-to-the-top

[6] Adam Lashinsky, "Nike's Master Craftsman," *Fortune*, November 12, 2015. http://fortune.com/2015/11/12/nike-ceo-mark-parker/.

[7] Justin Fox, "Netflix Has a Growth Problem," *Bloomberg News*, July 19, 2016.

[8] Leslie Patton, "MacDonald's Sales Growth Missed Estimates," *Bloomberg News*, July 28, 2016.

[9] Brian Deagon, "After 16 Quarters of Revenue Decline, When Will IBM Bounce Back?" *Investor's Business Daily*, April 25, 2016.

[10] Joan Schneider and Julie Hall, "Why Most Product Launches Fail," *Harvard Business Review*, April 2011.

[11] This point is subtle and requires elaboration. Most positioning frameworks that we're aware of focus on the benefits that the target customers would receive relative to the next best alternative (see the excellent article by James C. Anderson, James A. Narus, and Wouter Van Roosum (2006), "Customer Value Propositions in Business Markets, *Harvard Business Review*, March 2006). They may focus on one benefit, several benefits or a combination of benefits. Rarely do positioning exercises focus on the "barriers" to consumption that need to be removed. Thus, in this sense they're "one-sided" (focus on the positive or upside) but rarely are two-sided (position on upside and remove the downside barriers). Interestingly, there is consumer research on this "removal of the downsides"—but it has not worked its way into the positioning exercises themselves (see Kotler and Keller 2016 description on pp. 275–85).

[12] Rebecca Borison, "Amazon Prime Members Are Even More Valuable Than You Thought," *The Street*. February 27, 2016.

https://www.thestreet.com/story/13461916/1/amazon-prime-members-are-even-more-valuable-than-you-thought.html.

Chapter 2

13 We've disguised some of the facts in this example to maintain confidentiality. Throughout the case, we refer to the condition in question simply as ASD. As described here, the actual condition involved a degenerative disease that was largely diagnosed and treated by primary care physicians (PCPs). The drug that we're calling Terrafix provided a first-of-its-kind therapy for this disorder, which had previously gone undetected and untreated in many patients.

14 At the time that these events took place, new regulations had recently permitted direct-to-consumer advertising in the US pharmaceutical industry. However, the practice wasn't nearly as widespread as it has since become.

15 The discussion of segmentation presented here draws on concepts discussed in greater detail in Chapter 5.

16 The physician segmentation frame included a combination of physician characteristics and patient situations that, taken together, correlated with different levels of doctors' willingness to order a test. The unit of strategy and action in this case was a particular combination of patients and physicians treating those patients.

17 The team constructed a similar narrative for the target physician segment.

Chapter 3

18 See Kotler, Philip and Kevin Lane Keller (2016), *Marketing Management*, Boston, MA: Pearson. As Kotler and Keller note, "Marketers must develop activities and programs that reach consumers at all decision stages" (p. 173).

19 This issue is perfectly illustrated in a Harvard Business School case on Avaya (HBS case 9-508-048, David Godes, April 14, 2008). The key challenge in the case is how to best integrate the sales funnel and the marketing activities in order to spend money and resources across all phases of the buying process. In our view, this is the wrong approach.

20 See Kotler and Keller, pp. 172–80.

21 Note that the the awareness and consideration stages have been subsumed inside the information search stage.

22 There's a rich history of research on segmentation. In the overwhelming majority of cases markets are segmented first—then the follow on activity involves mapping the customer buying process by segment. We're advocating that one reverse the sequence. Begin with the buying process—then segment markets.

23 We could further extend this buying process to include post-purchase use and consumption of the product and re-purchase behaviors.

Chapter 4

24 We use the terms *characteristics* and *variables* interchangeably in this chapter.
25 The survey had been designed with this in mind and so included a lengthy section dedicated to questions about customers' location, organization, ownership and other variables.

Chapter 5

26 See Kotler and Keller (2016), "Identifying Market Segments and Targets," pp. 245–73. As they note, "Regardless of which type of segmentation scheme we use, the key is adjusting the marketing program to recognize customer differences" (p. 246).
27 See Kotler and Keller (2016), pp. 245–73.
28 The notion that situational variables are critical predictors of consumption behavior is well documented. See, for example, Pradeep Kakkar and Richard Lutz, "Situational Influence on Consumer Behavior: A Review," in Harold H. Kassarjian and Thomas S. Robertson, eds., Perspectives in *Consumer Behavior*, 3rd ed. (Glenview, IL: Scott, Foresman, 1981), 204–14. Peter R. Dickson, "Person-Situation: Segmentation's Missing Link," *Journal of Marketing*, 46 (Fall 1982), 56–64.
29 Technically, these behavioral objectives are unique to the sources of growth that most benefit the business.
30 In practice, we've found that large and medium segments are often further segmented by business model, that is distributor or user, and/or by industry vertical.
31 We fully recognize that this statement may be controversial. Several firms such as Claritas based their segments on a form of geographic clustering that classifies customers into 14 distinct groups and 66 lifestyle segments termed PRIZM Clusters (for example, Beltway Boomers). While these are interesting segments in their own right, they have little practical use in our methodology. Also, in practice we've found that firms that attempt to use attitudinal or values based measures to segment markets in the end look for "proxies" of these variables so that the salesforce can easily identify the target customers.
32 For B2B markets we adhere to the same logic—but recognize that the data collection process may be more complicated. In particular, B2B markets often have relatively few customers and it's impossible to do this kind of quantification. As a result, teams may have to use insights from qualitative research and logic to infer which of the actionable variables are most/best correlated.
33 As Peter Dickson (1982), noted "As demand results from an interaction of a person with his or her environment a segmentation perspective that includes both the person and the situation is needed to explain demand and target market strategy (p. 56). See full reference in note 28, Chapter 5.
34 Given the measurement error typical of survey work, cells whose propensity toward a behavior lie within a few percentage points of each other should be considered as having the same propensity.

Chapter 7

[35] There are various approaches to developing these personas. For example, http://www.buyerpersona.com/what-is-a-buyer-persona

[36] See, for example, a Forbes article that does a nice job of explaining the basics of being easy to do business with: https://www.forbes.com/sites/blakemorgan/2015/01/13/want-a-powerful-customer-experience-make-it-easy-for-the-customer/#7188698a6985.

[37] See Michael Solomon (2015). *Consumer Behavior: Buying, Having and Being*, Pearson: Upper Saddle River, NJ: Pearson. Or, Wayne D Hoyer, Deborah J. MacInnis, and Rik Pieters (2013), *Consumer Behavior*, Mason, OH: Southwestern.

[38] See, for example, Solomon (2015), Chapter 9, pp. 352–56.

[39] See, for example, a recent article on the power stories in digital marketing (https://sloanreview.mit.edu/article/the-power-of-consumer-stories-in-digital-marketing). Or, an excellent example from Gatorade (https://www.theguardian.com/media-network/media-network-blog/2012/may/23/storytelling-key-audience-consumer-engagement). There is also a rich body of work in academia on consumer stories, for example, see Jennifer E. Escales (2004), "Narrative Processing: Building Consumer Connections to Brands," *Journal of Consumer Psychology,* 14 (1–2), 168–80).

[40] Of course, the scope of the Behaviors and Outcomes section will be different for teams operating in B2C rather than B2B markets. In B2C markets, the focus is nearly always on the shopper, although attention should be paid to the presence and importance of influencers, for example, family members. In B2B markets, by contrast, while the behavioral objective will always concern an individual, the buying unit almost always contains multiple roles and individuals whose behaviors must be documented.

[41] There are markets whose modest number of customers makes it difficult or impossible to conduct a meaningful quantitative survey. In these circumstances, teams should still gather as much data about actual behavior as they can; they simply need to report it as absolute numbers rather than percentages.

[42] See Solomon (2015), Chapter 9, section on "shopping experience," 257–266.

[43] See Solomon (2015), Chapter 9, section on "situational effects of consumer behavior," 352–56.

[44] See Hoyer, MacInnis, and Pieter (2013), Chapter 4, "Memory and Knowledge," 99–115.

[45] Barsalou, Lawrence (1992), *Cognitive Psychology: An Overview for Cognitive Scientists*, Hillsdale, NJ: Lawrence Erlbaum.

[46] See Hoyer, MacInnis and Pieter (2013), section on "knowledge content: schemas and scripts", 106–108.

[47] Zaltman, Gerald (2003), *How Customers Think*, Boston: Harvard Business School Press.

48 Ariely, Dan and Jonathan Levav (2000), "Sequential Choice in Group Settings: Taking the Road Less Traveled and Less Enjoyed," *Journal of Consumer Research*, December (27), 279–90.

49 McKee, Robert (2003), "Storytelling that Moves People," *Harvard Business Review*, June, 5–8.

50 Schmitt, Philipp, Bernd Skiera and Christophe Van de Bulte (2011), "Referral Programs and Customer Value," *Journal of Marketing*, January, 46–59.

51 Lurie, Nicholas H. (2004), "Decision-Making in Information-Rich Environments: The Role of Information Structure," *Journal of Consumer Research*, March, 473–86.

52 See for example, Schau, Hope Jensen, Albert M. Muniz, and Eric J. Arnould (2009), "How Brand Community Practices Create Value," *Journal of Marketing*, September, 30–51. Also, Cova, Veronique and Bernard Cova (2001), "Tribal Aspects of Postmodern Consumption Research: The Case of French In-Line Roller Skaters," *Journal of Consumer Behavior*, June, 67–76. Of course the foundational work on consumer heuristics and biases is based on the work of Tversky and Kahneman (see Daniel Kahneman, Paul Slovic, and Amos Tversky eds. (1982), *Judgment Under Uncertainty*, Cambridge University Press).

Chapter 8

53 A key indicator of customers' willingness to invest new funds with a new advisor was the number of relationships those customers maintained with different financial institutions. Customers in Segment E tended to have multiple relationships (>3) with different institutions, while Segment K, for example, were more likely to have a single financial advisor relationship and to invest the majority of their portfolios with that one institution.

Chapter 9

54 The notion that a strong value proposition or "position" will result in growth is evident in the leading marketing textbooks. For example, Kotler and Keller (2016) note "All marketing strategy is built on segmentation, targeting, and positioning (STP). A company discovers different needs and groups of consumers in the marketplace, targets those needs it can satisfy in a superior way, and then positions its offerings so that the target market recognizes its distinctive offerings and images. By building customer advantages, companies can deliver high customer value and satisfaction, which lead to high repeat purchases and ultimately to high company profitability" (p. 275). Our view is that this approach sometimes works—and sometimes does not.

55 See Kotler and Keller (2016). Chapter 10 provides an overview of product positioning.

56 In *Simply Better: Winning and Keeping Customers by Delivering What Matters Most* (Boston: Harvard Business School Press, 2004), Patrick Barwise and Seán Meehan argue that most companies have taken differentiation so far that they've left their customers behind. Their key message is that customers don't want bells

and whistles, and they don't care about trivial differences between brands. What they really want are quality products, reliable services, and fair value for money. Yet most companies consistently fail to meet these basic customer needs. Barwise and Meehan argue that successful differentiation lies not in unique selling propositions, but in generic category benefits, such as good service, on-time delivery, and quality products, that any company can provide.

Chapter 10

[57]   Although a different context, see Kinley, Nik and Shlomo Ben-Hur (2015), *Changing Employee Behavior*, Hampshire, UK: Pelgrave MacMillan.

[58]   Deborah J. MacInnis, Christine Moorman, and Bernard J. Jaworski, "Enhancing and Measuring Consumers' Ability, Motivation, and Opportunity to Process Brand Information from Ads," *Journal of Marketing* 55 (October 1991), 32–53. The authors introduce the MOA model to explain how to increase the probability that individuals will attend to and process external stimuli.

[59]   See Kotler and Keller (2016), p. 170. Also, chapter 2 of Michael Solomon (2015), *Consumer Behavior* (Boston: Pearson) provides an excellent review of the information processing perspective on buyer behavior.

[60]   For a comprehensive review of the effects of advertising we recommend the following review article: Raj Sethuraman, Gerard J. Tellis, Richard A. Briesch (2011) "How Well Does Advertising Work? Generalizations from Meta-Analysis of Brand Advertising Elasticities," *Journal of Marketing Research*: June 2011, 457–71.

Chapter 11

[61]   We have chosen not to call out the special case of B2C markets in this chapter. A number of examples throughout the book illustrate the application of the principles to this type of market. In general, data on B2C markets also tends to be more readily available or easier to collect compared to the other types of markets profiled in this chapter.

[62]   See John Kotter (2012), *Leading Change*. Boston: Harvard Business School Publishing.

About the Authors

Bernie Jaworski and Bob Lurie have worked with hundreds of GMs and product managers to create and implement marketing and sales plans. This hands-on experience has given them a visceral understanding of what it takes to create and implement usable growth plans for the people responsible for "making things happen" in organizations. Their success with individual product lines has led to work with scores of CEOs and CMOs on how to deploy their novel methods and management routines throughout complex organizations.

Bernie Jaworski is the Peter F. Drucker Chair at the Drucker School of Management. He has published extensively in the most highly regarded marketing journals and has been ranked among the most highly cited scholars in the field of marketing. He has won all three major awards from the *Journal of Marketing*—the Maynard, Alpha Kappa Psi, and Jagdish Sheth Award—as well as several other awards. For 10 years he was a senior partner at Monitor Group, a global management consulting firm, where he helped lead several large-scale transformations of marketing at Fortune 500 firms.

Bob Lurie is Vice President, Corporate Strategy for Eastman. Prior to joining Eastman, he was co-managing partner of Monitor Group and a senior partner at Monitor Deloitte following the firm's acquisition by Deloitte Consulting in 2013. During his two decades as a management consultant, Bob worked with CEOs and other leaders of Fortune 500 companies in nearly every sector and part of the world to help them accelerate growth. He founded Monitor's marketing and growth practice, known as M2C, and led it through more than a decade of double-digit growth. He was the architect of the innovative approach to organic growth that fueled M2C's success and laid the groundwork for the *Organic Growth Playbook*. He has helped numerous organizations embed these ideas through large-scale marketing transformations and has published articles and white papers on growth strategy and building growth capabilities. Bob earned his PhD in economics from Yale University and has held positions in academia, as assistant professor of economics at Brandeis University, and in government, as a junior staff consultant on the President's Council of Economic Advisors.